'Gary Sheffield is one of Britain's foremost historians of the First World War – insightful, original and superbly informed.'

Max Hastings, bestselling author of *Catastrophe* and *All Hell Let Loose*

'In a book all the more impressive for its brevity, Gary Sheffield covers a remarkable amount of ground, from the war's causes to its consequences.'

Michael Neiberg, Professor of History at the University of Southern Mississippi

'One of Britain's foremost historians of the Great War offers here a clear and concise account of the great catastrophe of the 20th Century. Drawing on an enormous knowledge of secondary literature combined with many years of immersion in the archives, the result is a masterful mix of narrative and analysis that will prove both provocative and stimulating.'

Jeffrey Grey, Professor of History, UNSW Canberra

'Professor Gary Sheffield, one of the leading figures in the field, turns his considerable talent to providing the most up-to-date view of this most controversial of conflicts. The result is history at its very best; masterfully written, engaging and thought provoking.'

Andrew Wiest, Founding Director of the Center for the Study of War and Society, University of Southern Mississippi

'A compelling and original account that should become a set text for anyone wanting to understand the events of 1914-18.'

James Holland, bestselling author of *The Battle of Britain* and *Dam Busters*

'An excellent introduction to this vast subject which will be accessible to those beginning to study the conflict as well as a stimulating read for more experienced scholars.'

Brian Bond, Emeritus Professor of Military History, Kings College, London

About the Author

Gary Sheffield is Professor of War Studies at the University of Wolverhampton. He is President of the International Guild of Battlefield Guides and a Vice President of the Western Front Association. He has published widely on the First World War and regularly broadcasts on television and radio as well as contributing to numerous journals, magazines and newspapers. Previous books include the acclaimed *Forgotten Victory* and *The Chief: Douglas Haig and the British Army,* which was shortlisted for the prestigious Duke of Westminster's Medal.

A Short History of the First World War

Gary Sheffield

ONEWORLD

A Oneworld Paperback Original

Published by Oneworld Publications 2014

Copyright © Gary Sheffield 2014

The right of Gary Sheffield to be identified as the Author of this
work has been asserted by him in accordance with the
Copyright, Designs and Patents Act 1988

ISBN 978-1-78074-364-6
eISBN 978-1-78074-512-1

Typeset by Siliconchips Services Ltd, UK
Printed and bound by CPI Group (UK) Ltd.
Croydon, CR0 4YY

Oneworld Publications
10 Bloomsbury Street
London WC1B 3SR
England

Dedicated to the memory of my father-in-law, Clifford John ('Cliff') Davis (1924–2013), who served in the Royal Navy during the Second World War.

Contents

List of Illustrations and Maps

All illustrations are courtesy of the Spencer Jones collection.

All maps courtesy of Barbara Taylor.

Preface

The First World War was an event, or rather a series of events, of such importance that it can be a struggle to find words that adequately express its significance. It destroyed the German, Austro-Hungarian, Russian and Ottoman empires. It led to the establishment of a Marxist-Leninist state, the Soviet Union, and sowed the seeds of fascism in Italy and Germany. The British and French colonial empires were simultaneously driven to the zenith of their power, in the process creating the conditions that would, within a couple of generations, lead to their collapse. It killed millions and brought the world, albeit not directly, to an even greater conflagration.

The war also freed nationalities previously confined within larger states to establish independent countries: Czechoslovakia, Poland, Yugoslavia, Ireland. It facilitated the rise of the United States of America to global power and so made capitalist democracy an ideological force to contend with Soviet Marxist-Leninism, setting the scene for the Cold War. Britain, as a direct result of the war, became more thoroughgoingly democratic. The use of war to achieve political goals was discredited in the democracies, while being regarded as legitimate and even desirable by fascists and communists. Cultural life – literature, theatre, film, art, music – was irrevocably marked. After the guns of August opened fire, nothing was ever quite the same.

Harry Patch, the last surviving British soldier of the First World War, died in July 2009. His death, noted a distinguished historian, 'consigns Britain's part in the First World War into history'.[1] Technically, this is correct, but in reality, the scars are still too raw, passions still too high, for 1914–18 simply to slip away into history. One hundred years on, the meaning of the war, or whether the war had any meaning at all, is still bitterly contested. In the year of the centenary of the outbreak of the war, history wars were waged on page and screen. Scholarly controversies previously confined to seminars and learned journals became, to the bemusement of some academics, front page news.[2] The First World War still feels more like current affairs in much of the English-speaking world and in some parts of Europe.

Politicians, actors and pop stars felt compelled to share their views on the conflict. In May 2013, a letter from a group of actors, musicians, poets and politicians was published in the *Guardian*, a liberal-left British newspaper. It attacked the UK government's remembrance programme, declaring 'Far from being a "War to end all wars" or a "Victory for democracy" this was a military disaster and a human catastrophe'.[3] This promptly became known in some circles as the 'Luvvies' Letter'. Paul Lay, the editor of *History Today*, responded by tweeting 'Tell you what, instead of asking historians about remembering the war, let's ask the luvvies'. He followed it up with another tweet: 'Next: Jude Law, Kate Hudson & Brian Eno present paper on treating acute lymphoblastic leukaemia'.[4] Lay's point was exaggerated but typically astute. Historical research and analysis are highly specialised activities. More than most historical events, the First World War prompts people to go public with views based on emotion, limited knowledge and flawed understanding.

Anticipating the interest that the centenary was likely to cause (although not, I confess, either its scale or the venom with which some respond to their preconceptions being challenged), being asked to write an introductory book on the First World War appealed. Faced with the task of writing a short book on a huge subject, I decided to concentrate on three main themes. First, I consider the once-again contentious origins of the conflict. Then follows the largest section, devoted to the military history of the war: I make no apology for putting it centre-stage. Third, I consider the war as a 'total' conflict. Finally there is a brief coda that attempts to trace the influence of the First World War on the post-war world. I am well aware that this approach means some important topics are covered either very briefly or not at all. In the end, I had to be ruthless in my selection of topics and material. Nevertheless my hope is that, by integrating narrative with analysis and drawing upon up-to-date research, this book will give the reader a working understanding of not only what happened in 1914–18 but how and why.

Acknowledgements

My thanks go to Dr Michael LoCicero for providing initial drafts of some sections. It has been a pleasure working with Fiona Slater, my editor at Oneworld. Barbara Taylor drew the excellent maps. My new colleagues at the University of Wolverhampton have provided a wonderfully supportive working environment, and in particular I would like to thank Professor Stephen Badsey for sharing his expertise and Dr Spencer Jones for commenting on a draft of the text. Any mistakes that remain are, of course, my responsibility. The Sheffield and Davis families, as ever, provide a bedrock of love and support. My wife, Viv, has been as supportive as ever, uncomplainingly putting up with me writing yet another book. I thank her for that and so much more. This book is dedicated to the memory of her Dad.

Gary Sheffield
22 April 2014
Twitter: @ProfGSheffield
Website: http://www.garysheffield-historian.com

1

The Coming of War

Was anyone guilty?

Writing in his war memoirs in the 1930s, David Lloyd George asked 'How was it that the world was so unexpectedly plunged into this terrible conflict?' The man who had been Britain's Prime Minister in the second half of the First World War answered his own question: it had been a tragic accident. 'Nobody wanted war' but 'nations backed their machines over the precipice'.[1] Lloyd George reflected the view common at that time, eloquently expressed in 1929 by the American historian Sydney B. Fay: 'No one country and no one man was solely or probably even mainly, to blame'. Fay went on to condemn the so-called 'War Guilt clause' of the 1919 Treaty of Versailles, which stated that 'the aggression of Germany and her allies' was responsible for the war.[2]

These verdicts on the origins of the war represented far more than a semi-retired statesman sounding off in his memoirs or an academic pontificating from his ivory tower. They struck at the meaning of a conflict that had caused the death of millions. If the war was accidental, did that mean it was also preventable and, by extension, that those millions had died for nothing? The result of an appallingly destructive war was a post–1918 world that was less than ideal. This fed into a sense of futility, that the war had not been worth fighting. In 2012, a very influential book on the origins of the war was published by a respected academic that came to essentially the same conclusion as Lloyd George and Fay. In *The Sleepwalkers,* Christopher Clark argued:

The outbreak of war in 1914 is not an Agatha Christie drama at the end of which we will discover the culprit standing over a corpse in the conservatory with a smoking pistol. There is no smoking gun in this story; or, rather, there is one in the hands of every major character. Viewed in this light, the outbreak of war was a tragedy, not a crime.

Avoiding the allotting of war guilt is in vogue. In a newspaper polemic, another academic, Richard J. Evans, agreed with Clark that 'it's time to get away from the blame game' and went on to depict the war as futile: 'the end of the war in 1918 was a victory for no one... The [British] men who enlisted may have thought that they were fighting... a war to defend freedom: they were wrong'. Margaret MacMillan devoted over 600 pages of a book to discussing the origins of the war without coming to a firm view on who was to blame for causing it.[3] One review of *The Sleepwalkers* asserted that Clark's arguments 'effectively consign the old historical consensus to the bin'.[4] They do nothing of the sort: Clark's book is neither more nor less than a contribution – albeit one that has attracted much attention in lay circles – to a major historical debate. That debate goes on.

All historical writings must be judged in the context of the period in which they were produced. By the late 1920s, a reaction to the war had set in. The Treaty of Versailles was discredited in some quarters, reviled by British and American liberals as too harsh (an argument that of course appealed to Germany) and ruthlessly savaged by the economist John Maynard Keynes in his influential polemic of 1919, *The Economic Consequences of the Peace*. Lloyd George's war memoirs, no less than the writings of the war poet and former infantry officer Siegfried Sassoon, belong to the category of 'literature of disillusionment'. Fay was writing against a background of a general questioning of the wisdom of the USA's belated entry into the war. Similarly, in the second decade of the twenty-first century, as a decade-and-a-half of war in Iraq and

Afghanistan comes to an end, there is widespread disillusion with the use of armed force as an instrument of policy. But we should try to see the First World War as contemporaries viewed it and seek to avoid excessive use of hindsight and the imposing of twenty-first century values on individuals who lived one hundred years ago.

Reviewing *The Sleepwalkers* and another book that argues that the decision-makers of 1914 made errors of 'omission, not commission', the historian Holger Herwig pointed out that this line of argument 'dangerously leads us back' to Lloyd George's idea of the Great Powers somehow stumbling into war.[5] To take the 'stumbling' view is to ignore fifty years of research. Herwig is right. The evidence is compelling that Germany and Austria-Hungary bear the primary responsibility for beginning the war.

The rise of German power

The origins of the war stretch back at least to 1871. In that year, in the course of a comprehensive defeat of Napoleon III's France, which up to that point had been the continent's dominant military power, the German states (except Austria) were united into one state under Prussian leadership. The King of Prussia became Wilhelm I, Kaiser (Emperor) of Germany. Such a seismic shift in the balance of power often results in conflict or, at the very least, international instability; 1871 was an exception. Under the guidance of the 'Iron Chancellor', Otto von Bismarck, a new international equilibrium was created. Rather than seeing the unification of Germany as the platform for aggression, Germany became a status quo power. Although France was never reconciled to the loss of the provinces of Alsace and Lorraine as a result of 1871, Bismarck was adept at keeping France diplomatically isolated. Furthermore, Britain did not regard the emergence of the German Empire as a threat to its security and Berlin came to understandings with Austria-Hungary and Russia.

Figure 1 Wilhelm II, German Kaiser and King of Prussia (reigned 1888–1918).

Things changed with the accession of Kaiser Wilhelm II to the throne in 1888. A grandson of Queen Victoria, and so half English, Wilhelm was a destabilising influence in international affairs. He was possibly mentally unbalanced (on meeting him in 1891 the then British Prime Minister, Lord Salisbury, wondered whether the Kaiser was 'all there'), loved dressing up in fancy uniforms and had a mercurial personality. Wilhelm wanted to rule as well as reign. Dismissing Bismarck in 1890, Wilhelm rapidly proved, as the loosest of cannons, that he was not up to the job. His maladroit interventions on the international scene worsened a situation created by the new direction in German foreign policy that began in the 1890s. *Weltpolitik* (world policy) was a drive to gain colonies and expand German power and economic influence. In the process, Bismarck's carefully constructed system of alliances was sacrificed. The Reinsurance Treaty between Germany and Russia, a cornerstone of Bismarck's policy, was allowed to lapse by Wilhelm. Worse, in 1892, France and Russia became allies. Initially, this was, from the point of view of the two powers, simply a prudent counterpart to the Triple Alliance of Germany, Austria–Hungary and Italy. However, as international tensions intensified in the early years of the twentieth century, the Dual Alliance took on additional significance, especially because Britain emerged as a potential partner for France and Russia.

The security of Britain and its vast maritime empire was ultimately dependent on supremacy at sea. Traditionally, the British army had been relatively small and weak, the Royal Navy strong and powerful. Sensitivity about rival naval powers meant that the Low Countries of the Netherlands and Belgium were of particular strategic interest to the British and it was a long-standing policy aim that this area should not fall under the control of a hostile power. This was related to another tenet of British foreign policy, to oppose powers that attempted to achieve hegemony in Europe. Pursing this objective had seen Britain fight against the France of Louis XIV and Napoleon. In the second half of the nineteenth century, in the absence of such a threat, Britain could afford the luxury of 'splendid isolation', holding aloof from continental entanglements. The Empire, not Europe, was where potential threats lay and the most obvious likely enemies were France – the traditional foe – and Russia. France and Britain had almost come to blows in 1898, when rival imperial aspirations in Africa culminated in the Fashoda incident, a clash over a disputed area of Sudan. Russia and Britain were long-time rivals in the area of Afghanistan and Persia and fears of a Russian invasion of the Indian Raj never quite disappeared. Germany, on the other hand, before about 1900, was generally seen as a friendly state.

However, in 1898 Germany passed the first of its Naval Laws, which aimed to build up a powerful fleet, signalling the beginning of a naval arms race. The architect of the High Seas Fleet, Admiral Alfred von Tirpitz, playing on Wilhelm's jealousy of his mother's land, told the Kaiser that the plan was to mount such a challenge to the Royal Navy that Britain would 'concede to Your Majesty such a measure of naval mastery and enable Your Majesty to carry out a great overseas policy'.[6] The policy was disastrous. It poisoned relations with London, which accepted the challenge. In 1914, the Royal Navy was well ahead of its German rival in numbers of capital ships. Although there were other milestones along the path of the growth of enmity and suspicion between Britain and Germany, such as the Kaiser's noisy support for the Boers during the Second South African (or Boer) War (1899–1902), the avowed German challenge to British naval security was the most important single factor.

A high-profile mark of the diplomatic revolution that occurred in the first years of the new century came with the signing of the Entente Cordiale between Britain and France in 1904. This was a long way short of a military alliance and was not primarily aimed at Germany. The agreement was a largely successful attempt to settle long-standing problems, particularly colonial rivalries, but it was also highly significant in bringing together two states that as, the decade wore on, became increasingly fearful of German ambition and aggression. In 1905 and again in 1911, Germany sought to flex its muscles over Morocco, which France regarded as being in its sphere of influence. From a detached perspective, Germany's attempt to gain compensation from the expansion of French influence might seem to be on the same moral plain as French imperialism, if (inevitably) handled in a clumsy fashion by the Kaiser. But at the time, the two Moroccan crises were perceived as signs of Berlin's dangerous brinkmanship. And so, with Germany posturing against French imperialism and challenging British naval supremacy, France and Britain edged closer. Secret high-level negotiations

were initiated between the French and British military. The resulting plans provided for a British army to be deployed to France on
the left of the French army in the event of war in the west with
Germany, and for the French navy to concentrate in the Mediterranean, leaving the defence of France's northern coastline to the
Royal Navy. These agreements were achieved in the absence of a
formal, binding alliance, which caused the French deep anxiety in
early August 1914, when it briefly appeared that Britain would stay
out of the war.

In August 1907, Britain came to an agreement with another
colonial rival, France's ally, Russia. This helped ease tensions over
the competition for influence in Persia and Central Asia, which
suited Russia, as it allowed the Czarist government to concentrate
its energies on recovering from the twin disasters of defeat at the
hands of the Japanese in 1904–05 and the abortive 1905 revolution.
As the Liberal Foreign Secretary, Sir Edward Grey, commented in
1906, an agreement with Russia would 'complete and strengthen
the Entente with France and add very much to the comfort and
strength of our position'.[7] As with the Entente Cordiale, the new
accommodation with Russia fell well short of an alliance. Nonetheless, the Triple Entente of France, Russia and Britain increasingly
began to look like a power bloc. Superficial appearances, however,
were misleading. Britain would only support France under certain
circumstances. Furthermore, the British commitment was merely
moral – there was no treaty obligation.[8] Grey favoured a consensual
approach to resolving international disputes, along the lines of the
nineteenth-century Concert of Europe, whereby the representatives of the Great Powers would meet to defuse crises. For example,
after the 1912 Balkan War, Grey helped broker a peace settlement
at a conference in London during which he by no means always
favoured his Entente partners, siding with Austria over some key
issues.[9] The fact that Britain was to enter the war in August 1914,
and thus turn the Entente into a genuine power bloc, owed much
to the maladroit German strategy of invading Belgium.

The key role of Austria-Hungary

In recent years, the role of Austria-Hungary in bringing about the First World War has come to the fore. Germany had beaten Austria in a short war in 1866, but the defeated state soon accepted the status of junior partner to the victor and a treaty, inspired by distrust of Russia, was signed in 1879. Austria was a multi-national, multi-lingual empire, ruled by the House of Hapsburg. Nationalism was a force growing across Europe and it posed a particular threat to the Hapsburg Empire's internal cohesion and even its very exist-ence. The state became 'Austria-Hungary' in 1867, as important concessions were made in recognition of the strength of Hungarian nationalism. Hungarians were granted roughly equal status with the Austrians but there were many other nationalities, such as Czechs and Serbs, whose nationalist aspirations remained unfulfilled.

Shut out of its traditional spheres of influence in Italy in 1859 and Germany seven years later, Austria-Hungary increasingly looked to the Balkans. The decline of the Ottoman Empire (Turkey) had led to the weakening of its power in the Balkans, and in 1878, by the international Treaty of Berlin, the Austro-Hungarians were permit-ted to occupy the Ottoman provinces of Bosnia-Herzegovina. However, the Austro-Hungarians faced a rival force in the form of Balkan nationalism, centred on the independent state of Serbia, which aspired to rule over all Serbs, including the large number domiciled in Bosnia-Herzegovina. In the background was Russia, which saw itself as the protector of the South Slav people.

International tensions were heightened when in 1908 Vienna formally annexed Bosnia-Herzegovina. This was in part a response to the seizure of power in Constantinople by the Young Turks, a radical regime that intended to modernise and re-energise the Ottoman Empire. Such strengthening of the Ottoman state ran counter to the interests of Austria-Hungary, as well as those of pan-Slavists in Serbia and elsewhere: a rare example of the coincidence of interests.[10] The annexation of Bosnia-Herzegovina was seen by the Austro-Hungarian leadership as a way of forestalling the growth of Serbian power. In the face of German support for Austria-Hungary, neither Russia nor Serbia were willing to push the issue to the point of war (the former was weakened by its recent defeat at the hands of Japan and its Entente partners had proved unwilling to back Russia's stance).

So far, we have had a story of international tensions that stopped short of a war between the Great Powers. Because we know what happened in August 1914, it is all too tempting to read history backwards, with international history after 1871 merely an extended prologue to the outbreak of war. This is bad history. Posing the question of why general war came when it did, when it had previously been avoided, helps to sharpen the focus. What is clear is that developments in the four previous years led to the international situation being particularly unstable in the summer of 1914.

The 1908 Bosnia crisis was extremely destabilising.[11] Austria-Hungary's annexation of Bosnia-Herzegovina, an action which broke international law, marked a new and dangerous stage in international relations. It brought to an end Russia and Austria-Hungary's collaboration in keeping things calm in the Balkans, heightening Russian suspicion of Austrian intentions in the area. Moreover, two highly destabilising wars had taken place within the previous three years. Sensing Turkish weakness, Italy went to war with the Ottoman Empire in 1911, seizing Libya. The Italian action placed the world on alert that the Ottoman Empire, long regarded as the 'sick man of Europe', might be on the point of collapse. This possibility came a step closer in 1912, when a coalition of Balkan states (Serbia, Bulgaria, Greece and Montenegro) attacked Turkey and rapidly captured much of the Ottoman Empire's European territory. This was followed in 1913 by a second war. Bulgaria, dissatisfied with the peace brokered by Russia and Austria-Hungary, invaded Serbian territory but was swiftly defeated by the Serbs, Romanians, Greeks and Turks.

The Austrians could not but be alarmed at 'this new Serbia, this large, aggressive and antagonistic south Slavic state on their Balkan frontier', which still aspired to bring the Serbs in the Hapsburg

Empire within its borders.[12] No less than Austria–Hungary, Russia regarded the Balkans as its backyard and a long-standing Russian foreign policy objective was to control the Dardanelles, the Straits that separated Europe and Asia and allowed access from the Black Sea to the Mediterranean. The Balkan Wars raised fears in Russia that another state might seize the Ottoman capital of Constantinople and thus the Straits. The growth of German influence in Turkey, highlighted by the appointment of Liman von Sanders, a German general, to command Ottoman forces at the Straits, was a deeply worrying development for the Russians. Given Turkey's recent turbulent defeats in Libya and in the Balkan wars, the prospect of the Ottoman Empire disintegrating did not seem far-fetched. Austria–Hungary and, especially, Germany would be in the prime positions to take advantage. In early 1914, Russian fears were further stoked by evidence from intercepted secret German material. These suggested not only that Germany was indeed intent on taking Constantinople should the Ottoman Empire implode, but also, in an indication of Germany's wider aggressive intentions, that Berlin was undertaking an information campaign to prepare the German public for a war with France and Russia.[13]

THE INTERNATIONAL SYSTEM

The entire international system, the environment in which states relate to one another, has been put in the dock for failing to maintain the peace. While imperfect, the international system had accommodated Germany under Bismarck's rule: it was decisions of his successors to pursue more confrontational paths that led to its failure. Paul W. Schroeder has blamed the spirit of 'New Imperialism' that set in after about 1870, which often rewarded aggression, especially but not solely, in extra-European empire-building.[14] Following this logic, Austria-Hungary and Germany in 1914 were simply behaving as Britain had behaved towards the Boer republics in 1899, the United States towards Spain a year earlier and Serbia towards the Ottoman Empire and its Balkan neighbours in 1912–13. While imperialist mentalities probably contributed to the corrosion of the Concert of Europe, this argument is not entirely satisfactory. Contemporaries, influenced by attitudes that today would be seen as racist, saw a clear difference between behaviour of this sort beyond Europe, or a small power's activities in the borderlands of the Balkans, and a Great Power threatening the interest of its peers by aggressive activity in Europe proper. In particular, the fact that in the crises of 1905–06, 1908–09 and 1911–12 German leaders pursued a policy of brinkmanship by threatening war was seen by other states as destabilising.

The German perception of being 'encircled' by the Triple Entente was exaggerated (as we have seen, it was not the case that Britain would automatically support Russia and France in times of crisis) and was, in any case, a self-fulfilling prophesy. France and Russia had come together in 1892–94 out of fear of Germany. Subsequent German bellicosity had done nothing to relieve their anxieties and had served to add Britain to the Entente as a country member. Moreover, the choice of Germany and Austria-Hungary to reject Grey's numerous attempts to resurrect the Concert of Europe and thus settle Vienna's dispute with Belgrade by international co-operation points to the importance of decisions taken by individual statesmen and governments in the 'failure' of the international system, which can be made to work only if actors wish it. The Bulgarian crisis of 1878, which had been dealt with by an international conference, offered a clear precedent for coping with the crisis initiated by the Sarajevo assassination. While the strains placed upon the international system by the irreconcilable pressures of Serb nationalism and Austro-Hungarian interests in the Balkans should not be underestimated, it is not unlikely that a settlement could have been brokered by the Great Powers in July 1914, if Berlin and Vienna had wished for one. But as the leaders of these states sought to take advantage of the crisis to, at the very least, destroy Serbia, they were not interested in a peaceful resolution of the crisis.

Likewise, although an older interpretation held the existence of rival power blocs responsible for turning an essentially local dispute in the Balkans into a Europe-wide conflict, in reality alliances did not make a general war inevitable. Instead, such groupings can actually bring stability to a situation, not least through deterrence and the disciplines imposed by being a member of an alliance or coalition. However, in the case of 1914, a good case can be made that the problem was that coalitions were too weak. Italy, to the anger of its Triple Alliance partners, remained neutral in 1914 and compounded this betrayal by joining the Entente in 1915. Germany believed that the Triple Entente rested on foundations sufficiently insecure that the bloc could be broken apart over the July Crisis, with or without war. As Frank McDonough has argued, 'a fundamental problem which contributed to the outbreak of war was the *lack* of a fully effective balance of power in Europe – not its existence'.[15]

It was once fashionable to blame the outbreak of the war on imperialism, the drive to acquire colonies, raw materials and markets overseas. Following V.I. Lenin, Marxists saw German *Weltpolitik* in economic terms, with capitalists urging on foreign policy, which in turn led to a clash with other capitalist states whose capitalists also were a 'hidden hand' behind the foreign policies of the Great Powers. To again quote McDonough, 'In this view, millions of people were being sacrificed to ensure the future domination of one group of monopoly capitalists over another'.[16] Superficially, events such as the capture of German colonies in Africa and the Pacific by troops of the British and French empires, the carving of a vast German empire from the ruins of Imperial Russia and the dismemberment of the Ottoman Empire in the postwar peace process supported this theory. However such 'imperialism' was the by-product of a war begun for different reasons. The various empires picked up additional territories from defeated enemies almost out of force of habit, as for example the British had done in the Seven Years War a century and a half earlier. That was what empires did.

The 'imperialism' thesis is counterbalanced by the 'improbable war' argument recently propounded by the British-based German historian Holger Afflerbach. He argues that the outbreak of war took many people across Europe by surprise, including key military and political decision-makers, who took dangerous risks because of a belief 'that peace was secure'.[17] Certainly, there were many reasons why a major war might seem improbable. The economies of Europe were increasingly interdependent. In an influential book of 1910, Norman Angell argued that the notion that states could gain by war was a 'great illusion'. Rather, it was 'impossible' for a state to 'enrich itself by subjugating... another'. I.S. (Jan) Bloch's *Is War Now Impossible?* was also widely read, being published in an abridged English translation in 1899. Bloch argued that technology would lead to stalemate on the battlefield and an attritional struggle between economies that would tear societies apart.[18] In addition, other factors, such as international law, bound states together. While the 'improbable war' thesis has failed to gain universal acceptance, nonetheless it does an important service in reminding us that alongside the pressures that were to lead to war were others that tended towards stability. For all its faults, the international system did not make war inevitable.

The July Crisis

The immediate origin of the First World War was the murder of Archduke Franz Ferdinand by a young Serb, Gavrilo Princip, on 28 June 1914. Franz Ferdinand, the heir to the dual monarchy, was visiting Sarajevo, the capital of Bosnia-Herzegovina. The assassination was seen by Vienna as a direct challenge by Serbia. Actually, Princip was a Bosnian Serb and thus a subject of Austria-Hungary. Central authority in Serbia was weak. Dragutin Dimitrijevic (known as 'Apis'), the head of Serbian military intelligence, was also the leader of the Black Hand secret society and supplied a group of would-be assassins with weapons. This may have been an indirect attack on his political rival, Nicholas Pasic, the Serbian Prime Minister. But even the Black Hand could not control the activities of its members and it may have been a 'freelance' killing by local activists. In any case, Pasic got wind of a plot and gave a warning to the Austrians but the advice was too opaque to be useful.[19]

It is arguable that the fact that Pasic could not stop the semi-renegade Apis from sending death squads on to Hapsburg territory puts Serbia in the category of a rogue, or at least failing, state.[20] This line of thinking legitimises the Austro-Hungarian attack of July 1914. However, the shooting of the Archduke was not an example of state-sponsored terrorism, nor was the connection between Apis and the assassins clear during the July Crisis. Apis's nephew later stated that had his uncle's role been known, it would have appeared that 'the whole Serbian General Staff and probably the Belgrade government itself was involved in the crime', which would have done 'untold damage' to Serbia.[21] Austria-Hungary's behaviour, doing little for three weeks and then delivering a draconian ulti-matum to Serbia, most of which Belgrade promptly accepted, also diminished the Great Powers' sense that Serbia was a rogue state. While superficially plausible, the idea that Serbia was a rogue state that deserved punishment by an Austro-Hungarian invasion ignores the high probability that, as already noted, had there been an international conference, Serbia would most certainly have been punished, but without war. Moreover, the Sarajevo crisis did not override the security concerns of other powers about the situation in the Balkans to the extent of France, Britain and above all Russia being willing to give Austria-Hungary a free hand.

In Vienna, hawks such as General Conrad von Hötzendorf and Count Leopold von Berchtold, the Foreign Minister, and even the aged Emperor Franz Josef were determined to seize the pretext offered by the Sarajevo assassination to deal with Serbia.[22] The chance to go to war with Serbia had been missed during the Balkan Wars of 1912–13. Suddenly, unexpectedly, there was another opportunity to strike. To this end, in spite of the fact that Serbia largely accepted the draconian demands of the Austrian ultimatum of 23 July, which would have turned it into a virtual satellite state, Austria–Hungary declared war on 28 July. Vienna sought nothing less than eradication of an enemy by the destruction of the Serbian state and, fearing even at this late stage that international mediation might prevent war, bombarded Belgrade to make war a fait accompli. If any country behaved as a rogue state in the summer of 1914, it was Austria–Hungary. It wanted a local war with Serbia, even though there was no guarantee that it would not drag in Russia and escalate into a general conflict. This was a gamble that the Austro–Hungarian decision-makers were willing to take. It is clear that a large measure of the responsibility for bringing about the First World War belongs to Austria–Hungary.

Germany was also culpable in starting the war. If we step back and review the July Crisis in greater detail, Germany's critical role is laid bare. When Austria–Hungary's leaders decided to respond to the Sarajevo assassination by attacking Serbia, they looked to its ally for support. Without Berlin's backing it is extremely unlikely the Austro–Hungarian Empire would have gone ahead with its dangerous course of action. Berlin was just as eager for war as Vienna. Emperor Franz Josef wrote to Kaiser Wilhelm on 4 July 1914 that Austria–Hungary wanted to 'eliminate Serbia as a power factor in the Balkans'.[23] On the following day, Count Hoyos, from the Austrian Foreign Ministry, and the Austro–Hungarian ambassador, Count von Szögyény-Marich, had high level discussions in Berlin. Their request for support had a sympathetic hearing from the Kaiser and Arthur Zimmerman from the German Foreign Office. Later, Wilhelm convened a meeting with General Erich von Falkenhayn, Theobald von Bethmann Hollweg, the Chancellor and

Baron Moriz von Lyncker, the head of the Kaiser's Military Cabinet.
The meeting 'considered the question of Russian intervention and
accepted the risk of general war'.[24] That evening Szögyény-Marich
sent a telegram to Vienna:

> [T]he Kaiser authorised me to inform our gracious majesty that
> we might in this case, as in all others, rely upon Germany's full
> support… [but] this action must not be delayed. Russia's attitude
> will no doubt be hostile but for this he had for years prepared and
> should a war between Austria-Hungary and Russia be unavoid-
> able, we might be convinced that Germany, our old faithfully ally,
> would stand by our side. Russia at the present time was in no
> way prepared for war and would think twice before it appealed
> to arms.[25]

Thus on 5 July 1914, Wilhelm II issued what has become known to
history as the 'blank cheque' of unconditional support for Austria-
Hungary, a decision rubber-stamped by Zimmerman and Bethmann Hollweg on the following day.

Germany and Austria-Hungary were united in seeking a decisive confrontation with Serbia, no matter what the risk. Count
Forgách of the Austrian Foreign Ministry wrote privately on 8 July
that Berchtold was:

> determined… to use the horrible deed of Sarajevo for a military-
> clearing up of our impossible relationship with Serbia… With
> Berlin we are in complete agreement. Kaiser & Reich Chancellor
> etc. more decided than ever before; they take on board complete
> cover against Russia, even at the risk of a world war which is not
> ruled out, they consider the moment as favourable & advise to
> strike as soon [as possible]…[26]

At first, the crisis was slow burning, in part because Tisza, the
Hungarian Prime Minister, had to be persuaded to support

military action against Serbia. With some reservations, he agreed on 14 July. Alarmed at the developing situation, on 18 July S.D. Sazonov, the Russian Foreign Minister, told Austria-Hungary that Russia would not tolerate the undermining of Serbian independence. This clear warning to Vienna was reinforced by the French President, Raymond Poincaré, on 21 July, when he pointedly reminded the Austrian ambassador in St Petersburg of the friendship between Russia and Serbia and that France was allied to Russia. This clearly drawn red line was ignored by the Austro-Hungarians, who on 23 July delivered their draconian ultimatum to the Serbian government, the terms of which were so severe that Sazonov's reaction on hearing them on the 24th was 'It's the European war'.[27] Nevertheless, to the surprise of the statesmen of Europe, on 25 July Pasic accepted all but one relatively minor clause. In spite of inflicting national humiliation on Serbia and achieving what any disinterested observer would regard as more than adequate revenge for the assassination, on 28 July Austria-Hungary declared war. On the following day, Belgrade was shelled. The British Foreign Secretary, Sir Edward Grey, deeply alarmed at the turn of events, called in the German ambassador on 29 July to urge mediation and to warn that Britain might get involved in a general war on the side of France and Russia.

Russia responded to Vienna's action by mobilising on 30 July. The next day, Germany issued an ultimatum to Russia and followed that by declaring war on Russia on 1 August and France on the 3rd. Germany demanded that neutral Belgium allow German troops to cross its territory. When the request was refused, the German army invaded Belgium on 4 August. This was the trigger for Britain's declaration of war. With the exception of the Ottoman Empire, which joined the Central Powers (the name given to the German-led coalition) in late October, and Italy, which initially remained neutral, 5 August 1914 found all Europe's Great Powers at war.

It is one thing to lay out what happened in July–August 1914, but quite another to discern the motives of the actors. In the case

Figure 2   Field-Marshal Conrad von Hötzendorf, Chief of the Austro-Hungarian General Staff, 1912–17.

of Austria–Hungary, it seems there was a sense that the credibility, perhaps the very existence, of the Empire was at stake. The wars of 1912–13 had gravely weakened its position in the Balkans, which was the only sphere of influence that it had left. To strike against the newly-powerful and confident Serbia gave Austria–Hungary a chance to stop the rot. Recent research has shown that Vienna had no concrete war aims and powerful individuals such as Conrad were pessimistic about the chances of success. But Austria–Hungary's decision-making elite wore blinkers, focusing on the reckoning with Serbia at all costs. For Austria–Hungary and Germany, 'war had become an aim and an end in itself'.[28]

The Fischer debate

One man above all has shaped the debate on the origins of the First World War over the last fifty years: the German historian Fritz Fischer. His work proved incendiary, particularly in Germany, when it was published in 1961. Fischer broke the consensus that Europe slid into war in 1914 by arguing that the war was caused, in the uncompromising German title of his first book, by 'Germany's grab for world power' (Griff nach der Weltmacht).[29] The local dispute in the Balkans, in which Germany had given firm backing to Austria-Hungary, was escalated in spite of Berlin clearly understanding it was likely to lead to Russian involvement and hence a general European war. In a later book, *War of Illusions,* the July Crisis was placed in context of pre-war German foreign policy, particularly in the four years immediately preceding the war.[30] Fischer gave prominence to the so-called 'War Council' of 8 December 1912, at which, he argued, the decision was taken that war would be launched about eighteen months later. Worried by the rise of the Social Democrats, which to Wilhelm's dismay did well in the Reichstag elections of 1912, the Imperial government took the time-honoured path of war against a foreign enemy to unite the population behind the government. Fear of domestic turmoil thus played a major role in Germany's decision to launch the First World War. In Fischer's words, 'The war provided an opportunity to assert and strengthen the old social and political order and to assimilate the Social Democrats as well'.[31]

Key to Fischer's views was his depiction of Bethmann Hollweg as bent on waging aggressive war. This included showing that the Chancellor took a leading role in formulating the 'September Programme' of territorial annexations designed to cement Germany's domination of the continent. This was quite a turnaround from earlier views of the German Chancellor, who was previously seen as a 'pusillanimous compromiser and appeaser'.[32] As a British historian commented in 1966, 'it is the new view of Bethmann Hollweg's character and purposes as it emerges from the documents Professor Fischer has discovered that has upset people most'.[33] Fischer set out clear continuities between the foreign policies of the Kaiser's Germany and those of the Third Reich. Although the idea of Bethmann Hollweg as a precursor of Hitler seemed far-fetched to some, in the course of the First World War Germany did in fact carve out an empire in the east that, minus the genocidal aspects, prefigured the drive for *Lebensraum* (living space) of the Nazi era. Fischer's thesis was put forward at a time when Germans were still coming to terms with the Second World War. Many saw the Nazi regime as an aberration, with the *Kaiserreich* (empire) representing the true, decent Germany. 'For historians schooled in this tradition', Fischer admitted, 'my book was nothing short of treason'.[34]

Fischer's ideas no longer command support in their entirety. The idea that a deliberate decision to defer war for eighteen months was taken at the so-called War Council of 8 December 1912 has been rejected by many historians,[35] although what happened there is at the very least indicative of the German decision-making elite's willingness to contemplate aggressive war. Similarly, the central role Fischer ascribed to domestic concerns in Germany's path to war has largely been debunked. But Fischer's arguments about the belligerence of German foreign policy before the war, the readiness of the German leadership to court war in pursuit of diplomatic objectives and its decision to initiate aggressive war remain fundamentally sound. German leaders, trusting in their military strength, were set apart from their opposite numbers in the other Great Powers by their willingness to threaten to unleash a European conflict to obtain foreign policy goals.[36]

By manipulating the crisis, Germany hoped to divide the three Entente powers.[37] In previous Balkan crises, Britain and France had been reluctant to support Russia and there appeared to be an opportunity for Germany to break up the Entente without war. Bethmann Hollweg believed that Britain could be kept out of the war. German behaviour from 5 to 30 July can be characterised as a policy of 'calculated risk' or 'brinkmanship'. The blank cheque gave the go-ahead to the Austro-Hungarians to launch a limited and local Third Balkan War but Germany was probably, in this period, prepared only to risk a general conflict, rather than actively create one. In the end, the leadership in Berlin decided to take that fatal extra step, in an extraordinary display of chaotic decision-making (the Kaiser several times changed his mind whether or not to go to war). By issuing an ultimatum to Russia on 31 July, Germany initiated a general European war.[38]

Germany's prophylactic war?

Many historians agree with Fischer's contention that Germany went to war out of pessimism about the future, summed up in the title of one of his books: *World Power or Decline*. In Herwig's words, the leadership in Berlin in July 1914 had a 'strike-now-better-than-later' mentality. Niall Ferguson, among others, has argued that Germany began a preventive war in August 1914 from fear of Russia.[39] In October 1913, Russia had begun its 'Great Military Programme'. This involved a substantial build-up of troop numbers as well as continued growth of the system of strategic railways.[40] Russian military expansion undoubtedly caused anxiety in Berlin: on 18 July, Gottleib von Jagow, the German Secretary for Foreign Affairs, privately stated that 'Russia is not ready to strike at present' but 'According to all competent observation, Russia will be prepared to fight in a few years. Then she will crush us by the number of her soldiers; then she will have built her Baltic fleet and her strategic railroads'.[41] However, there is simply no credible evidence that Russia was planning a war of aggression.[42] The context of the Great Military Programme was the rebuilding of the reputation and strength of the Czarist state after the twin catastrophes of defeat at the hands of Japan and the failed 1905 revolution. Armed forces are symbols of national power and prestige and can be used as instruments of diplomacy and deterrence that can increase the international standing of a state and add weight to a state's diplomacy. Put simply, the possession of large and effective armed forces is not necessarily an indication that a state intends to use them aggressively. The question attributed to Josef Stalin – 'The

Pope? How many divisions has he got?' – was equally relevant to the situation before the First World War. A weakened Russia had been humiliated during the 1908 Bosnian Crisis. The Russian leadership was determined that that should not happen again.

The role of Russia and France

Attempts to assign equal responsibility to Russia, Germany and Austria-Hungary for the outbreak of the First World War ignore the fact that there was a world of difference between Russia's decisions in July 1914, which were backed by France, and those of the Central Powers. Russia responded defensively to the crisis provoked by the Austrian ultimatum to Serbia on 23 July 1914. The Russian reaction was governed by the determination not to let its vital national interests in the Balkans be attacked. Sazonov, the Foreign Minister, saw the threat in stark terms, warning in a ministerial meeting on the following day that Russia's very status as a Great Power was at risk if Austria-Hungary was allowed to get away with this flagrant attempt to reduce Serbia to vassal status. The influential Agriculture Minister, A.V. Krivoshein, recognised the risks involved but believed that only 'by making a firm stand' was there a chance of deterring Germany.[43] French support – and it happened that President Poincaré and his Prime Minister, René Viviani, were in St Petersburg from 20 to 23 July on a prearranged visit – was forthcoming, unlike in 1908, and was important in stiffening Russian resolve. Poincaré was a keen supporter of the agreement with Russia. Shortly after becoming President, he informed the then Russian Foreign minister that he would 'not fail to use [his influence] to ensure... the sanctity of the policy founded on the close alliance with Russia'.[44] During the July crisis, Poincaré viewed supporting Russia as vital to keeping that country out of the arms of Germany and avoiding the nightmare of an immensely strong power bloc, a revival of the nineteenth-century League of Three Emperors, which would leave France isolated and marginalised. Thus Austria-Hungary's bid to halt its decline as a great power by attacking upstart Serbia was resisted by both Russia and France, which feared for their future as great powers if they did nothing.[45]

Russian preliminary moves towards mobilisation on 26 July were not intended to trigger a war: rather, in line with Krivoshein's advice, they were warning shots intended to underline the seriousness of the Austrian move against Serbia and to help persuade Vienna and Berlin, even at this late stage, to step back. It was also a necessary step in preparing Russia for war should the worst happen. Initially the plan was to mobilise only in certain areas, to underline that this was a response to Austria, so pre-mobilisation moves were not extended across Russia. It was hoped that Germany would read this limited move as evidence that the Czar's government was seeking to avoid provocative measures. In the event, on 30 July, St. Petersburg ordered a full mobilisation in response to the Austrian attack on Serbia. As one official explained, 'a partial mobilization could be carried out only at the price of dislocating the entire machinery of general mobilization': should the war spread beyond the Balkans, the Russians 'would be powerless to defend ourselves on the frontiers of Poland and East Prussia'.[46] Russian mobilisation proved a gift to the German government, as it allowed it to portray the war as defensive. This was important in rallying otherwise wavering members of German society behind the government.

British entry into the war

There was nothing inevitable about the British entry into the war. In late July and at the beginning of August 1914, the Liberal government, led by H.H. Asquith, was deeply divided over the issues of war and peace. This reflected the state of opinion in the country as a whole. Various church groups, and the Labour movement, had no love for the Czar's regime and there was a widespread belief that a quarrel in the Balkans was no concern of Britain's. While

Figure 3 David Lloyd George, British Prime Minster, 1916–22.

some Cabinet ministers, such as Grey and Lord Haldane, believed that Britain should uphold the balance of power by supporting France, others took a contrary view. Even Asquith initially thought that Britain should stay out of the war. One of the most influential members of the Cabinet was David Lloyd George, Chancellor of the Exchequer and the radical Welsh conscience of the still-powerful non-conformist lobby. If Lloyd George had pushed his opposition to British participation in the war to the point of resignation, the government would probably have collapsed. And yet on 4 August, Asquith's government, with Lloyd George remaining a prominent member, brought a largely united nation into the war.

What changed the situation was the German invasion of Belgium. Both Britain and Germany (the latter through its predecessor state of Prussia) had guaranteed the independence and neutrality of Belgium in a treaty of 1839. That a major power should simply rip up an international agreement was regarded as a moral outrage, causing genuine anger.[47] Before 1914, German war planners had been aware of the likely consequences of violating Belgian neutrality but had chosen to ignore them. It is well within the realms of possibility that, had Germany attacked France without marching through Belgium, Britain would have stayed out of the war, or at least that it would have caused a political crisis that delayed British support for France. This could have had catastrophic consequences for the French. German strategic myopia thus gratuitously added an enemy to the forces ranged against them and threw away an opportunity to gain a major advantage in the initial campaign in the west.

Sir Edward Grey has been harshly criticised for not making it clear, early in the July Crisis, that Britain would stand by France and Russia. If he had done so − or so the argument goes − Germany could have been deterred from starting the war.[48] This is unfair on two counts. First, the realities of British party politics meant that Grey was unable to give this assurance. Second, it is bizarre to assign war guilt to a man who strenuously worked for peace, proposing an international conference or mediation on six occasions during the July Crisis.

Niall Ferguson has put forward the argument that the British were wrong to fight in 1914. Had they stayed out, Germany would have won and a 'Kaiser's European Union' would have emerged. This Panglossian view has not achieved much acceptance among historians. In reality, quite apart from the moral dimension of failing to resist blatant aggression and breaches of international law (in 2013 a prominent academic theologian argued persuasively that according to the Christian principles of just war, Britain was right to fight in 1914),[49] the consequences of a German victory would have been cataclysmic for Britain. The British had every reason to be concerned about the German invasion of Belgium. Maintaining maritime security by keeping the coast of the Low Countries out of the hands of a hostile power had been a staple of British foreign policy for centuries. German occupation of Belgium posed a similar threat to that of the occupation of the same territory by another naval rival, Revolutionary and Napoleonic France, a century before and provoked the same response. Similarly, opposition to attempts to achieve hegemony by continental powers had led Britain to join many coalitions to restore the balance of power. Had Britain turned its back on France and Russia in 1914, Germany probably would have won the war. Britain would have been isolated, friendless, facing a continent controlled by a neo-autocratic and aggressive foe in which democracy had been largely snuffed out. Britain could well have been faced with war with Germany some time after 1914, which the British would have had to fight without allies. For Britain, the war that broke out in August 1914 was a very traditional conflict. The Germany of Wilhelm II joined the Spain of Philip II and the France of Louis XIV and Napoleon on the roll-call of aggressors that Britain had opposed over the years.[50]

THE ROLE OF MILITARISM IN CAUSING THE WAR

Many historians have moved away from detailed examinations of the diplomacy and decision-making of the July Crisis to analyse the underlying causes of the war. One popular explanation between the two world wars was the role of 'great armaments'. However, there is no evidence that arms races necessarily lead directly to conflict; the US–Soviet nuclear arms race is a case in point. Certainly, the Anglo-German naval building competition before the First World War destabilised relations between the two states but the German army's invasion of Belgium was the *casus belli* for Britain. The context of military build-up helped create an atmosphere of uncertainty and distrust between the powers that fed into the wider mood of militarism; not just readiness to use armed force in support of state policy but the excessive admiration of military culture, deference to armed forces, belief in the benefits of war and Social Darwinist thinking (that is, the idea of the 'survival of the fittest' applied to international relations).[51]

The so-called 'war by timetable' thesis argues that rigid military plans tied the hands of politicians during the crucial days of July and

August 1914. There was a general fear that being slower to mobilise than the enemy would set an army at a disadvantage from the
start, as had happened to the French in 1870. When, on 1 August,
the unpredictable Kaiser suddenly demanded that the German armies
be sent against Russia alone, sparing France, General Helmuth von
Moltke, the Army Chief of Staff, had to say 'no'. There was no alternative to the Schlieffen Plan, by which the bulk of the German army
would be deployed in the west, and it was logistically impossible to
unpick it at that stage.[52] In that armies were dependent on carefully-
choreographed mobilisation plans that rested on the use of inher-
ently inflexible railways, the 'war by timetable' idea contains some
truth. Russia, seeking to send a clear signal of its alarm at Austro-
Hungarian and German policy in the Balkans, mobilised its armies on
31 July 1914. The original idea of mobilising solely against Austria was
scrapped because it was unworkable. The unfortunate side-effect of
this defensive move was to ratchet up tension and play into the hands
of the Germans: as already noted, it allowed the war that Berlin was
about to launch to be depicted as defensive and thus helped unite the
population against the Russian bogey.

However, the notion that civilian leaders were, to use an apt
term, 'railroaded' into war by 'gung-ho' generals does not bear scrutiny. Both Moltke and his Austro-Hungarian counterpart Conrad von
Hötzendorf had been urging war for some years, but only in summer
1914 were their strident demands finally aligned with the decision of
the politicians to go to war. While these men were far more influential than their counterparts in France, Russia and Britain, their views
were not decisive in tipping the deliberations of the decision-making
elite in Vienna and Berlin in favour of war.

The verdict

The view that the outbreak of war was avoidable is absolutely
correct. Abstract forces such as 'nationalism', 'imperialism' and
'militarism', and issues such as Anglo-German naval rivalry and
domestic tensions within the Great Powers did not cause the war,
although they all may have made it more likely. However, as the
British historian David Stevenson has written, 'The European
peace [in 1914] might have been a house of cards, but someone
still had to topple it'.[53] The First World War came about because
key individuals in Austria–Hungary and Germany took conscious

decisions to achieve diplomatic objectives, even at the cost of conflict with Russia and France. The responses of Russia, France and eventually Britain to the events in the Balkans and their consequences were essentially reactive and defensive. The actions of the Great Powers in limiting the damage from previous Balkan crises strongly suggests that had the Austrians and Germans wished it, the crisis of summer 1914 could have been resolved by the action of the international community, which would have isolated and punished Serbia but left its independence and security intact. On this occasion, however, Austria–Hungary and Germany wanted war. To return to but invert Clark's 'whodunit' metaphor, there *is* a smoking pistol in this story; or rather, there are two, in the hands of Austria–Hungary and Germany. The outbreak of war was certainly a tragedy but it was also a crime committed by the leaders of two aggressor states.

2
From Clash of Arms to Stalemate, 1914–15

Western Front 1914[1]

The military operations that commenced in August 1914 were on a scale that dwarfed even those of the Franco–German War of 1870–71. Both the Germans and the French were seeking to emulate the rapid and decisive victories achieved by the Prussian-led armies forty years earlier. However, other recent wars – such as the American Civil War (1861–65) and the Russo-Japanese War (1904–05) – had shown how difficult it could be to achieve swift and decisive victory. While a large French force had been surrounded and forced to capitulate at Sedan in September 1870, the armies of late-nineteenth century industrialised states were increasingly resilient, not least because they were larger. The German states had initially put 462,000 men into the field in 1870 but about 1.4 million in August 1914. The growth of the population of Europe in the nineteenth century, from 187 million in 1800 to 468 million in 1914, created a much larger pool of manpower, which states could draw on for their armies. Two other developments aided the trend toward gigantism of European armies. The first was the development of popular nationalism; the second was increasing control of the state over the individual. At the end of the Napoleonic Wars, the French state's increasingly desperate attempts to conscript men into the army led to ever larger numbers of men successfully dodging the draft. Across Europe, a hundred years later, it was both more difficult to avoid the clutches of the military, and in most cases socially unacceptable to do so, as the rights of citizenship were increasingly seen to be linked to the obligation to defend the state.[2]

Over the last two centuries, rapid, decisive victories on land have only occurred when an army had a significant advantage over the enemy. In 1870, Prussian organisation, generalship and staff work were all hugely superior to that of the French. No army had such a marked advantage in 1914. As the guns of August sounded, the combination of broadly similar, huge armies with plentiful reserves of men, backed by societies that supported the war effort of the state to a greater or lesser degree, combined with destructive modern weaponry, pointed, for those with eyes to see, towards attrition.

Generals were not completely blind to these developments. The increasing lethality of weapons, especially artillery, had been manifest in recent wars, especially the campaigns fought in Manchuria between Japan and Russia a decade earlier and the Balkan Wars of 1912–13. But the 'lessons' were less obvious than they appear a century later. In spite of the temporary deadlock and huge casualties in Manchuria, it seemed that a lesson was that well-motivated troops who possessed the willpower to cross the danger zone to get to grips with the enemy would prevail, albeit at a heavy cost in life. By no means all generals believed the war would be short. In Britain, both Field Marshal Lord Kitchener, the Secretary of State for War and Lieutenant-General Sir Douglas Haig, who would go on to command the British Army on the Western Front, believed the struggle would be lengthy. France's Chief-of-Staff, General Joseph Joffre, prepared the French army for a brief conflict with Germany but was well aware that such a war could last well beyond the initial clashes.[3] In part, it was a case of what the market would bear. The collapse of Russia into revolution after defeat at the hands of Japan was a very recent warning of what might happen to societies under the strain of a prolonged war. Suspicions of the reliability of the working classes lurked not far below the surface. The German military elite harboured doubts about whether the war really would end in six months but given the fact that they faced powerful enemies on two fronts, they chose to pin their hopes on, in Moltke's words, 'ending the war… as quickly as possible by way of a few great strikes'.[4]

KEY COMMANDERS IN THE EARLY BATTLES OF THE WAR

Helmuth von Moltke (1848–1916)

General Helmuth von Moltke ('the Younger') is best remembered for his inability to retain control of his rapidly advancing armies during the invasion of France and Belgium in summer 1914. He was the nephew of the nineteenth century military commander Field-Marshal Helmuth von Moltke 'the Elder' (1800–1891). His family connections did his career no harm. Succeeding Field-Marshal Alfred von Schlieffen (1833–1913) as Chief of the German General Staff in 1906, it was Moltke's task to revise the former's carefully devised 'Schlieffen Plan' to meet the changing conditions of modern warfare. This earned him great criticism, which was not wholly deserved. He was a pre-war 'hawk', who favoured the waging of a pre-emptive war by Germany.[5] Moltke's personality and temperament combined to make him totally unqualified to handle the inherent stresses and strains of a war on two fronts. Above all, he lacked self-confidence. Command and control failures resulted in the decisive strategic reverse at the First Battle of the Marne (5–12 September 1914). This clear Allied victory, followed by the precipitate retreat of the German armies and the onset of trench warfare, led to Moltke's dismissal on 14 September. He died a broken and embittered man in June 1916.

Joseph Joffre (1852–1931)

The steadfast and imperturbable commander of the French armies on the Western Front from 1914 to 1916, Joseph-Jacques Césaire Joffre assured his place in history with his victory on the Marne in September 1914. Joffre was born of humble parentage in the Pyrénées commune of Rivesaltes and graduated from the *École Polytechnique* in 1870. Active service in the Franco-Prussian War was followed by colonial postings to Indochina, West Africa and Madagascar. Joffre was appointed Chief of the General Staff in 1911, a position that automatically led to him becoming Commander-in-Chief when war broke out. In the three years prior to the war Joffre devised 'Plan XVII' which called for a series of all-out offensives across the Franco-German border. This proved a bloody failure in August 1914 and was thrown out of joint by the German Schlieffen Plan. Caught unaware and faced with retreat and imminent defeat, Joffre showed that he possessed an abundance of iron nerve and force of character – exactly the traits that his opponent Moltke the Younger lacked. Joffre's strategy of attrition once the Western Front deadlock began was basically correct but his series of costly and barren offensives during 1915, coupled with apparent lack of preparation to meet the German offensive at Verdun in 1916, caused politicians to become disillusioned with him.

In December 1916 he was created Marshal of France and elevated to a meaningless position. Joffre's career was over and he sat out the rest of the war, a sad figure lacking power or even influence, and formally retired in 1919.

Sir John French (1852–1925)

Field-Marshal Sir John Denton Pinkstone French commanded the BEF (British Expeditionary Force) on the Western Front until December 1915. Commissioned in 1874, he gained professional recognition and national fame for his dynamic leadership of the British cavalry during the Second South African War (1899–1902), where Douglas Haig was his Chief of Staff. Appointed Chief of the Imperial General Staff in 1912, his leadership of the BEF in mobile battles on the continent was uninspired. The long, difficult retreat to the environs of Paris demonstrated that French was out of his depth and lacked the talents to thrive as a commander in a coalition. During 1914 and 1915, French steadily lost the confidence of key figures: the King; Lord Kitchener, the Secretary of State for War and a long-term rival; the influential staff officer, Lieutenant-General Sir William Robertson; and Haig, once French's protégé but now disillusioned with his leadership. French's tenure of command came under increased scrutiny during the costly and strategically barren battles of 1915, during which he was often ill and inaccessible. The failure of the Loos offensive in September and especially his clumsy attempt to make a scapegoat of Haig over the mishandling of the reserves forced French to resign in December of that year. He went on to hold a number of important home commands, including Viceroy during the unsuccessful campaign to reassert British rule in his ancestral homeland, Ireland.

Erich von Falkenhayn (1861–1922)

General Erich von Falkenhayn was one of the most thoughtful but also the most ruthless soldiers of the war. Early on, he recognised that Germany was unlikely to prevail in a long-drawn out war with the Entente. Therefore he was unusual among senior commanders on either side in being willing to settle for a less than complete victory.[6] A personal favourite of Kaiser Wilhelm II, Falkenhayn gained active military experience in China during the Boxer Rebellion (1900). Serving in the important post of Prussian Minister of War from 1913–15, Falkenhayn replaced the discredited Helmuth von Moltke as Chief of the General Staff following the First Battle of the Marne in September 1914. Convinced of the Western Front's strategic primacy, he nevertheless could see the war as a whole, and so grudgingly sanctioned major operations against Russia during 1915 when he would have preferred a separate peace with Russia or France. This strategic policy was continued in 1916, much to the consternation of the Eastern

Front commanders Hindenburg and Ludendorff. Falkenhayn instead concentrated Germany's main offensive effort at Verdun, with the object of forcing France to the negotiating table.

However, Falkenhayn's strategy unravelled. The fighting at Verdun gained unstoppable momentum, the Russians attacked on the Eastern Front and the British and French on the Somme, and his woes were capped by Romania's declaration of war. Falkenhayn was summarily dismissed in August 1916. Replaced by the seemingly more dynamic partnership of Field Marshal Paul von Hindenburg and General Erich Ludendorff, he spent the remainder of the war commanding, with some success, armies in Romania, Palestine and Lithuania. A characteristically cool and dispassionate war memoir was published three years before Falkenhayn's death at Potsdam in April 1922. Unlike his successors, who abandoned his limited strategy for the path of defeat and destruction, Falkenhayn showed a bleakly realistic appreciation of Germany's situation and formed his plans accordingly.

German war strategy was based on the plan devised by Field-Marshal Alfred von Schlieffen, Chief of the General Staff until 1906. The Schlieffen Plan, as modified by Moltke, was a massive offensive by seventy-three divisions, intended to knock France out of the war in six weeks.[7] Following this, forces would be shifted from west to east to face the invading Russian Army. The key to this huge gamble was the circumvention of the heavily fortified portion of the French frontier between Luxembourg and Switzerland by violating the neutrality of Belgium. Faced with having to fight a general war on two fronts, it appeared to German planners to be the only option. The invasion of Belgium would, if all went according to plan, bring about a right-wing sweep by three armies to encircle Paris. The remaining French defenders, having been driven eastward, would be forced back on to their frontier fortress area and be annihilated. Moltke clearly identified the likely British reaction to such blatant aggression but discounted it; the war would be over before the British strength of naval and financial power could make a difference. Some debate over whether or not the Schlieffen Plan was a post-war construct to explain away German defeat in the First

Figure 4   General Erich von Falkenhayn, Chief of the German General Staff,
1914–16.

World War has contributed to controversy over the last decade.[8]
This viewpoint, however, has failed to attract much support.

French war strategy was embodied in Plan XVII, a gigantic
general offensive by five armies (823,000 men) designed to liber-
ate Alsace and Lorraine and then invade Germany. This scheme,
despite the fact that French military planners clearly recognised
that Belgian neutrality might be violated by the Germans in a bold
attempt to bypass their fortified frontier zone, failed to take into
account the extent of the territorial violation or the possibility that
Germany would employ military reserves to increase the strength
of its peacetime regular army. Thus, having underestimated both

Figure 5   Field-Marshal Sir John French, Commander-in-Chief of the British Expeditionary Force, 1914–15.

enemy intentions and the size of the German army, the French left flank, with the small British Expeditionary Force (BEF), originally comprising four infantry and a cavalry division under Field-Marshal Sir John French, extending the Allied line, would remain open as three of the five armies advanced to regain the lost provinces.

The war in the west opened with the German invasion of Luxembourg and Belgium on 2 August 1914. Spirited resistance by the 265,000-man Belgian army, especially at the fortress of Liège and the great city-port of Antwerp, delayed but ultimately failed to stem the relentless enemy advance that over-ran over three-quarters of the country, including Brussels and Antwerp.

Meanwhile, France's Plan XVII, underpinned by the doctrine of *offensive à outrance* (all-out attack) stalled in the face of fierce opposition. Wearing colourful uniforms of blue coats and red trousers, in actions such as Morhange-Sarrebourg and Virton and Semois in mid-August, the French army suffered appalling casualties. On 22 August, for instance, two Colonial divisions sustained losses of 11,650 men.[9] German attacks were also hugely costly.

Further to the north, the French were forced into a two week-long retreat, although they turned and temporarily blunted the advance of the German right wing at the Battle of Guise (28 August). The British fell back in parallel. General Sir Horace Smith-Dorrien's II Corps carried out a defensive action at Mons on 23 August. It fought well but was forced back by superior numbers. The British losses, of about 1,600 men, were small by later standards but caused shock at home, leading to a surge of enlistments in the army. Three days later, II Corps, by now separated from Lieutenant-General Sir Douglas Haig's I Corps, was forced to turn and fight again, at Le Cateau. This battle was much more serious, with heavier British casualties. Smith-Dorrien was able to do sufficient damage to the Germans to allow him to disengage and resume the retreat, although it took several days for II Corps' cohesion to recover.

Moltke, sensing victory, sought to carry out a double envelopment to crush the Allied armies. It was not to be. Joffre, radiating energy, abandoned Plan XVII and carried out a far-reaching purge of failed generals. Constantly in contact with his commanders in the field, he scraped together forces to create a Sixth Army. General Alexander von Kluck, the commander of German First Army, played into Joffre's hands by swinging his army to pass to the east rather than the west of Paris, thus exposing its flank. Joffre launched a counter-offensive from the environs of Paris. The decisive Battle of the Marne (5–12 September 1914) halted the German advance on the French capital and thus destroyed Germany's best chance of winning the First World War. The Germans were left with no alternative than a general strategic retirement, with the Allied armies in pursuit. The Germans turned and fought along the heights above

Figure 6   Field-Marshal Helmuth von Moltke the Younger, Chief of the German General Staff, 1906–14.

the River Aisne. In heavy fighting (13–16 September), the BEF came close to breaking through. German forces arrived in the area just in time and the fighting soon turned into primitive trench warfare, characterised by barbed wire obstacles, crude entrench-ments and supporting artillery concentrations. Although no one at the time knew it, the struggle on the Aisne set the stage for the deadlock to come.

Germany's great military gamble in the west had broken down due to adherence to overambitious strategic objectives, inadequate logistic support primarily based on horse-drawn transport and failure to take into account consequent Allied use of the French railway system as an effective means of shifting troops when and where required. Joffre's dynamic generalship, his finger constantly on the pulse of his armies, contrasted strongly with Moltke's hesitant performance. Just as the military thinker Carl von Clausewitz had argued a century before, battle remained a contest between the wills of opposing commanders. Whereas Joffre had personally taken the decision to attack on the Marne, the German decision to withdraw in the face of the Allied assault was made by an Army commander and a middle-ranking officer from Moltke's staff without reference to Moltke himself.[10]

Moltke suffered a nervous breakdown and was replaced by General Erich von Falkenhayn, who reinvigorated the German offensive, beginning the so-called 'Race to the Sea' (October–November 1914) during which both sides attempted to escape the impasse on the Aisne and re-establish a war of manoeuvre by exploiting the open flanks to the northeast. Heavy but inconclusive fighting in Picardy and Artois was but a prelude to the long drawn-out struggle in Flanders, where British, French and Belgian forces successfully withstood a series of German offensives aimed at breaking through and capturing the strategically vital Channel ports. The Belgians protected the Allied flank by deliberately breaching the sea defences at Nieuport, thus inundating the land. The climax of the fighting came at the First Battle of Ypres in late October to early November. Although French and Belgian forces were heavily involved, the two German attacks that came closest to succeeding were launched against Haig's British I Corps, on 31 October and 11 November 1914. On both occasions the line held – but only just.

By mid-November 1914, the armies were temporarily exhausted and primitive trench warfare had emerged across the stalemated Western Front that extended some 400 miles from Switzerland to the sea. The numbers of dead, wounded, missing and prisoners were staggering. In August–September, the Germans and French each suffered around 333,000 casualties. Germany, fighting of course a

Figure 7 Marshal Joseph Joffre, Commander-in-Chief of the French Army, 1911–16.

two-front war, lost 800,000 men between August 1914 and January 1915. Officially, 116,000 of those casualties were killed and 85,000 of these fatalities occurred in the west, but record-keeping could be inaccurate; the actual number of German dead might have amounted to some 240,000. French casualties between August 1914 and January 1915 amounted to 528,000 and perhaps as many as 300,000 were killed. The British had losses of around 90,000 by the end of 1914 and the Belgians lost 50,000 in the fighting in October–November 1914 alone.

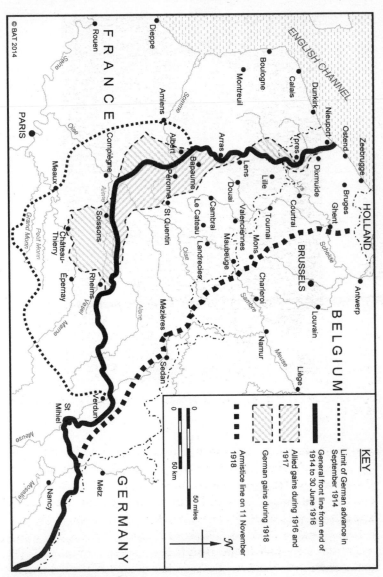

Map 1   The Western Front

Eastern Front 1914

The fighting on the Eastern Front, extending from the marshes of East Prussia to the Carpathian mountains, remained comparatively fluid compared to that in the western theatre, which was hemmed in by the sea on one flank and mountains on the other. The vast spaces in the east meant that there was always a flank to turn or a weakly held front to penetrate. The reverse side of the coin was that, in comparison to France and Belgium, Eastern Europe's infrastructure was under-developed, meaning that it was much more difficult to support large modern armies in prolonged campaigns. Operations took on a pre-modern character: 'State of the art weapons depended for their ammunition on wagons without springs hauled by oxen along barely-marked tracks'.[11]

Franco-Russian war plans were dependent on the latter deploying and striking with its massive army to divert German strength from the west. Germany would remain on the defensive whilst Austria-Hungary, which lacked the strength to conduct two major offensive operations simultaneously, responded to Russian mobilisation by making operations against Russia the main effort, while downgrading the importance of the campaign against Serbia. Operations began with the invasion of East Prussia by two Russian armies in mid-August 1914. Russian ineptitude, including the broadcast of radio messages *en clair* (unencrypted),[12] geographical circumstances and superior leadership of the defending German Eighth Army combined to inflict a crushing defeat (122,000 casualties and the loss of 500 artillery pieces or guns) on the Russian Second Army at the Battle of Tannenberg (23–30 August). German losses were approximately 15,000 killed, wounded and missing. Eighth Army, commanded by the victorious duo of Hindenburg and Ludendorff, then wheeled northwards in a bold attempt to engage the neighbouring Russian First Army. The resultant Battle of the Masurian Lakes (9–14 September) forced the invaders back to the Russian frontier. German soil had been cleared of the enemy.

On 16 August, Conrad launched four Austro-Hungarian Armies against the Russians. Opposed by 1,200,000 Russian defenders, the advance made considerable progress, with victories at Krasnik (23–26 August) and Komarow (26–31 August). However, the Germans failed to mount a supporting offensive into Poland. The Austrian push was brought to a standstill in mid-September and then reversed by the Russians in three weeks of fighting, with the staggering loss of 300,000 men and 300 guns; like the armies in the west, the Austrians and Russians learned the price of attacking in the face of modern weapons. The key fortress town of Lemberg was abandoned and the equally important fortified town of Przemysl left to be invested by the Russians.

The end of September saw fresh offensives flare into life. The Germans attacked first in Poland on 29 September, the newly-formed Ninth Army attaining the line of the River Vistula by 9 October. A Russian scheme to invade Silesia was halted during the twin battles of Lòdz and Lowicz (16–25 November), after which they retired to secure river defences west of Warsaw. To the Germans, Russian soldiers seemed 'easy to defeat but hard to kill'.[13] The armies of the Central Powers had had the best of the encounters but the Russians were far from decisively defeated. Thereafter, the Eastern Front lapsed into temporary deadlock as winter set in.

Serbian Campaign 1914

Austria-Hungary sent three Armies (about 460,000 men), commanded by General Oskar Potiorek, against Serbia. The 400,000-man defending army of twelve divisions, under General Radomir Putnik, could only rely on neighbouring Montenegro for immediate military support. The invasion opened with the bombardment of Belgrade by Austrian gunboats on 29 July 1914; ground forces crossed the Serbian frontier on 12 August. The subsequent fighting resulted in a 'David and Goliath' outcome that smashed the Austrians and surprised the world. The Serb victory, however, proved short-lived. Short of ammunition and supplies and facing a hugely superior enemy, they successfully repelled attempts to seize the capital before its abandonment on 2 December. Belgrade was nevertheless regained two weeks later and Hapsburg forces were pushed back over the frontier in a startlingly successful counter-offensive (5–15 December). Austro-Hungarian losses from 12 August to mid-December amounted to 227,000 men killed, wounded and missing and 179 guns. Serbian losses were an estimated 85,000 killed, wounded and missing but they had beaten back the Austro-Hungarian offensive – for the moment.

War at sea 1914–15[14]

Before 1914, when people thought about naval power, they thought about battleships. The pre-war naval competition between Britain and Germany had been concentrated on these mighty armoured beasts. In 1906, the British First Sea Lord (the professional head of the Royal Navy), Admiral of the Fleet Sir John 'Jacky' Fisher, launched HMS *Dreadnought,* a revolutionary 'all big gun' design, with ten 12-inch guns and steam turbine propulsion that gave her, for the time, the exceptionally fast speed of twenty-one knots. Older 'pre-Dreadnoughts' became obsolescent. The French battleship *Bouvet,* for instance, commissioned in 1898, had only two 12-inch guns, a substantial secondary armament and a speed of eighteen knots. *Bouvet* was sunk off Gallipoli in 1915. In 1908–09 Fisher introduced a new category of capital ship: the 'battlecruiser'. These had a battleship's firepower but even greater speed, which was the trade-off for the potential vulnerability of thinner armour. When war broke out, the Royal Navy had twenty-two dreadnoughts, with another thirteen building, and nine battlecruisers and one under construction. Germany had fifteen dreadnoughts, with five building, and five battlecruisers, with another three being built. Furthermore, a new generation of 'super dreadnought' battleships, such as HMS *Queen Elizabeth,* had been launched, moving the arms race to another level.

Both popular and naval opinion was shaped by interpretations of the theories of the influential American thinker, Alfred T. Mahan. He held that that navies should seek to control the sea, which involved decisive victory over the enemy fleet. The victorious power would then be in a position to starve the opponent into surrender or bring about economic collapse by disruption of the enemy's trade. Against this background, it is not surprising that many expected that shortly after the outbreak of war between Britain and Germany there would be a 'new Trafalgar', a clash of dreadnoughts in the North Sea. There was some disappointment and surprise when this did not happen. When eventually the two battle fleets met, off the coast of Jutland in May 1916, the outcome was indecisive and a full-scale battle did not reoccur.

This did not mean the navies were inactive. In fact, a new Trafalgar proved superfluous, as the Allied – mainly British – navies had an effective margin of dominance at sea from the beginning to the end of the war. It did not go unchallenged – in particular, German submarines posed a major threat. This British naval dominance at sea was of the greatest possible significance, a primary factor in ensuring that the Entente and not the Central Powers won the First World War. Exercising this dominance mainly took the form of escort duties, blockade enforcement and anti-submarine warfare rather than clashes of battleships. Two hugely significant strategic successes were achieved by the Royal Navy within the first few days of the war, without a shot being fired. The first was the severing, in the early hours of 5 August by a British cable ship, *Alert,* of the trans-Atlantic cables that connected Germany with the neutral United States.[15] This placed Germany at a severe disadvantage in the battle with the Allies to disseminate propaganda in the USA and forced the Germans to communicate with their diplomats in the USA by cables that touched British territory or by wireless messages – both of which could be intercepted and deciphered, as was to be the case with the 'Zimmermann Telegram' in February 1917. The German Foreign Office made a clumsy attempt to entice Mexico into joining Germany in a future war against the USA by bribing them with territory lost in the Mexican–American War in the 1840s. The British passed on the message to Washington. When the telegram was made public (and obligingly confirmed as authentic by the German Foreign Minister, Arthur Zimmermann himself) it caused outrage and did much to swing the American people behind the US declaration of war a few weeks later.

The second strategic success was that the BEF was safely conveyed to France without a single transport ship being lost. Indeed, troop and supply ships crossed the English Channel unmolested throughout the war. Sea power thus enabled expeditionary warfare, giving the Allies great strategic 'reach' and flexibility. In 1914, it allowed Australian and New Zealand troops to be conveyed from the Antipodes first to Egypt (escorted part of the way by the navy of Britain's ally, Japan) and then to France. In the following year, sea power allowed the campaign to be fought at the Dardanelles and an Allied force to be transported to the Balkans and subsequently sustained at the Greek port of Salonika. In the latter cases, it might be said that sea power gave the Allies rather too many options.

In a naval war with Germany, Britain had strategic geography on its side. The British Isles lay squarely across Germany's access to the wider world. The English Channel could be made impassable by minefields and the Grand Fleet, based at Scapa Flow in the Orkney Islands, blocked the way through the North Sea. The senior leadership of the Royal Navy was not anxious to risk their capital ships in open battle. Merely by remaining undefeated, the Royal Navy was achieving strategic success.

Some German naval strategists had similar views about risking 'Wilhelm's mechanical toy', as one German officer called the High Seas Fleet. These were reinforced by a small-scale British victory fought close to the German coast (the Battle of Heligoland Bight, 28 August 1914)[16] but a strategy emerged of wearing down the Royal Navy by a series of small probing attacks into the North Sea. The object was to isolate and destroy elements of the British fleet. Before the war it was hoped that such operations could be carried out close to the German coast, but the British decision to retaliate through the use of distant blockade, (that is, deploying ships far out at sea rather than inshore, to prevent merchant shipping from reaching German or neutral ports) put paid to this idea. Instead, hoping to lure out and defeat small portions of the British fleet, the German High Seas Fleet raided the east coast of England in December 1914, shelling the coastal towns of Scarborough, Hartlepool and West Hartlepool, and Whitby.

British codebreakers (based in Room 40 in the Admiralty building) were intercepting and reading German naval wireless signal traffic. While not fool-proof, this gave the Royal Navy a huge potential advantage. On 24 January 1915, the codebreakers of Room 40 discovered the German fleet was making another sortie and Vice-Admiral Sir David Beatty's battlecruisers sailed to intercept it. The old German cruiser *Blucher* was sunk and, but for command confusion among the British, the German losses in the Battle of Dogger Bank could have been even greater.

The British decision to mount a distant blockade meant that merchant vessels of all nationalities approaching the British Isles ran the risk of being stopped and boarded by the Royal Navy. Contraband – which amounted to anything that could aid the German war effort – was seized. While it was possible for ships to sneak through the blockade and reach German ports, in practice Germany was rapidly deprived of seaborne commerce. The consequences soon manifested themselves in the form of food shortages in German cities, in large part the product of British ruthlessness and naval efficiency.

However, naval affairs did not go entirely smoothly for the Allies. The escape of two German warships to then neutral Constantinople in October 1914 was an embarrassment for the British and helped bring the Ottomans into the war on the side of the Central Powers. The outbreak of war found some German warships on the oceans, with no hope of reaching Germany. They were gradually hunted down and eliminated but in the meantime acted as commerce raiders. Admiral von Spee's East Asia Squadron was cut off from Germany but Spee was determined to do maximum damage before it was destroyed. At the Battle of Coronel, off the coast of Chile, on 1 November 1914, the Squadron destroyed a weaker British force. However, a squadron of modern ships was sent from Britain and Spee's force was crushingly defeated at the Battle of the Falkland Islands, 8 December 1914.

THE BEGINNINGS OF WAR IN THE AIR

The exploitation of the sky for military purposes long predated 1914. During the 1790s, the French used balloons for reconnaissance on campaign and in 1849 the Austrians attempted to use them to drop bombs. A major step in the development of air power arrived in the 1870s, when balloons began to be combined with engines to produce 'airships', with one or more 'gondolas' for the crew. A further breakthrough came with the invention of the rigid airship, which enclosed the gas-filled 'envelope' in a metal frame. At the beginning of the twentieth century, Germany in particular embraced the airship for both military and civil use with enthusiasm, launching a programme presided over by Graf (Count) Ferdinand von Zeppelin. It seemed to some that the future of military aviation belonged to airships. It is significant that in his 1908 novel *The War in the Air,* the British writer H.G. Wells portrayed cities being destroyed by fleets of airships rather than aeroplanes.

Orville and Wilbur Wright had succeeded in getting a primitive aeroplane briefly airborne at Kitty Hawk, North Carolina in 1903. In the eleven years before the outbreak of the First World War, the heavier-than-air craft emerged as a serious rival to the airship, especially from 1908, when the Wright brothers began to demonstrate their invention. By the time war came, the major powers had all invested, to a greater or lesser degree, in aircraft. The implications for British security of Louis Blériot's 1909 flight across the English Channel were profound. Potentially, the Royal Navy's dominance at sea was no longer enough to keep Britain safe from invasion.

The aircraft available to the armies and navies of Europe in August 1914, such as the Blériot XI used by both the British and the French and the German Taube, were rudimentary. The main use of aircraft was for reconnaissance, and the role of Allied airmen in detecting the German manoeuvre in early September 1914 that led to the Battle of the Marne demonstrated to any remaining doubters the utility of the aeroplane in war. Likewise, German reconnaissance machines proved invaluable during the Tannenberg campaign on the Eastern Front. As one historian has commented, 'The age of armies marching blindly around Europe was gone for good and the aeroplane was the reason for this change'.[17] When trench warfare began in the west in 1914, the roles of aircraft were adapted to spot for artillery. By spring 1915, photographic reconnaissance by aircraft enabled accurate maps of enemy trenches to be created. The beginning of what historians have called a 'Revolution in Military Affairs' was underway.

Although air combat had been foreseen before the war, early aircraft had no fixed armament and aerial combat consisted of observers attempting to shoot at aeroplanes with carbines or revolvers. As the value of air reconnaissance became apparent, things began to change. It became imperative to prevent the 'eyes in the sky' from crossing the lines, and so aircraft began to be armed. There was a breakthrough in early 1915 when Raymond Saulnier, a Frenchman, attached 'deflector plates' to the blades of a propeller, which allowed a machine gun to be fired straight down the nose of an aircraft. This was a major step forward in the creation of a true fighter aircraft and the French formed *Escadrilles de Chasse* (hunting squadrons), with the discrete role of destroying enemy aeroplanes. Roland Garros, flying a Morane-Saulnier Type L, achieved the first 'kill' using this device. However, in the summer of 1915, the Germans were using a superior device fitted in the Fokker E1 monoplane. This was an interrupter gear, which meant that the machine gun could only fire when the propeller was not in alignment with the gun muzzle. The Fokker gave the Germans a crucial margin of superiority over the Western Front in the second part of 1915. The Allies responded with new aircraft types and the Battle of Verdun, which began in February 1916, saw history's first concerted struggle between air forces to achieve air superiority as part of a wider ground battle. Initially the Germans had the advantage, but it swung to the French in March 1916, 'a situation that had great and perhaps decisive influence on the outcome of the battle'.[18]

The activities of 'aces' such as Garros, the German Max Immelmann, a pioneer air tactician, Albert Ball, an introverted Englishman who was a highly effective fighter pilot and later Manfred von Richthofen, the 'Red Baron' who, with eighty kills, was the highest-scoring ace, have come to dominate the popular memory of the air war of 1914–18. It is important to remember, however, that they were enablers: their activities were designed to allow the slow reconnaissance and artillery co-operation aircraft to carry out their tasks. Which side had superiority in the air varied from period to period. During the first part of the Somme campaign in 1916, the Allies had the upper hand but the period of the Arras offensive in 1917 was known to British pilots of the Royal Flying Corps (RFC) as 'Bloody April'. Neither side was able to move up a notch from gaining 'air superiority' to gaining 'air supremacy'. Even during the great Allied offensive of 1918, the Germans 'never totally lost control of their airspace'.[19] Generally speaking, the Germans preferred to act on the defensive, while the Allies carried the fight to the enemy. Major-General Hugh Trenchard, head of the RFC on the Western Front for much of the war, shared Haig's vision of a relentless offensive.

Western Front 1915

The year 1915 was marked by failed Allied offensives in the west. For the most part, the Germans were content to sit on the defensive. They were prepared to sacrifice territory for tactical advantage, meaning that the Germans generally held the high ground, forcing the Allies to attack uphill. Conversely, the Allies were obliged, by the politics of honour, to defend as much friendly ground as possible. Thus the British defended the vulnerable Ypres Salient (a salient is a position surrounded on three sides by enemy-held territory). Although it would have made military sense to fall back to a more defensible position, it was politically impossible to abandon the last sizeable Belgian town to the Germans. On the defensive on the Western Front, the German army made effective use of elaborate entrenchments protected by barbed wire entanglements, machine-guns and masses of artillery. The Allied armies undoubtedly learned from the battles they fought and French and British assault methods improved over the course of the year. At the Second Battle of Artois (May–June 1915), for instance, the French became the first army to make extensive use of 'stormtrooper' infiltration tactics, seeking the weak spots in enemy positions, by-passing centres of resistance that were then dealt with by troops following the lead troops.[20] However, the Germans succeeded in developing their defensive techniques at a similar rate. The beginnings of defence-in-depth, which made use of strong points with counter-attack troops operating in the spaces between them, rather than relying strictly on linear trenches, is a case in point. Thus the Germans maintained a technological and tactical edge in the west.

The Western Front was a form of siege warfare. There were no available flanks to exploit and turn along the 400-mile front extending from the Swiss border to the Belgian coast. The mountains of neutral Switzerland anchored one flank. In principle, the Allies, using British naval power, could have mounted an amphibious landing on the Belgian coast. In reality, such an operation posed considerable challenges and the Royal Navy was very reluctant to risk ships so close to shore. Thus every land assault had to be made frontally. The first major attempt by the French to break the deadlock began as early as 20 December 1914, on the Champagne front. It made little progress, although the French continued to batter away until mid-March.

The vast bulk of Allied troops on the Western Front were French. The Belgians took little part in offensive operations until late 1918 and the BEF was small (six infantry divisions and a cavalry division were in theatre by early September 1914), although it steadily grew in size during the course of 1915 as volunteer Territorial and New (or 'Kitchener's') Army units, and some Canadians, reached the front to join the Regulars. Indian troops had also arrived toward the end of 1914. As the junior partner in the coalition, the British had to accede to French demands to take the offensive. Although the BEF was short of men and guns, Haig's First Army carried out the first British major offensive, Neuve Chapelle (10–13 March). This 'set-piece' operation was characterised by a brief artillery bombardment followed by infantry advancing in a succession of 'waves'. Some ground was gained and a breakthrough seemed possible, before the defenders closed the gap and the stalemate resumed. With the substitution of a lengthy for a short bombardment, Neuve Chapelle set the general pattern for British operations until the end of 1917.[21]

Figure 8   Troops of the British Indian Army in France, *c.*1915.

Battles such as Neuve Chapelle, or the French attack on Vimy Ridge on 9 May 1915 that captured the crest of this formidable position, demonstrated that while it was relatively straightforward to break *in* to enemy lines, it was exceedingly difficult to break *through* the trenches and break *out* into open ground. Time after time, an initially promising attack foundered as the defender rushed up reserves more quickly than the attacker could send forward reinforcements to capitalise on initial success. The problem was essentially one of communication. Armies were too big and too widely dispersed to be commanded from horseback, as in years past. Although there was a comprehensive field telephone network, to all intents it came to a halt at the edge of No Man's Land. Lacking 'walkie-talkie' radios, commanders were denied the information they needed to make timely decisions. Out of date scraps brought back by 'runners', messengers who physically travelled from the front line, were generally all that was available. Reserves almost invariably arrived when the window of opportunity had closed. The defenders, however, were able to use their field telephone network to summon reserves to the threatened spot.

Other factors weighted the dice in favour of the defender. At its simplest, a man in a trench was difficult to hit, while a man advancing across open land to attack a trench was a much more vulnerable target, especially given the accuracy, range and volume of fire produced by up-to-date artillery, machine guns and even the infantryman's standard bolt-action rifle. Barbed wire in front of the trench further protected the defender. Moreover, traditionally, once the infantry started to give way, cavalry had been unleashed to travel more quickly than the retiring enemy, get in among them and convert a retreat into a rout. Under trench warfare conditions, cavalry, while by no means as useless as commonly believed, nonetheless found it very difficult to carry out this role. In the Second World War, armoured vehicles were used for this purpose but when the first tanks appeared in 1916, they were too slow and unreliable to be used for pursuing retreating infantry. The story of the next few years was of attackers gradually discovering, by trial and error, the way to overcome the advantages that trench warfare bestowed on the defenders. By the end of 1917, they had succeeded. But in 1915 this was in the future and the Germans were able to reduce their troops on the Western Front to a bare minimum and make their main effort against Russia.

The only German offensive in the west in 1915 occurred near Ypres in a murderous month-long battle (22 April–25 May). The battle began when a greenish-grey cloud began to roll across No Man's Land towards the Allied trenches. It was chlorine gas, the first major use of a deadly chemical weapon in modern warfare. The gas caused panic among some French North African troops but others, including Canadians, stood firm. German troops proved reluctant to advance into their own gas cloud and, bizarrely, German High Command had neglected to provide substantial reserves to follow up the initial success. Thus the opportunity to capitalise on the unrepeatable surprise caused by the initial use of gas was thrown away. The Germans gained a mere tactical success, when there was a real possibility of a strategic victory. Both sides rapidly improvised anti-gas equipment. By the end of the war, the pad soaked in chemicals and tied across the nose and mouth that had been used in the spring of 1915 had been succeeded, in stages, by sophisticated respirators. Overall, Allied losses in Second Ypres, primarily sustained in a series of fruitless counter-attacks, amounted to 70,000; German casualties totalled 35,000 before the battle was brought to an inconclusive end. The pronounced salient held by the Allies at the beginning of the battle had been flattened somewhat but the Germans had failed to break through.

The same basic pattern of disappointment seen at Neuve Chapelle in March 1915 was repeated, with variations, during the French offensives of 1915: Woëvre (5–30 April), Second Artois (9 May–18 June), Third Artois (15 September–4 November), Champagne (25 September–6 November). The British had no better luck. Aubers Ridge (9 May), a rare complete disaster (12,000 casualties for no gains), was succeeded by Festubert (15–25 May) and Loos (25 September–14 October). The latter was the biggest British effort thus far, in support of Joffre's autumn offensive in Champagne and Artois. Haig's First Army of six divisions was given the daunting task of securing the myriad mine villages, collieries and slagheaps of the Pas-de-Calais commune of Loos-en-Gohelle. The assault opened in the early hours of 25 September. The British plan, for the only time in the war, centred on the use of poisonous gas.[22] It was the first time that the British had used gas on a large scale and the unreliable nature of the weapon (the chlorine gas was released from canisters; to be effective it needed the wind to blow strongly enough in the right direction) brought varied results. In some places, the gas blew back on the attacking troops but elsewhere it assisted First Army to achieve some significant local gains before stiffening German resistance and fierce counter-attacks halted the advance.

An attack by reserve divisions on the following day failed, thanks to the troops being held back too far from the battlefield and thus having to endure a punishing and mismanaged approach

march. These tired and untried New Army formations, vainly hurling themselves against the now solidified enemy defences, suffered over 8,000 casualties in just four hours. This costly trag-
. edy set the stage for bitter recriminations between French and the man who would shortly replace him as the BEF's Commander-in-Chief, Haig. Subsequent fighting degenerated into an inconclusive slogging match. The final attack, launched against the notorious Hohenzollern Redoubt on 13 October, cost the attacking division 3,643 casualties, the majority sustained in the first ten minutes. BEF losses at Loos amounted to 62,000 killed, wounded and missing; German casualties were approximately 26,000.

Increasingly in 1915, generals came to see sheer weight of shellfire as the way to success. They were not entirely wrong, but effective use of artillery, all too often lacking in 1915, and combining artillery with other arms, especially infantry, was also of critical importance, as was to become increasingly clear in 1916–17. However, it would be wrong to think that the Allied armies learned nothing from these attacks: new techniques and weapons were developed in a process of trial and error (see box: 'Revolution in Military Affairs' page 81).

French and British losses for the year 1915 amounted to 1,571,000; German losses to 612,000. The close of the year found the Allied High Command heartened, despite the inability to achieve a sustained breakthrough, by what was believed to be the formula for final victory: more guns, lengthier bombardments, improved staff work and communications were all expected to play their part in a great offensive for 1916. An Anglo-French programme for producing heavy guns was agreed in spring 1915 but not until 1918 were unlimited supplies of guns and ammunition available.[23] Germany's High Command, having focused previous efforts on the Eastern Front, planned what was hoped to be a fatal blow against France. These Allied and German strategies would result in Verdun and the Somme, two major campaigns that became synonymous with attrition.

ATTRITION

The First World War is regarded as the quintessential attritional conflict. In popular use, 'attrition' is regarded as the consequence of at best a failure of imagination, at worst the murderous incompetence of the generals. This is highly misleading. All wars and battles contain elements of attrition: it is inherent in the very nature of warfare. The Second World War, often regarded as the mobile antithesis of the 1914–18 War, had its share of attritional land battles, some of which had phases of static fighting: Stalingrad, Alamein, Okinawa, Cassino, Normandy. The strategic bombing campaigns against Germany and Japan were attritional to the core. So, in both world wars, were the naval battles of the Atlantic.

The tactical conditions of the Western Front from late 1914 to spring 1918 meant that the battles tended to be static, which magnified the attritional aspect. In the absence of substantial gains of ground, what commanders of a later war would call the 'body count', was the primary means of measuring success. While some campaigns began with an attempt to re-open warfare that became attritional clashes when breakthroughs failed to materialise (the Allied offensives of September 1915, for instance), others were designed to be attritional from the beginning (for example the German attack at Verdun in February 1916). An older generation of historians tended to regard deliberate attrition as 'degeneracy in the art of war'.[24] More recently, historians have begun to see controlled attrition in a rather different way. In a total war fought between roughly equal adversaries on a deadlocked front, wearing out enemy strength and degrading enemy morale by killing or incapacitating enemy soldiers can be an effective strategy, although double-edged if the attrition is reciprocal. Some historians see the limited, 'bite and hold' methods of British generals such as General Sir Herbert Plumer (commander of Second Army) and General Sir Henry Rawlinson (Fourth Army) as a viable alternative to Haig's strategy. In fact, Haig's favoured approach of combining attrition with manoeuvre was a sensible attempt to get the best of both worlds by being ready to take advantage of fleeting opportunities for advances.[25] General (later Marshal) Ferdinand Foch has been lauded for his attritional methods. One of his subordinates, General Marie-Eugène Debeney, averred that on the Somme in 1916 Foch had 'reawakened the spirit of the offensive in our army and given it the confidence that success would follow from careful preparation and bold execution'. Recent writers have supported this view. Such attrition was appallingly costly in human life but ultimately effective.[26]

Attrition was not confined to the battlefield. The Allied naval blockade and the German U-boat campaigns, and even the embryo

> strategic bombing of civilians, were all part of attritional strategies to strike at the willingness and ability of states and societies to wage war. Victory eventually went to the side that on battlefront and home front was able to outlast the enemy.

Eastern Front 1915

At the beginning of 1915, German High Command's preferred strategy was for the resumption of major operations in the West. However, the crippling defeats and enormous loss of manpower sustained by Germany's chief ally, Austria–Hungary, coupled with thorny political considerations based on the need to further exploit territorial gains obtained during the 1914 campaign, determined that the primary offensive effort for 1915 would be directed against Russia. The first attack, launched on the northern front, resulted in the Second Battle of the Masurian Lakes (7–22 February) during which the Russians lost 200,000 men – killed, wounded or captured – before retiring some 70 miles. Austro-German attempts to relieve Przemyśl in the south stalled due to harsh terrain, poor weather and primitive roads. The fortress capitulated to the Russians on 22 March after a six-month siege. The failed Carpathian offensives in January, February and March 1915 put the Austro-Hungarian army under terrible strain: Conrad's ambitions outran the ability of his forces to deliver.[27] Many of the pre-war trained soldiers who had survived the initial campaigns had now gone, meaning that the Hapsburg armies were weakened in experience as well as numbers. Subsequent Russian efforts to advance to the Carpathian Mountains became bogged down in the face of determined enemy resistance.

The arrival of spring heralded the start of the most successful operation of the year, indeed one of the most successful of the entire war. Falkenhayn planned a great offensive. To this end, the capable General August Mackensen's Eleventh Army (formed of units from the Western Front) was to mount a surprise attack in the Gorlice-Tarnow sector, southeast of the Galician capital of Cracow,

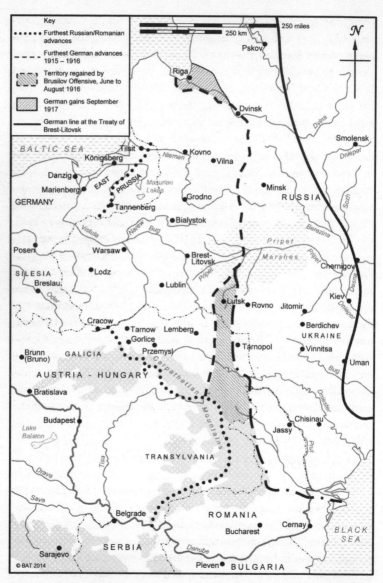

Key

• • • • Furthest Russian/Romanian advances

- - - Furthest German advances 1915 – 1916

▨ Territory regained by Brusilov Offensive, June to August 1916

▦ German gains September 1917

— German line at the Treaty of Brest-Litovsk

250 km　250 miles

N

Pskov

Riga

Dvinsk

Smolensk

Dvina

BALTIC SEA

Tilsit

Königsberg

Kovno

Vilna

Niemen

Danzig

Marienberg

EAST PRUSSIA

Masurian Lakes

Grodno

Minsk

RUSSIA

Sozh

GERMANY

Tannenberg

Bialystok

Berezina

Vistula

Narew

Bug

Posen

Warsaw

Brest-Litovsk

Pripet Marshes

Chernigov

SILESIA

Breslau

Lodz

Lublin

Pripet

Lutsk

Rovno

Jitomir

Kiev

Desna

Oder

Dnieper

Cracow

Tarnow

Gorlice

Lemberg

Tarnopol

Berdichev

UKRAINE

Vinnitsa

Przemysl

Brunn (Bruno)

GALICIA

Carpathian Mountains

Uman

Bug

AUSTRIA - HUNGARY

Bratislava

Budapest

Lake Balaton

Chisinau

Jassy

Dniester

Drava

Tisa

TRANSYLVANIA

Prut

Sava

Belgrade

ROMANIA

Cernay

BLACK SEA

Bucharest

Sarajevo

SERBIA

Danube

Pleven

BULGARIA

© BAT 2014

Map 2　The Eastern Front

supported by Austro-Hungarian Second and Fourth Armies. Early on 2 May, 950 German guns commenced a devastating bombardment of the Russian positions. Masses of German infantry then closed to overwhelm the surprised and shattered defenders. Russian Third Army was, by the end of the second day, practically annihilated, 120,000 men having been captured. The relentless eastward advance pressed on against crumbling resistance. The fortress city of Przemyśl was retaken by the Austro-Hungarians on 3 June and Lemberg fell on 22 June. Mackensen, now reinforced by the Austrian-Hungarian Third Army and German forces, turned north towards Brest-Litovsk, 120 miles east of Warsaw. It was with this prize in mind that Falkenhayn ordered German Ninth and Twelfth Armies to march against Warsaw. On 4–5 August the Polish capital fell, with Brest-Litovsk captured ten days later. By late September, in one of the greatest of the Central Powers' victories of the war, the Russians had, in addition to being swept out of Poland, been driven back to a 600-mile line stretching from Lithuania to the border of neutral Romania. The five-month long campaign cost them a colossal two million casualties, of which half were prisoners. German casualties amounted to approximately 87,000; Austro-Hungarian losses are unknown. Gorlice-Tarnow was notable, not only for the scale of the Central Powers' success but also for command and control that was much superior to that of the Russians and an innovative combination of artillery and air power.[28]

Turkish Fronts 1914–15

The Ottoman Empire (Turkey), announced its entry into the war on the side of the Central Powers with a surprise naval bombardment of Russian Black Sea ports in October 1914. By becoming a belligerent, Turkey changed the character of the war. The huge, multi-ethnic and multi-lingual Ottoman Empire had a common frontier with Russia and lands in British and French colonial spheres of interest. Both London and Paris were capitals of great empires and it was inevitable that the war would be seen as an opportunity for imperial expansion at Turkey's expense. Thus the Allied campaigns against the Ottomans had a dual purpose: to contribute to bringing about victory in the larger war and to achieve imperial objectives.

The Ottoman land war against the Allies commenced with an initially successful but ultimately disastrous winter offensive in the Caucasus (November 1914–January 1915). Fighting in mountainous terrain, in harsh winter weather, the poorly-equipped Turkish Third Army, commanded by the Ottoman Minister of War Enver Pasha, caused sufficient alarm for the Russians to appeal to the British and French to launch a diversion (this was a factor in the genesis of the Anglo-French Dardanelles/Gallipoli campaign in spring 1915). However, Enver was thrown back by the Russians and forced to retreat to the Ottoman territory. The fighting at Sarykamish (27 December 1914 to 4 January 1915) was the turning point. This battle led to the Ottomans scapegoating the Armenians, which resulted in the genocidal destruction of the Armenian population. In the Caucasus campaign, the Turks suffered nearly 50,000 fatalities, the Russians nearly 30,000. Far away in the Middle East, the Turks opened another front by sending VIII Corps across the Sinai Peninsula to attack the Suez Canal in British-controlled Egypt. This was heavily defeated in a single day of fighting (3 February 1915).

For the Entente, and especially the British, attacking the Ottoman Empire was extremely attractive. A war against the Turks appeared to offer the opportunity to strike an important strategic blow against the Central Powers as a whole: thinking that led to the ill-fated Dardanelles/Gallipoli campaign. More parochial reasons – securing British oil interests – were behind the landing of Indian army troops to secure the Mesopotamian port of Basra in November 1914. A classic case of 'mission creep' led the British Indian government – responsible for this theatre of operations – to sanction a campaign inland, which by stages led to an attempt to capture Baghdad with an inadequate force of one reinforced division under Major-General Charles Townshend. The steady advance (May–November 1918) up the Tigris was brought to a standstill by a heavily reinforced Turkish Army at the Battle of Ctesiphon (22–26 November), after which Townshend's weak and exhausted force retired downriver to the town of Kut-el-Amara, where it would undergo an epic five-month siege that began on 7 December.

THE DARDANELLES/GALLIPOLI CAMPAIGN

The Allied attempt to open the heavily-defended Dardanelles straits that ultimately connect the Mediterranean and Black Seas and capture the Turkish capital of Constantinople was deeply flawed from the very beginning. In late 1914, with the Western Front stalemated and British leaders casting around for an alternative strategy, the Russians, attacked by the Turks in the Caucasus, appealed for help. This helped to germinate the seeds of a plan being sown by Winston Churchill, the political head of the Royal Navy, to strike at the Ottoman Empire by attacking the Dardanelles and then Constantinople. It seemed possible that this use of British naval power would tip the Ottoman Empire into collapse. A key German ally would have been knocked out of the war, the Russians assisted and important British strategic and foreign policy objectives achieved. All this proved to be wishful thinking. Initially, the Allies launched a purely naval attack. On 18 March 1915, an Anglo-French fleet was defeated as it attempted to force its way through the Straits, which were defended by shore batteries and minefields. Three battleships were sunk and three more badly damaged by mines.

Following this serious defeat, Allied policy-makers decided to commit ground forces to a risky amphibious assault on the Gallipoli peninsula, aiming to roll up the western defences of the Straits from the land. Consequently, an expeditionary force of 75,000 British, Australian, New Zealand, Indian and French troops was assembled under a British general, Sir Ian Hamilton. On 25 April, landings were made in two locations on the peninsula, with a diversionary landing across the Straits. They met fierce resistance from the Turkish Fifth Army of 60,000 men commanded by a German general, Liman von Sanders, deployed in small groups along the coastline to defend likely landing sites, with reserves held inland. British 29th Division came ashore on five beaches on the southern tip of the peninsula at Cape Helles. The initial waves suffered heavy casualties. Poor Allied command and co-ordination, and stubborn defending by the Turks, combined to confine the invaders to the landing beaches throughout the first day. On the west coast, the untried men of ANZAC (Australian and New Zealand Army Corps) landed a mile north of their projected landing at Ari Burnu. Pressing inland over a confused landscape of circuitous valleys and steep ridges, the disorganised Australian and New Zealand advance was checked by a decisive counter-attack under the command of Colonel Mustapha Kemal, the future founder of the Turkish republic. Inconclusive fighting left the Allies unable to press far enough inland on both the Helles and ANZAC fronts. By 8 May, a disheartening deadlock similar to that experienced on the Western Front prevailed, Hamilton having lost almost a third of his force to enemy action and disease.

An attempt was made to re-energise the operation in August. Additional forces were dispatched to Gallipoli and two more divisions were prepared for a new landing just north of Anzac Cove, at the remote and relatively undefended Suvla Bay. The offensive began on 6 August, with a barren and costly diversionary attack at Helles. The main assault at Anzac Cove reached the heights of the tactically important Sari Bair range before being hurled back by a timely Turkish counter-attack. At Suvla Bay, however, Lieutenant-General Sir Frederick Stopford's inexperienced force achieved surprise and pushed inland. However, he failed to capitalise on his advantage and a three-day delay on the beaches allowed the Turks to rush up reinforcements and halt a resumption of the offensive on 9 August. The new trench stalemate dragged on into autumn. Hamilton was replaced by General Sir Charles Monro, who recommended an evacuation, regardless of the fact that serious casualties might be incurred. London concurred with this proposal. Suvla and ANZAC were evacuated by sea on 20 December; Cape Helles on 9 January 1916. Not a single life was lost during the withdrawal.

Combined British Empire and French casualties amounted to 252,000 killed, wounded and missing. Turkish losses were an estimated 218,000–251,000. In overall strategic terms the campaign was an unremitting failure that damaged British prestige. The Gallipoli adventure was not, as often claimed, a brilliant conception poorly executed; from the very beginning it was wildly over-ambitious and founded ultimately on a gross underestimation of the resilience and fighting power of the Ottoman forces.[29] For years to come, Churchill's reputation was stained by his involvement in 'the Dardanelles'.

Italian, Serbian and Salonika Fronts 1915

On 23 May 1915 another front opened when Italy, which had chosen neutrality in August 1914, declared war on Austria-Hungary.[30] The Italian government had been courted by both the

Entente and the Central Powers but was persuaded by the prospect of making territorial gains at the expense of the Hapsburg Empire. The mountainous terrain of the northern or Trentino sector precluded any immediate offensive action by the Italians. This left the eastern or Isonzo front as a possible gateway into the regions of Dalmatia and Slovenia. These lands contained some Italian-speakers and the annexation of these territories was a key war aim of the government in Rome. During the First Battle of the Isonzo (23 June–7 July 1915), two Italian Armies attacked across the high, stone-strewn wilderness of the Carso. Their objective was Gorizia and ultimately the great port city of Trieste. The Austrian position was immensely strong, with their trenches cut out of the rock. The poorly-trained Italian forces were badly hampered by inadequate artillery. Their morale was low and they lacked cohesion, a reflection of the regional and social tensions within wider Italian society. The Second (18 July–3 August), Third (18 October–3 November) and Fourth (10 November–2 December) Battles of the Isonzo were further Italian offensives characterised by heavy losses for miniscule gains. Italian casualties (killed, wounded and missing) totalled 386,547; Austro-Hungarian losses amounted to 129,050. Twelve Austrian divisions were diverted from the Russian front to fight the Italians but this made no difference to events in the east.

Grand strategic considerations influenced the Central Powers' decision to crush Serbia. Turkey's entry into the war on their side and the consequent necessity to re-open the section of the Berlin to Constantinople railway, which traversed Serbian territory, led to a combined Austro-German-Bulgarian offensive (the Bulgarians entered the war on 23 September, hoping to take Macedonia from Serbia). The Central Powers captured Belgrade and drove the Serbian forces and a substantial portion of the civilian population over the mountains into Albania. The two-month (October–December) campaign and a harrowing winter retreat reduced the Serbian army from an estimated pre-war establishment of 330,000 men to 75,000 effectives by the end of the year. Thus, Vienna's objective in launching the war in July 1914 was achieved but the fact that the Germans dominated the coalition forces that destroyed Serbia highlighted Austrian weakness. For Conrad, the man who had done so much to bring about the cataclysm in the summer of 1914, this was a 'bitter pill'.[31] The Allies attempted to assist their beleaguered Balkan ally by dispatching French and British troops to the seaport of Salonika in neutral Greece. It was a case of too few forces dispatched too tardily to help the Serbs but it established a potentially exploitable Entente toehold in the Balkans.

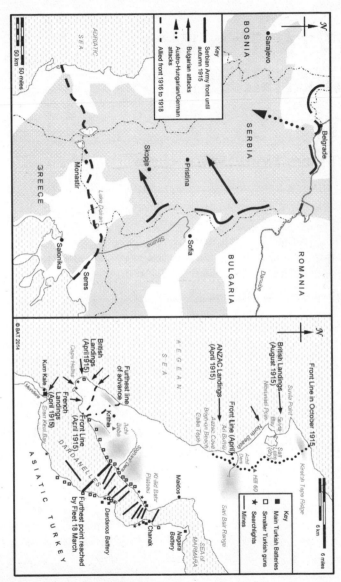

Map 3   The Balkans and Gallipoli

3

1916: The War Intensifies

Western Front 1916

At the Chantilly conference in late 1915, France, Great Britain, Russia and Italy agreed upon a series of sequential co-ordinated offensives, starting in the following spring, which would overwhelm Austro-German defences on three fronts. German High Command, satisfied with the succession of spectacular victories in the East during 1915, decided to shift its main offensive effort to the west. The result was the battle at Verdun. Meanwhile, on the Western Front the British army steadily expanded in size. The initial four infantry divisions sent to France in August 1914 had grown to fifty-six by June 1916. But most of the troops were inexperienced and poorly trained civilians in uniform, consisting of New Army and Territorial units raised following a nationwide appeal by the Secretary of State for War, Lord Kitchener, in August 1914.

The Battle of Verdun

The Battle of Verdun was the product of a pessimistic but realistic assessment of the strategic situation in late 1915, carried out by the German Chief of the General Staff, Erich von Falkenhayn. He recognised that in the long term the formidable power of the Allies was bound to prevail. Therefore Germany should strike at the cohesion of the coalition ranged against Germany by forcing France to the negotiating table and bringing about a separate peace. Falkenhayn believed that the French would be forced to fight at all costs for Verdun, the loss of which would badly damage French prestige. Although Falkenhayn's motives and intentions are controversial among historians, it seems that he planned a deliberate campaign of controlled attrition, based on artillery fire, designed to bleed the French Army white among the belt of fortresses and so destroy France's willingness and ability to fight on. With 'England's best sword' eliminated, the coalition would disintegrate. However, Falkenhayn's subordinates, who actually conducted the offensive, did not accept his concept of operations and fought it in a more traditional way. In any case, battles have a nasty habit of acquiring momentum and it soon span out of control.[1]

The Fifth Army, nominally commanded by the Kaiser's son, Crown Prince Wilhelm, was the primary instrument of Falkenhayn's plan. The offensive opened on 21 February 1916 with a bombardment by 1,400 guns on an 8-mile front east of the River Meuse. Advancing German infantry, preceded by specially trained stormtroops armed with flamethrowers, eventually forced the stunned defenders back southwards along the entire front. Fort Douaumont, denuded of guns to support earlier offensives, fell on 25 February. It was at this moment of crisis that Joffre appointed General Henri-Phillipe Pétain to take over at Verdun. Pétain quickly succeeded in reorganising and inspiring the hard-pressed defence. The phrase associated with him, '*Ils ne passeront pas!*' ('They shall not pass!'), was actually coined by his subordinate General Robert Nivelle, but it sums up Pétain's philosophy. The culmination of his early efforts was the establishment and maintenance of the *Voie Sacrée* (Sacred Way), a forty-mile stretch of road that carried an endless stream of reinforcements and vital supplies to the front. The failure of the Germans to interdict this artery is evidence of Falkenhayn's attritional strategy, that he did not intended to take Verdun, rather to make the French fight for it. French resistance, ably supported by increasingly accurate artillery support, managed to halt the southward German thrust by the end of February.

Following this, Falkenhayn broadened the attack to include two strategically important hills (*Le Mort Homme* – the Dead Man – and

Côte 304) on the left bank of the Meuse. French resistance in this sector was also extremely determined. The great offensive designed to inflict unsustainable loss of life on the enemy was taking a heavy toll on the attackers, as the measured strategy of attrition gave way to costly efforts to seize the forts (the Germans captured Fort de Vaux on 7 June). Throughout spring and summer, the campaign continued, with ceaseless artillery fire placing the infantry under the most appalling strain. A subsequent summer offensive (23 June–11 July), tasked with seizing the Meuse heights, was only narrowly repulsed before the Anglo-French offensive on the Somme put an end to further German attacks. Three French counter-attacks, launched against the now exhausted Fifth Army during the autumn and winter, managed to regain most of the lost territory, including Forts Douaumont and Vaux, before the fighting died down in mid-December. Nivelle, who was to play a major role in early 1917, made his name in this phase. In the 10-month long struggle, 377,000 Frenchmen became casualties. German losses were an estimated 337,000. Verdun has a deserved reputation as one of the most terrible of all First World War battles.

The Battle of the Somme

An Anglo-French campaign on the Western Front had been part of the general agreement to attack on all fronts arrived at during the Chantilly Conference in November 1915. The chosen ground for the great summer offensive was the junction of French and British armies near the River Somme. The experienced French were initially intended to take the lead in the battle but Verdun forced the French progressively to downgrade their contribution, making the early part of the Somme a predominately British battle.

The Somme was the first battle fought by the BEF under its new Commander-in-Chief, Sir Douglas Haig. His aspiration was to achieve a major breakthrough of the enemy defences and thus re-open mobile warfare, but there was a Plan B of limited advances

Figure 9   Field-Marshal Sir Douglas Haig, Commander-in-Chief of the British Expeditionary Force, 1915–19.

and attrition. Haig's principal operational commander on the Somme was the Fourth Army's General Sir Henry Rawlinson, who favoured a modest 'bite and hold' approach of lengthy bombardments and limited tactical advance, followed by immediate consolidation and destruction of enemy counter-attacks. The eventual plan was an uneasy compromise between the two approaches, with Rawlinson choosing to ignore Haig's clearly stated concept of operations, resulting in highly unfortunate effects on the first day of the battle.[2]

The Somme sector had been competitively quiet during 1915 and, by the eve of the battle, General Fritz von Below's German Second Army had constructed an impressive complex of trenches, fortified villages and deep dug-outs. Many of the dug-outs were forty feet below ground. Protected by wide belts of barbed-wire obstacles, the Germans awaited the anticipated enemy assault, the preparations opposite being all too apparent. The British tactical plan of attack was based on the principle of 'the artillery conquers and the infantry occupies'. Unfortunately, the British lacked the necessary numbers of heavy guns and had insufficient stocks of high-explosive shells. Field guns firing man-killing shrapnel were a poor substitute and Haig made matters worse by ordering the guns to fire on a large number of targets across the depth of the German defences rather than concentrating fire on key areas. The week-long artillery bombardment that commenced on 24 June was a terrible ordeal for the Germans cowering in their dugouts but it failed to neutralise their artillery and machine guns.

At 7:30a.m. on 1 July 1916, when thirteen British infantry divisions attacked, they met fierce resistance and in some places uncut barbed wire. Some of the attackers were weighed down with extra kit such as sandbags to consolidate the trenches 'conquered' by artillery. Most displayed exemplary courage but suffered appalling losses. The myth is that they were all ordered to advance at a slow walk. Some did, according to the non-prescriptive advice passed on by High Command, but local commanders were free to come up with their own tactics. One formation that used more imaginative tactics was 36th (Ulster) Division. Initially it made a spectacular advance, only to be driven back. Ultimately, the precise infantry tactics used by different units were irrelevant, because the artillery failed to do its job, thus ensuring the defeat of the foot soldiers in the northern part of the battlefield.

However, in the south, the opportunity for a substantial advance did occur. On the right flank, the raw British troops of 18th and 30th Divisions took all their objectives. Rawlinson, who simply discounted the possibility of a major advance, spurned the chance. Had Haig's original concept of pushing mobile reserves through the assault troops been followed, an advance of perhaps three to five miles could have been achieved. In the context of 1916, this would have been a substantial success salvaged from the wreck of Fourth Army's plans. French Sixth Army on the British right made a major advance for very low losses that contrasted with the 57,000 (including 19,000 fatalities) suffered by the BEF in the bloodiest single day in British military history. The Germans, too, were badly battered. Moreover, incessant British attacks over the coming weeks to capture ground prior to the next major push gave German commanders food for thought about the British Empire's ability and resolve to engage in a lengthy battle of attrition. The next main assault occurred on 14 July, when six divisions over-ran a portion of the German second line in a risky dawn attack. During the first part of the Somme offensive, the Germans added to the 'butcher's bill' by a policy of immediate counter-attacking when ground was lost. Painfully slowly, the BEF and the French drove the Germans back. The entry of Romania into the war tipped the balance against Falkenhayn: he was replaced on 29 August 1916 by Hindenburg and Ludendorff.

In mid-September the Allies launched their next major offensive. The French attacked on 12 September, the British three days later. Canadian and New Zealand formations took part in this attack; earlier, Australian and Indian forces had been in action. Attacking on a ten-mile front, twelve BEF divisions, assisted for the first time by a recent British invention, tanks, pressed forward for about a mile. The offensive resumed on 25 September with some notable gains and intense fighting before autumn rains turned the battlefield into a quagmire. Various reasons, not least the pressure being placed on Haig by Joffre, ensured the long drawn-out battle of attrition would go on. A final seven-division attack was launched on both sides of the River Ancre on 13 November. Three-quarters of a mile were gained and the fortified village of Beaumont-Hamel captured before the campaign ended on 18 November.

The Somme offensive was a crucial battle for the BEF. A mixture of top-down and bottom-up tactical and doctrinal development (including infantry fire-and-movement based around the Lewis light machine gun, the creeping artillery barrage, the introduction

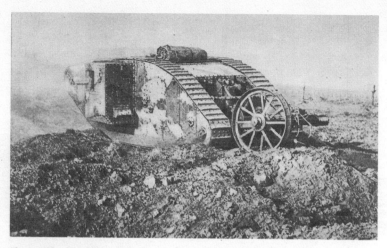

Figure 10   British Mark I tank on the Somme battlefield, 1916.

of a practical armoured fighting vehicle and use of effective air power) allied to valuable experience gained at every level from GHQ downwards meant that, heavy casualties notwithstanding, the British army was a much more formidable fighting force at the end of the Somme than it had been at the beginning. Strategically, relief of the pressure on Verdun was achieved and the German army, worn down by heavy losses, was deprived of the majority of its pre-war officers and NCOs. The maintenance of the gruelling and costly offensive for months on end and the consequent short- and long-term results remain a heated source of controversy to this day. British Empire casualties amounted to 420,000 killed, wounded and missing; French 195,000. German losses were perhaps as high as 600,000.

Eastern Front 1916

The year 1916 proved to be the last gasp of Imperial Russia as a functioning member of the Entente coalition. Verdun led to urgent French requests for a relief offensive, so Russia mounted an assault

east of Vilna in the Lake Naroch sector. The Russians had a significant advantage in manpower (of the order of 5:2) and ordered a
two-day preliminary artillery bombardment, unprecedented on the
Eastern Front, but the 'artillery preparation troubled the defence far
less than when most ineffective on the Somme'.[3] The attack began
on 18 March but soon broke down in the face of German artillery
fire and the saturated ground. The battle dragged on until mid-
April. Many of the 122,000 Russian losses were caused by frostbite.
German casualties were around 20,000.

Later that year, in the summer, continued German and Austrian
attacks on Verdun and the Trentino led Czar Nicholas II to order a
major offensive to assist his hard-pressed French and Italian allies.
On the sector of the Southwest Front (Army Group), four Armies
(forty infantry and fifteen cavalry divisions), under the command
of General Aleksei Brusilov, attacked on a 300-mile front from
the Pripet Marshes to the Romanian border. Facing them were
four Austro-German Armies consisting of thirty-nine infantry
divisions (all but two of which were Austro-Hungarian), and ten
cavalry divisions. The offensive opened on 4 June with an effective
bombardment. Because the Russians attacked across such a broad
front, rather than concentrating on a small number of sectors, the
Central Powers' commanders were unable to identify an obvious
build up. Thus the Russians achieved a large measure of surprise.
The defenders fell back fifty miles, losing some 700,000 men
killed, wounded and missing in the process.

Thereafter, the offensive began to stall as the iron law of logistics
– armies advancing from their bases find it increasingly difficult to
keep in supply while armies falling back on their bases find it easier
– began to kick in. The Central Powers, making use of a superior
lateral railway network, shored up their defences with twenty-three
divisions dispatched from other fronts: with campaigns raging in Italy
and at Verdun and with the Somme about to begin, the Germans and
Austro-Hungarians were coming under extreme pressure from the
Entente coalition. However, General Aleksei Evert, commander of
Northwest Front, failed to launch a timely offensive in the northern
sector of the Eastern Front, deploying an array of excuses: his attack,

delivered on 13 June, was both too little and too late.[4] Conceivably, if, following Brusilov's operation, sequenced offensives had been launched by Evert and by General Alexei Kuropatkin's Northern Front, a decisive victory would have resulted. As it was, Austro-German forces held the line – even though by the time Brusilov's forces finally ran out of steam on 20 September, the Russians had recaptured much of the territory lost in previous campaigns, once again threatening the Carpathians.

Casualties on both sides were enormous: perhaps 1.4 million Russians and 750,000 Austro-Hungarian troops. It was another blow to the combat effectiveness and cohesion of both armies and states, although the impact on Russia was more immediate. In one sense the campaign was a victory for the Germans, as they secured unity of command on the Eastern Front. Effectively, German generals took control of the Hapsburg armies, paying only lip service to Austro-Hungarian sovereignty and autonomy.

THE BATTLE FOR GERMANY'S OVERSEAS EMPIRE

When war began, Germany's overseas possessions were cut off from the *Kaiserreich* by British naval superiority, making it extremely difficult to reinforce them. In some areas, it was simply a matter of the Allies mopping up German colonies almost at will. Australian and New Zealand troops quickly occupied the German Pacific islands and the British and Japanese co-operated in capturing Tsingtao, a German colony in China. The capture of wireless (radio) stations was of strategic significance and, as in the case of the war against the Ottomans, the British and French sought to expand their empires, partly to achieve security for existing territories.

On 7 August 1914, only three days after Britain entered the war, German Togoland was invaded by British and French forces (largely European-officered African troops) and conquered in a brief campaign that lasted less than a month. German South-West Africa (today, Namibia) was attacked in September 1914 by forces from the Union of South Africa. The South African forces were distracted from the campaign by a rebellion at home against the Union by 12,000 Boer 'bitter enders'. These men resented the peace settlement at the end of the Second South African War, concluded in 1902, and took the opportunity of the outbreak of war with Germany to strike. Thirty thousand Union troops were used to defeat the insurgency, which was over by the end of January 1915. Union forces resumed the offensive in South-West Africa and by mid-July 1915 the German colony was in South African hands.

The conquest of the German colony of the Cameroons, in West Africa, involved British, French and Belgian troops, again, mostly Africans officered by Europeans. The fighting lasted from September 1914 to February 1916. Things were even more difficult for the British Empire forces in German East Africa (Tanganyka). A German officer, Lieutenant-Colonel Paul von Lettow-Vorbeck, commanding a force of Asakris (African troops), waged a brilliant guerrilla campaign against admittedly often leaden-footed opposition that had overwhelmingly superior numbers. He kept the war going until two weeks after the German surrender in Europe: when Lettow-Vorbeck heard about the Armistice in November 1918, he voluntarily capitulated, undefeated.

In all the African campaigns, losses from sickness were very high. Vast numbers of African 'porters' were used to carry supplies. They suffered particularly badly, especially from the tsetse fly that transmitted trypanosomosis (sleeping sickness) to animals and humans. The ratio of battle casualties to non-battle casualties (that is, those caused by sickness and accidents) in the East African campaign (1916 to 1918) was 1 to 31.40 among troops and an astounding 1 to 140.83 among indigenous 'followers', which included the porters. Approximately 3,650 soldiers and 700 porters were killed, died of wounds, posted missing or taken prisoner in 1916–18, the figures for 'died of disease or injury' were 6,300 troops and 43,200 followers.[5]

Italian and Balkan Fronts 1916

In 1916, the strategy of the Italian Commander-in-Chief, General Luigi Cardona, was essentially that of the previous year. He mounted five more battles of the Isonzo (the fifth to ninth, fought between March and November 1916). These brought one solid gain, the capture of the important town of Gorizia in August, but Austro-Hungarian defenders and nightmarish terrain blocked any further advance. The other Italian front, the Trentino, flared into life with a major Austro-Hungarian offensive (15 May–17 June). This followed

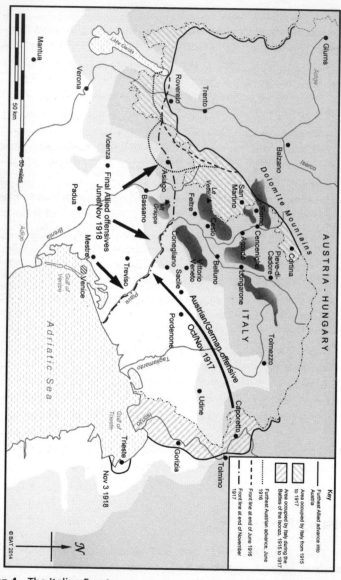

Map 4   The Italian Front

the pattern of so many Great War offensives: initial success, then increasing difficulty for the attackers in struggling forward against congealing resistance. The Italians were aided by the Russian Brusilov offensive, which forced the Austro-Hungarians to withdraw troops and send them to the apparently collapsing Eastern Front.

Russian successes, along with the slow but steady Anglo-French advance on the Somme and the Italian capture of Gorizia, encouraged neutral Romania at last to declare war against the Central Powers in August. Taking the offensive, the Romanians made inroads into Transylvania but were met by a devastating counteroffensive by German, Austro-Hungarian, Bulgarian and Ottoman forces, commanded by none other than the recently demoted Falkenhayn. Ill-trained and incompetently led, the Romanian army was crushed, Bucharest, the capital, captured and the Romanian government forced to sign a humiliating peace. It was a dazzling display of how effective the German army could be in mobile warfare, albeit against a decidedly third-rate opponent.

Romania, with its highly desirable agricultural land, was a strategic prize. The same could not be said of the Allied enclave at Salonika. By 1916, Allied forces had been reinforced by Russian and Italian contingents and the reconstituted Serbian Army. The Salonika front was in large part maintained because French domestic politics demanded that a sizeable command be found for General Maurice Sarrail, much to the disgust of many senior British leaders. Sarrail mounted the Battle of Dorian in August. He achieved some success until counter-attacking German and Bulgarian forces forced the abandonment of the meagre territorial gains. Another push by Sarrail's forces in October secured Monastir.

Turkish Fronts 1916

The Ottoman war took a new turn in January 1916 when the British and French cut their losses and finally evacuated Gallipoli, in spite of the resulting blows to their prestige within the Muslim world (both the French and British Empires had millions of Islamic subjects). This was followed by disaster in Mesopotamia, when Townshend's beleaguered garrison in Kut was forced, after the failure of four relief efforts, to capitulate to besieging Turkish forces in April. Some 2,700 British and 6,500 Indian soldiers were taken prisoner, along with Townshend. While the general had a comfortable imprisonment, ordinary soldiers suffered badly at the hands of their captors through a combination of neglect and deliberate cruelty.

On the Caucasus Front, the Russian army managed to capture the fortress town of Erzurum and the Black Sea port of Trebizond in January and April, respectively. Subsequent encroachments in Anatolia and Mesopotamia during March to July were stalled by a revitalised Turkish defence, after which the fighting lapsed into stalemate. British concerns for the safety of the Suez Canal were at the heart of an advance into the Sinai. In a major engineering project, a railway was built from the main bases in Egypt into the Sinai peninsula. An Ottoman force led by a German commander, Colonel Kress von Kressenstein, attempted to halt the advance but was soundly defeated at Romani on 4 August. The Suez Canal and Red Sea thus secured, open support for the Arab revolt in the Hejaz (which began in June 1916 with the capture of Mecca), provided Britain with the opportunity to disrupt the Turkish rear.

THE BATTLE OF JUTLAND

The commander of the German High Seas Fleet, Admiral Hugo von Pöhl, was replaced by Admiral Reinhard Scheer in January 1916. Scheer discarded the caution of his predecessor and returned to the attritional strategy of attempting to catch and eliminate elements of the British Grand Fleet. On 31 May 1916, five battlecruisers commanded by Admiral Franz von Hipper were dispatched north along the west coast of the Jutland peninsula. This was the bait to attract British ships on to the guns of Scheer's main force, of sixteen new and eight old battleships, some 50 miles behind. The separate groups also included a combined total of eleven light cruisers and sixty-three destroyers.

Admiral Sir John Jellicoe's Grand Fleet, having received advanced notice of the anticipated German sortie from Room 40's cryptographers, was already at sea and steaming eastward in two divisions towards Scheer's force. The southern group of four fast battleships and six battlecruisers was commanded by Vice-Admiral Sir David Beatty. Jellicoe's Grand Fleet of twenty-four battleships and three battlecruisers kept pace 70 miles to the north. A combined total of thirty-four light cruisers and eighty destroyers provided escort for the capital ship groups.

Hipper and Beatty's battlecruiser squadrons spotted each other at about 2.20p.m. Hipper immediately turned towards Scheer. Beatty followed as both sides, steaming in a parallel course, exchanged long-range gunfire in a murderous ship-to-ship duel that quickly turned to the advantage of the Germans. The British battlecruisers *Queen Mary* and *Indefatigable* were sunk with heavy loss of life before Scheer's main force came into view. Beatty, recognising that he now faced the entire enemy battle fleet, immediately turned about and doubled back north towards the Grand Fleet with Scheer and Hipper in close pursuit. Jellicoe deployed eastward to come between the enemy and the Jutland coast as the opposing fleets approached each other.

The main battle commenced at 6p.m. HMS *Invincible* was lost with 1,026 men, while Hipper's flagship *Lützow* was crippled by shellfire. Reeling from severe losses in ships and men, Jellicoe was nevertheless able to position his fleet astride Scheer's van (leading ships) by implementing the classic naval manoeuvre known as 'Crossing the T', allowing the maximum number of guns to come to bear. The German admiral was left with no choice but to execute a 'battle turn around' and retire southwest. The British followed and were again able to Cross the T but Scheer escaped under the cover of smoke and a torpedo barrage. Jellicoe prudently turned away from the torpedoes. Confused fighting raged until nightfall. Situated between the High Seas Fleet and its base at Wilhelmshaven, the British now held a distinct tactical advantage. Exploiting the onset of darkness and the prevailing confusion, the emboldened Scheer managed to make his escape by rushing the light forces covering Jellicoe's rear with the loss of the previously damaged *Lützow* and one old battleship. Following this, the Grand Fleet returned to its bases.

More than 250 ships were involved in the Battle of Jutland. The Royal Navy lost three battlecruisers, three light cruisers, eight destroyers and 6,945 men killed, wounded and captured. German losses amounted to a battlecruiser, a pre-dreadnought, four light cruisers, five destroyers and 3,058 killed and wounded. Royal Navy tonnage losses were almost twice that of the High Seas Fleet. All this lead to a sense of disappointment in Britain and bitter recrimination in the Royal Navy, with cliques focused around Jellicoe, the cautious 'regulator' and Beatty, the aggressive 'ratcatcher'.[6] In reality, Britain had gained the success that mattered: the strategic situation was unchanged and remained so, despite subsequent German sorties into the North Sea. An American journalist neatly summarised the results of Jutland: 'The prisoner has assaulted his jailer but he is still in jail'.

The weary stalemate

The year 1916 ended with the stalemate intact. The campaigns of that year had done immense damage to the armies of Austria-Hungary and Russia and the extent to which the authority of the Czarist government had been undermined was to be fully revealed during the March Revolution of 1917. Germany clearly had the upper hand on the Eastern Front. In the west, Falkenhayn's Verdun strategy had failed: France was still in the war and Falkenhayn himself had been replaced by Hindenburg and Ludendorff. Although the French army had taken a terrible battering, it had ended the year on a note of victory. From the German perspective, the worst moment had come in August–September, when a combination of Allied pressure on all fronts raised the prospect of the Central Powers' defence collapsing somewhere. Perhaps if Romania had entered the war earlier, it would have been the straw that broke the camel's back. Certainly, the decline in the purchase of war bonds indicated a failure of resolve among the middle-classes on the German home front.[7] The crisis was weathered but another worrying development was the emergence of Britain as a power with a major army deployed on the Western Front. The BEF was far from a perfect instrument but it was improving, had high morale and was present on the Western Front in large numbers. The new team at OHL (*Oberste Heeresleitung*, Supreme Army Command) feared a repetition of 'Somme fighting' and so determined on a new and highly risky strategy for 1916: a resumption of unrestricted submarine warfare.

4

The Year of Strain: 1917

Western Front 1917

As 1916 ended, Allied High Command intended to continue the Somme offensive in the new year. This strategy was blown off course when Joseph Joffre, who had finally exhausted his credit with French politicians, was appointed Marshal of France and 'kicked upstairs'. His replacement was General Robert Nivelle, who had established his reputation in the latter stages of Verdun. Nivelle's concept of operations was very different from Joffre's. He believed that the tactical methods that had worked well during the French fightback at Verdun – using massed artillery to enable infantry to capture limited objectives – could be used in an altogether more ambitious way, to smash through the enemy positions, which would lead to a breakthrough, the destruction of the German army in the west and decisive victory.

The main blow would be delivered by the French army on the *Chemin des Dames*, the Ladies' Road, in the Aisne sector. Before that, the British would mount an attritional offensive around Arras, with the aim of pinning German divisions to their front. Haig's BEF was subordinated to French general headquarters (GQG) while these operations were being conducted. This was the compromise reached after David Lloyd George, who had become Prime Minister at the end of 1916, had conspired with Nivelle (who spoke fluent English and had won over Lloyd George) permanently to subordinate the BEF to GQG. This plan, suddenly announced at a conference in Calais in February 1917, caused the most serious crisis in British civil-military relations of the entire war.

German High Command also rethought its strategy in the west. Recognising the damage its forces had sustained at Verdun and on the Somme, OHL ordered withdrawal across a broad front, to a newly built, heavily fortified defensive position, the *Siegfried Stellung,* which the British called the 'Hindenburg Line'. This retreat took place between 16 March and 5 April and shortened the length of line held by the German army by some twenty-five miles, allowing 13 divisions to be released to the reserve. Allied forces gained a brief taste of mobile warfare, pursuing the retreating enemy over ground that had been systematically and ruthlessly devastated. The experience did nothing to dispel the impression of the Germans as barbaric 'Huns'.

On Easter Monday, 9 April 1917, the BEF's Arras offensive opened with striking success. General Sir Edmund Allenby's Third Army penetrated deep into the German positions, demonstrating the effectiveness of the new tactics that had emerged through hard experience on the Somme and through discussions with the French. One infantry formation, 9th (Scottish) Division, advanced 3.5 miles, the greatest advance yet seen under conditions of trench warfare, while 12th (Eastern) Division actually captured enemy artillery in Battery Valley. On the left flank, Lieutenant-General Sir Julian Byng's Canadian Corps, with crucial support from British artillery, stormed and captured the dominating heights of Vimy Ridge. Unfortunately, Allenby became carried away with the initial success. Believing that, at long last, mobile warfare had returned to the Western Front, he gave orders that 'Third Army is now pursuing a defeated enemy and that risks must be freely taken'.[1] In reality, the British were not yet capable of seamlessly moving from a 'set-piece' operation to open warfare; the infantry were advancing beyond the range of supporting field guns and the Germans rushed reinforcements to the Arras sector. The result was that the BEF's advance was contained and although there were further limited advances, notably of a mile on 23 April, the battle became one of attrition that continued into May. BEF casualties amounted to 159,000 – the daily loss rate was the highest of the entire war – while German losses were around 180,000.

THE REVOLUTION IN MILITARY AFFAIRS

The First World War saw a change in the conduct of warfare so profound that it has become known among historians as a Revolution in Military Affairs (RMA). This was not the product of the employment of tanks, or machine guns, or chemical weapons, or submarines, important as they undoubtedly were. Rather, the RMA was produced by the combination of three pieces of existing technology: artillery, radio (wireless) and aircraft. In 1914, the latter two were in a very primitive state. Broadly speaking, before the war, in order to fire at a target with any chance of hitting it, gunners needed to be able to see it. Effective use of gunnery was also hampered by inadequate maps and failure to take into account wear and tear on gun barrels (calibration).

On the Western Front, indirect artillery fire (shooting at targets not visible from the gun battery) became possible because aeroplanes flew over enemy positions and identified targets. Gunners, aided by accurate maps produced by aerial photography, were guided by airmen who used radio to direct the fire of guns until the shells were landing accurately on the target. Battles were now conducted 'in depth': forces, headquarters, logistic centres, railway facilities and the like, which had previously only been vulnerable to random shelling as long as they were in the range of artillery, could now be deliberately and accurately targeted. Counter-battery work – neglected before 1914 – became fundamental. Armies invested in heavy guns and ammunition, especially howitzers and high-explosive shells, rather than man-killing shrapnel.

The implications of this RMA were profound. War was now conducted in three rather than two dimensions. Further advances in mapping, aerial photography, survey, calibration and communications, allied to innovations such as sound ranging and flash spotting by 1917 helped produce 'predicted' artillery fire. Sophisticated developments in command and control transformed artillery into a decisive weapon, used effectively by the Germans, British and, to some extent, the Russians.[2] Jonathan Bailey, an historian who pioneered the idea of artillery and air power producing an RMA, argued that this was the birth of the 'Modern Style of Warfare'; the type of conventional warfare conducted ever since has its roots on the Western Front between 1914 and 1918.[3]

Before the French offensive opened on the Aisne on 16 April, Nivelle promised to capture the city of 'Laon in twenty-four hours then break out'.[4] If the breakthrough had not occurred by the time that forty-eight hours had elapsed, the offensive would be halted. Although buoyed up by the anticipation of victory, French soldiers' morale was brittle. Nivelle had boasted openly about the forthcoming offensive, with details even appearing in French newspapers, which badly compromised operational security, but he grew less confident as the offensive neared. The German withdrawal had partially derailed his plans and there were some high-level sceptics who saw the flaws in Nivelle's plan. After a tense meeting of senior French military and political leaders on 6 April, Nivelle was left in post but with his authority in tatters.[5]

Like its German and British counterparts, by spring 1917 the French army was well-versed in advanced tactics based on effective use of artillery and light machine guns. When the attack went in on 16 April, the assaulting French formations did well by the standards of 1917, advancing as much as three miles. However, the Germans stubbornly refused to relinquish possession of the Chemin des Dames ridge. The fighting went on until the 25th, making April 1917 the bloodiest month experienced by the French army since November 1914: there were 134,000 casualties, including 30,000 killed. The Germans, too, had suffered badly, including having 28,500 of their men taken prisoner and 187 guns captured. But for the French troops, led to expect decisive victory, limited gains were no longer enough. The realisation that Nivelle's promised breakthrough was no more than a chimera, and of his failure to keep his promise to break off a faltering attack quickly, tipped the long-suffering troops into mutiny.[6]

Fifty-four French divisions were affected, with mutineers refusing to obey their officers' orders (particularly orders to attack), singing anti-war and revolutionary songs and, occasionally, assaulting officers. The mutinies were not in the main caused, as was once thought, by pacifist propaganda and subversion. The key factors were the soldiers' sheer fatigue, their disillusionment with the endless, apparently fruitless offensives, concern for their families and chafing at discipline. Such symptoms of war weariness were combined with mundane issues that could be put down to failures of leadership, such as poor food and lack of leave. A soldier of the 5th Infantry Division wrote to his uncle in June, listing the demands of his comrades:

> Peace and the right to leaves [sic], which are in arrears.
>
> No more butchery, we want liberty.
>
> [Better] food, which is shameful.
>
> No more injustice.
>
> We don't want the blacks [i.e. French colonial troops]…mistreating our wives…
>
> We need peace to feed our wives and children and to be able to give bread to the women and orphans.

Pétain, who replaced Nivelle, was careful to address these problems and used the ultimate punishments cautiously; probably between forty and sixty-two mutineers were executed, out of more than five hundred-fifty condemned to death. Fortunately, the Germans did not attack during the period of the mutinies, which had ended by the beginning of July. Later in 1917, Pétain was to launch some limited and successful assaults at Verdun (20–26 August) and Malmaison (23 October), under favourable conditions, to ease the French army back into the habit of attacking, but for the rest of the year the main burden of taking the offensive passed to the BEF.[7]

Third Battle of Ypres

Britain's main effort on the Western Front in 1917 took the form of a major offensive around Ypres. Operations began with the capture of Messines Ridge (7–14 June) by Plumer's Second Army. This was a highly successful set-piece attack assisted by nineteen mines (tunnels packed with high explosive) that were detonated under the German trenches. Although it delivered key high ground to the British that had been lost some time before, it was logistically impossible to switch the attack immediately to the Ypres Salient. Haig then changed his command team, giving the task of launching the main attack to General Sir Hubert Gough's Fifth Army, seemingly believing that the operation required a 'thruster' rather than a more cautious commander like Plumer. Gough's planning of the offensive was poor and Haig was at fault for failing to 'grip' his subordinate. Haig aimed to clear the horseshoe of ridges overlooking Ypres, secure the vital enemy railway centres at Roulers and Thourout, capture the hostile naval bases at Ostend and Zeebrugge and force the enemy out of Belgium. Ever since he had become C-in-C Haig had wanted to fight around Ypres. Here were the strategic objectives that had been lacking on the Somme, and concerns about the effectiveness of the German U-boat campaign gave an additional reason to make clearing the Belgian coast a priority. A British division was sent to the so-called 'Hush Camp' on the coast to train for an amphibious landing behind German lines, complete with tanks, which would be launched once the main attack broke out of the Ypres Salient.[8]

On 31 July 1917, Fifth Army, supported on the flanks by Second Army and General François Anthoine's French First Army, jumped off north-eastward out of the Ypres Salient. Fifth Army advanced 2,500 to 4,000 yards on the left and centre. General Sixt von Armin's German Fourth Army's defensive plan was based on 'elastic' defence-in-depth, with a series of pillbox-studded defensive zones. In many places, the initial Allied gains of 31 July were lost because the Germans allowed the Allies to advance before hitting the off-balance forward troops with specialist counter-attack units. On the right, the offensive stalled opposite the Gheluvelt plateau. This important tactical feature masked a formidable concentration of German artillery that effectively enfiladed any advance to the northeast. Subsequent heavy rainfall before dusk, inundating the thousands of shell holes created by the ten-day preliminary bombardment, turned the battlefield into the infamous folk-memory nightmare of mud and floodwater that would continue, with little reprieve, throughout August. All this aided the determined resistance of the German defenders. The shattered village of Langemarck, five miles northeast of Ypres, was captured on 16 August. The Gheluvelt plateau, its defenders thwarting all attempts to seize it, remained a significant obstacle.

With Fifth Army bogged down, literally and figuratively, Haig tacitly admitted his original error by replacing Gough as the principal operational commander. Gough's successor was Plumer, who, with his Chief of Staff Major-General 'Tim' Harington, formed a formidable command team at Second Army. In contrast to the ambitious operations of Fifth Army methodology, they decided on 'bite and hold': the assaulting infantry would not advance beyond the range (approximately 2,000 yards) of its supporting artillery. This limited approach allowed the attackers to occupy, consolidate and readily defend an objective from the inevitable counterattacks. Coinciding with good weather, the subsequent battles of Menin Road Ridge, Polygon Wood and Broodseinde (20 and 26 September and 4 October) were highly successful. The Gheluvelt plateau was cleared and a footing gained on the southern and central portions of the main Passchendaele Ridge. If this could be captured, the British would be well-placed to carry out a subsequent advance and take Roulers, Thourout and the Brugge basin. From the perspective of German High Command the strategic situation seemed so alarming that they considered a general retirement from the Ypres Salient. Haig was on the brink of a major operational, rather than simply attritional, victory.

At this critical stage, the weather broke once again and transformed the ground into a quagmire. The very success of the heavy British bombardments destroyed the drainage in the Salient and made it more difficult to drag the field guns over broken ground to get them into range for the next attack. Yet to keep up the tempo of the operation and to ensure that the defenders did not have time to recover, it was necessary that each blow was succeeded rapidly by the next. Thus preparations were rushed and insufficient attention was paid to building roads and tracks. All this contributed to the failure of the battles of Poelcappelle (9 October) and First Pass-chendaele (12 October).[9]

Haig was forced to scale back his ambitions, cancelling the amphibious operation and settling for the capture of the remaining portion of Passchendaele Ridge as a jumping-off point for a fresh offensive in 1918. The Canadian Corps was brought up: its commander, Lieutenant-General Sir Arthur Currie, predicted that the Ridge could be taken but at the cost of 16,000 casualties. He was correct on both points. From 26 October to 10 November, four attacks led to the ruins of Passchendaele village falling into Allied hands. A small part of the Ridge was retained by the Germans. One more unsuccessful attack, launched to extend the vulnerable salient created during the campaign's final stage, occurred on 2 December.

After the war, 'Passchendaele', as the entire campaign became known, was hugely controversial. This battle, rather than the Somme, became the principal charge against Haig and the generals. Losses were huge – perhaps 260,000 on each side.[10] In attritional terms, the Germans were less able to bear the losses: one historian has suggested that, arguably, 'the German citizen army, the reservists and wartime conscripts, was eviscerated at Passchendaele'.[11] It is untrue that British High Command was simply unaware of battlefield conditions: the story that a senior officer burst into tears on seeing the ground is highly unlikely. A compelling case for the battle can be made, at least up to the end of the third of Plumer's victories on 4 October (substantial successes that have vanished from popular memory). Thereafter, there were three rationales for continuing to fight. First, the continuation of attrition and second, to relieve pressure on the French army, recovering from the mutinies. While the need for this has been disputed, Haig certainly believed it to be necessary and he was supported in this by General Hermann von Kuhl, Chief of Staff to Crown Prince Rupprecht's Army Group, who argued 'that the British had to go on attacking until the onset of winter ruled out a German counter-attack… The sacrifices that the British made for the Entente were fully justified'.[12] Third, as Harington noted, there was no secure line where the offensive could be halted short of Passchendaele Ridge.[13] Either the BEF pushed on or cut its losses and fell back towards Ypres – an option that was politically and psychologically unthinkable.

THE EXPERIENCE OF TRENCH WARFARE ON THE WESTERN FRONT

By the time the Western Front had stalemated in late 1914, rudimentary trench systems extended approximately 400 miles from the English Channel to the Swiss border.[14] The intensity of fighting varied from sector to sector. Some, like Ypres or Verdun, had evil reputations, whilst others remained relatively quiet. A pervasive spirit of 'live and let live' frequently developed in those quieter areas, although the seemingly passive state of affairs could be upset by the unwelcome arrival of an aggressive enemy unit or the start of a local or general offensive. In any case, the often close proximity of the opposing trenches set the stage for tacit truces and consequent fraternisation. The Christmas Truce of 1914 was the most famous example but it was far from the only one. A German lieutenant, Ernst Jünger, recalled a remarkable episode resulting from bad weather:

> One morning, when, thoroughly wet through, I went up out of the dugout into the trench, I could scarcely believe my eyes. The field of battle that had hitherto been marked by the desolation of death itself had taken on the appearance of a fair. The occupants of the trenches on both sides had been driven to take to the top and now there was lively traffic and exchange going on in schnapps, cigarettes, uniform buttons, etc., in front of the wire. The crowds of khaki-coloured figures that streamed from hitherto so deserted English trenches had a most bewildering effect.[15]

A typical trench system in 1915–16 showed considerable development from the early days of positional warfare. It consisted of front, support and reserve lines connected by communication trenches. The daily routine began with morning 'Stand To'. During this time both sides clambered on to the 'fire step' (the ledge that soldiers stood on to be able to see and fire over the lip of the trench) as a preventive measure against surprise attack during the dangerous hour before dawn. Machine-gun and rifle fire, and/or brief bombardments by artillery, trench mortars or rifle grenades, formed what was known to the British as 'Morning Hate', a form of mutual ritualised aggression that emphasised the presence of the combatants whilst relieving accumulated tensions of the previous night. H.A. Foley, a British soldier, recorded:

> As the light slowly grew, we could feel just the glimmering of hope that perhaps this morning they would rest and let the day dawn in peace. And then those dreaded flashes and in a moment hell would be loosened all round. This morning, in full blaze of the strafe, as seven of us sat crouched in the little shelter under the parados of our fire-bay, a high-explosive shell pitched just in front of the parapet, blowing it to fragments. The air was filled with smoke and debris and we had the sensation of experiencing a dozen concentrated earthquakes. Our doorway luckily was not blocked and we scrambled out, in spite of the entreaties of James, a miner from Wales, to 'hold the roof, for God's sake, hold the roof'. We squirmed out, over the tumbled ruins of our parapet, round into the neighbouring bay and there awaited the next instalment. It came but not so close; and gradually slackened.[16]

Sentries remaining in place, both sides carried out various inspections followed by a welcome breakfast. The troglodyte existence was essentially a nocturnal one, so daylight hours were spent below ground on a series of domestic fatigues undertaken by work details tasked with repairing trenches, filling sandbags and dozens of other chores that contributed to overall efficiency and order. This beehive-like activity was interspersed with periods of much-needed rest and the preparation of the midday and evening meals. Snipers were a constant menace and the exposure of heads or limbs above the parapet was a risk best avoided. Increased activity commenced shortly after evening 'Stand To' in the hour before dusk. Sentry duty, with each man spending up to two hours at a time on the fire step, the repair and strengthening of trenches or barbed wire obstacles, patrols and carrying parties constituted the majority of night-time work details.[17] A British corporal, Geoffrey Husbands, remembered:

> All the nightly activities of trench life were carried on for our benefit. Some of the platoon were told off for a ration party, to fetch up the company's grub; others had the more exciting role of going 'over the bags' on patrol, or listening post, returning to relate marvellous stories of misadventures in flooded shell holes or among barbed wire entanglements. Those of us detailed for guard duties took their turn with the Jocks [Scottish soldiers] on sentry posts and grimly endured the cold.[18]

The length of trench tours varied. One to two weeks in the front line was the norm but this could be exceeded or reduced depending on circumstances. This was followed by similar periods in support and reserve before the rotation started again. Exchange of units normally occurred under cover of darkness; the new arrivals, heavily encumbered by a multitude of necessary trench stores (ammunition, picks, shovels, barbed wire, corrugated iron, etc.), settling in before daybreak. Shelling or indirect machine-gun fire on known trench junctions or rear crossroads almost always inflicted casualties. A unit considered itself fortunate to undertake a relief without interruption. In a conflict dominated by artillery, the 'poor bloody infantry' were always at the mercy of the guns.[19]

Cambrai

The final offensive of 1917, the Battle of Cambrai, was to demonstrate the remarkable resilience of both the British and German armies on the Western Front. On 20 November, the first large-scale tank battle was launched by Byng's British Third Army. Less well-known, but equally important, is that Cambrai saw the first use of a 'predicted' artillery bombardment. By making use of advanced gunnery techniques, the Royal Artillery obviated the need to sacrifice surprise by carrying out extensive preliminary shoots.[20] Tanks and infantry pierced the Hindenburg Line to a depth of five miles. More than 400 tanks were used, and all, even the latest Mark IV types, which were a distinct improvement on the Somme vintage model, were slow, vulnerable to enemy fire and mechanically unreliable: 180 were out of action by the end of the first day of the battle. Cavalry were passed through the gap but too late, on a short winter day, to make much impression before night fell. Tough German resistance in the key sector of Flesquières also prevented the British capitalising on the initial success. The defenders recovered and the fighting degenerated into inconclusive attrition.

Then, on 30 November, the Germans sprang a surprise of their own by counter-attacking, using some of the tactics that were to appear again in the 1918 Spring Offensive. Much of the ground lost in the first days of the battle was recaptured and Haig reluctantly abandoned most of his remaining gains. Ending on 5 December, overall the battle was a draw, with roughly 45,000 casualties on each side. However, there was a deep sense of disappointment in Britain, where for the first time in the war, church bells had been rung to celebrate a victory. Haig's support at home, which had emerged from the Somme and Passchendaele offensives substantially intact, began to peel away, the victim of disappointed expectations. Nonetheless, both the initial British assault and the German counter-offensive demonstrated that dynamics of the battlefield were changing. For the first time since the beginning of trench warfare on the Western Front, defenders were finding it difficult to hold their positions against a well-organised, determined attack.

Eastern Front 1917

The liberal March revolution in Russia raised hopes in Britain and France that the Russian war effort would be rejuvenated. That was certainly the intention of the new Provisional Government. Arguably, by failing to make peace with Germany and instead loyally sticking by its allies, the Provisional Government sacrificed its only real hope of holding on to power, as the general population and the army were war-weary. With something of the spirit of the French revolutionaries of 1792 about them, Russia's new leaders began a major offensive, later named after the War Minister, Alexander Kerensky. Launched in Galicia in early July, under the able command of General Brusilov, the Russian armies achieved some notable initial successes across a broad front. The Austro-Hungarian forces in the path of the advancing Russians fared particularly badly before the old problems reasserted themselves: the offensive ran out of impetus as logistic problems increased. The German counter-offensive, begun on 19 July, was brutally effective. The discipline of Russian troops was undermined by the reforms of the regime and the

Russian forces crumbled before the remorseless German advance. Brusilov denounced the 'instability of our troops and discussions as to whether to obey or not orders of commanders' and 'the criminal propaganda of the Bolsheviks'.[21] A separate German offensive, up in the Baltic provinces, captured Riga in early September and an amphibious assault took some islands in the Baltic. The results of the Kerensky Offensive were catastrophic. It left the Russian army in chaos, the Provisional Government's authority being stripped away almost daily and the road to the capital, Petrograd, wide open In November the Provisional government fell when the Bolsheviks seized power in Petrograd in a coup.

Italian and Balkan Fronts 1917

For Cardona's Italian Army, the first part of 1917 saw more of the same: costly offensives that attempted to drive back the Austro-Hungarian forces. The Tenth Battle of the Isonzo in May was inconclusive but in the Eleventh Battle, in August 1917, the Italians advanced five miles on to the Bainsizza plateau. However, this achievement was almost immediately wiped by the Twelfth Battle of the Isonzo, launched not by Cardona but by the Central Powers. Under the command of a German commander from the Western Front, General Otto von Below, seven German and eight Austro-Hungarian divisions were formed into the Fourteenth Army. Below deployed his forces opposite Caporetto, a small garrison town located on the northern flank of General Luigi Capello's Italian Second Army. Two Austro-Hungarian armies attacked on the flanks against Italian Third and Fourth Armies. Central Powers' aircraft achieved local command of the air, a fact that was of great importance to the outcome of the battle.

The offensive took the form that would become all too familiar to the Allied armies over the next few months: an intense six hour 'hurricane' artillery bombardment in the early hours of 24 October was followed by infantry using infiltration tactics. In many places, with surprise having been achieved, the defence crumpled, with Italian soldiers being over-run, fleeing or surrendering. There were some pockets of resistance and the Austro-Hungarian armies on Fourteenth Army's flank had a harder time than others. Italian Second Army was all but destroyed and Italian Fourth and Third Armies were forced back by the flanking Austrian armies. Cardona attempted to make a stand on the Tagliamento River, forty miles from the original front line, but on the night of 2–3 November, Below's advance guards forced a crossing. The Italian retreat continued for some seventy miles before a last stand was made behind the Piave River. Here, the Central Powers' forces, having out-run their supplies, stalled on 12 November. Following this, the Italian defences along the river barrier were improved on the orders of General Armando Diaz, who had superseded Cardona on 8 November.

Caporetto cost the Italians 320,000 men, including an astounding 265,000 prisoners. It was a savage blow, yet it was not decisive. Remarkably, the Italian Army recovered its cohesion and survived to fight on in 1918, albeit bolstered by a force of six French and five British divisions, commanded by two men with good Western Front records, Generals Marie Émile Fayolle and Sir Herbert Plumer. These troops were rushed to Italy in the wake of Caporetto, from fear that the Italians would collapse altogether, but only arrived after the military situation had stabilised. Austro-German losses were approximately 70,000.

The debacle was caused in part by the skill of the attackers but also because of the poor state of the Italian army. A young German officer who took part in the battle, Erwin Rommel, the future Field-Marshal, was amazed to be greeted by 'enemy' troops throwing away their weapons and greeting him as a liberator. Rommel was convinced that 'even a single machine gun operated by an officer could have saved the situation'. As Mark Thompson has commented, Rommel 'could not conceive the condition of infantry who had been bundled to the top of a mountain and ordered to defend it to the death against some of the best soldiers in the world, without the benefit of proper positions, artillery support, communications or confident leadership' and having endured a terrible ordeal since 1915. 'The seeds of the Salerno Brigade's defeat [at Caporetto] were sown long before October 1917'.[22]

At Salonika, there was an Allied offensive (11–17 March 1917), in the Monastir sector. This was launched to support Nivelle's offensive on the Western Front, which was to begin in mid-April. The Monastir offensive failed, not least because of the problems of co-ordinating a multi-national force that by this stage included Serbian, Russian and renegade Greek formations, as well as British and French. The German and Bulgarian defenders held on and by May the offensive had ground to a halt, with the Russian and French forces affected by mutiny. The unsatisfactory military situation was slightly offset by the Greek entry into the war on the side of the Allies in June.

Ottoman Fronts 1917

For the British, 1917 was a year of achievement in the Middle East. The military situation north of Basra remained stalemated until the arrival of a new theatre commander, Lieutenant-General Sir Stanley Maude, in August. In sharp contrast to Townshend, Maude's leadership of the by now reinforced and re-equipped forces in 'Mespot' was founded on the logistic art of the possible. Maude carried out a series of prudent advances supported by heavy artillery firepower. He was able to retake Kut in late February 1917 and capture Baghdad on 11 March, after which the Mesopotamian campaign was prolonged by a series of extended operations designed to strengthen British control of the region. In November, Maude died of cholera, the second senior commander to die of disease during this campaign (the German commander of the Ottoman forces, Field-Marshal Colmar von der Goltz had succumbed to typhus in April, coincidentally in the same house as Maude). General Maude was succeeded by Lieutenant-General Sir William Marshall, one of his corps commanders.

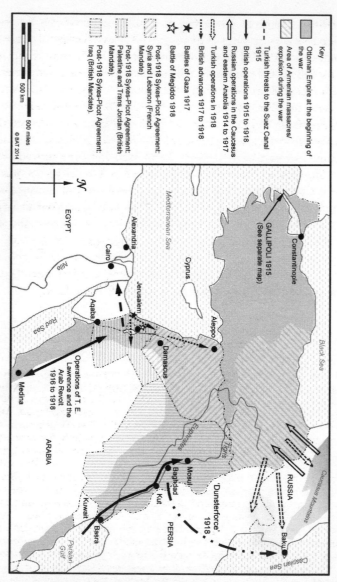

Map 5   The Middle East and Caucasus Fronts

British attempts to advance into Ottoman-held Palestine suffered serious reverses during the first two Battles of Gaza in March–April 1917. The performance of British Empire troops on the battlefield did not match the meticulous logistic arrangements, which included the construction of a railway across the Sinai desert. The second failure to breach the Gaza Line was, foolishly, reported by General Sir Archibald Murray to London as a success. When this was shown to be an empty boast, Murray was replaced by a new Commander in Chief, General Sir Edmund Allenby, moved sideways after his relative failure at Arras. Allenby received reinforcements; Lloyd George, quick to see the advantages of success away from the Western Front, wanted the capture of Jerusalem to boost the morale of the British people.[23] Allenby took his time in preparing the next offensive, the carefully-orchestrated Third Battle of Gaza (1–2 November 1917). This finally breached the formidable Gaza defences and compelled the abandonment of Jerusalem by the Turks. The Holy City fell to the British on 9 December.

THE AIR WAR INTENSIFIES

Under the pressure of war, aircraft development was accelerated. Aircraft such as the Fokker D.VII or the British Sopwith Snipe of 1918 were immensely more sophisticated than the types available at the beginning of the war. Specialised aircraft were developed, for instance bombers such as the British DH-4, the French Caudon G-4 and the German A.E.G. G-IV, and planes used primarily for artillery observation, such as the British R.E.8 and the German Albatross C.III. Likewise, methods of employing air power grew very sophisticated. *Jagdgeschwader 1*, (Richthofen's Circus), a large grouping of fighter aircraft, was a famous example of the tendency towards greater centralisation of air assets and, increasingly, the air battle became an essential part of ground offensives. The toll on airmen was high. The casualty rate among British pilots was in the order of fifty percent, a reflection of Trenchard's offensive strategy; for the French, the figure was thirty-nine percent for air crew (pilots and observers). It is possible that the percentage of German losses was even higher than that of the British.[24] In addition, there was the mental strain of combat flying, which is unquantifiable but very real. This was the central theme of one of the finest novels to emerge from the air war, *Winged Victory* (1934), written by V.M. Yeates, a British pilot who had been assigned to ground attack duties in 1918.

In 1917, it became common to employ aeroplanes against ground targets. Such attacks had occurred since early 1915 in an unsystematic fashion, the Germans being impressed by the effect of British aircraft on the Somme. Two varieties of ground attack emerged. The first, akin to what is today called close air support, saw aeroplanes shooting and bombing ground targets in direct support of the infantry. The second was similar to modern battlefield air interdiction, seeking to isolate the battlefield. On 8 August 1918, the first day of the Battle of Amiens, British planes suffered heavy losses in attempting to destroy the bridges over the River Somme. Both the British and Germans used ground attack extensively during the Battle of Cambrai (November–December 1917), which can be seen as its 'coming of age'.[25] For aircrew, ground attack, or 'strafing' became highly dangerous as anti-aircraft guns proliferated. Their most high-profile victim, Manfred von Richthofen, was killed in April 1918, very probably by ground fire from an Australian machine-gunner. He was not on a ground attack mission but while flying low he became vulnerable to weapons primarily intended for use against strafing aircraft.

Tethered balloons had a key role on the battlefield. Equipped with a telephone and binoculars, from their baskets observers could see very long distances into enemy-held territory – fifteen miles from 4,000 feet – and so were a valuable source of information. As such, they tended to be both a priority target for attacking aircraft and heavily defended. The American pilot, Lieutenant Frank Luke, specialised in such targets, earning the nickname of the 'Arizona Balloon Buster'. Flying a French aircraft, a Spad XIII, in just *eight* days, in September 1918 he accounted for fourteen balloons and four aircraft. He had a total of twenty-six kills when he was killed later that month. Luke was awarded the highest US decoration, the Congressional Medal of Honor.

War at sea 1917–18

In the last two years of the war, the British and German battle fleets maintained their stand-off in the North Sea. The overall strategic situation remained unchanged: as long as it remained undefeated, the Royal Navy was winning, and control of the wider oceans gave the Allies a huge strategic advantage. The Second Battle of Heligoland Bight (17 November 1917) was the final clash of the war that involved British and German capital ships, albeit on a small scale and with no losses on either side. The last venture by the German High Seas Fleet into the North Sea, in April 1918, did not result in contact with its British counterpart. Very close to the end of the war, in late October 1918, with the situation growing worse by the hour, Germany's naval High Command ordered the High Seas Fleet to sea. Seeing defeat and death as more honourable than continued inaction, the admirals sought the climactic battle that had eluded them so far. On learning of the plan, mutiny broke out among the ships' crews at Wilhelmshaven and Kiel and eventually the fleet fell into the mutineers' hands.

In the Mediterranean, where the combined fleets of Great Britain, France and Italy (which entered the war in May 1915) outnumbered those of Austria-Hungary and Ottoman Turkey, there was no major fleet action. The Austro-Hungarian fleet in the Adriatic Sea declined to offer battle, instead behaving as a classic 'fleet in being'. It posed a threat that the Allies had to take seriously and thus deploy major warships to the Mediterranean just in case. They were in support of the Otranto Barrage, a blockade of the Adriatic by drifters. Otherwise, the naval war off southern Europe was mostly conducted by submarines and light surface vessels, which from the spring of 1915 included German U-boats. The torpedoing of battleships such as the pre-dreadnought HMS *Triumph* off Gallipoli (25 May 1915) demonstrated the threat that submarines posed to capital ships. The German-Austrian submarine campaign was stepped up in 1917–18, with some success. In the Baltic, the German and Russian navies were the primary combatants but large-scale offensive and defensive mining ensured naval operations had a limited impact on the Eastern Front. Operations in the Black Sea were confined to skirmishes, coastal bombardments and mining by opposing Russian and Ottoman naval forces.[26]

U-BOAT WAR

The German U-boat (*Unterseeboot,* submarine) fleet showed its potential from the earliest months of the war. Three obsolete British cruisers (HMS *Aboukir*, *Cressy* and *Hogue*) were sunk in rapid succession by *U-9* on 22 September 1914. Such successes suggested a counter to the British blockade.

Seizure and internment of merchant ship crews was mostly out of the question. The German leadership concluded that the interminable enemy blockade had exceeded the limits prescribed by international law (they were probably right) and so in February 1915 the first unrestricted submarine warfare campaign began. All ships approaching the British Isles, regardless of nationality, could be attacked. The campaign turned out to be short-lived. Events such as the loss of the Cunard liner RMS *Lusitania* off the coast of Ireland on 7 May 1915, when more than 1,000 people died, including 128 American citizens, resulted in strong protests from the United States and played into the hands of British propagandists. In the face of international criticism and terrible publicity in neutral and Allied countries, the German leadership eventually ended unrestricted sinkings and returned to a focused campaign directed at Allied shipping. However, the abortive campaign had enjoyed some success: during 1915, 885,471 tons of shipping had been destroyed, with a further 1.23 million tons in 1916.

For the remainder of 1916, the majority of German submarines were confined to North Sea operations in conjunction with the High Seas Fleet. Those operating from Flanders and Mediterranean bases used torpedoes and mines to engage enemy warships and transports. The second unrestricted submarine warfare campaign opened on 1 February 1917. Germany's leaders, fearing a resumption of Somme-style attritional campaigns, gambled on the resumption of unrestricted U-boat warfare, combined with bombing of southern England, being enough to force Britain out of the war by sinking the merchant ships that carried food and other vital supplies across the oceans at such a rate that the country would starve. German leaders had few illusions about the likely reaction of the United States to further attacks on neutral shipping. However, it was believed that 600,000 tons of hostile shipping per month could be sunk before American manpower and resources made a serious impact. With Britain out of the war, it was hoped that it could quickly be won.

The renewed campaign was at first very successful: 520,000, 565,000 and 860,000 tons of shipping were sunk in the months of February, March and April 1917, respectively. Britain did indeed seem to be facing defeat. The introduction of the convoy system by the Admiralty in May 1917, in which groups of merchant ships sailed escorted by warships, reduced losses dramatically. A mere 27 of 8,894 merchant ships were lost while under escort, as opposed to 356 sailing independently.[27] The German gamble failed to break Britain's resistance and gratuitously added a major power – the USA – to the list of its enemies, just at the time when Russia was on the point of being forced out of the war. Of course, when the United States entered the war the Allied blockade became even more effective. The renewed submarine campaign continued until the end of the war, with 310,000 tons of shipping sunk as late as August 1918.

Meanwhile, the struggle for control of the English Channel continued unabated with submarines and light surface warships based in the German-occupied ports of Ostend and Zeebrugge threatening Great Britain's direct communications with the continent. The Royal Navy responded by coastal bombardments and the laying of a mine barrage across the entrance to the English Channel, but the threat remained very real. In response, British naval forces launched coastal raids, including during the famous St George's Day attack on Zeebrugge (23 April 1918). However, the only solution to the U-boat menace proved to be the capture of the Belgian coast by the land forces that broke out of the Ypres Salient in late September 1918, compelling the Germans to abandon their positions. A British naval force occupied Ostend unopposed in early October. In the last full month of the war shipping losses to U-boats had declined to 116,000 tons.[28]

Germany's U-boats proved to be of much greater value than the battlefleet that had done so much to poison relations with Britain prior to the war. They had sunk 12.5 million tons of enemy shipping in exchange for the combined loss of 178 vessels by the time of the Armistice. As dangerous to the Allies as the submarine campaign undoubtedly was, it was not enough to deliver victory to Germany. Great Britain and her allies were always able, despite moments of supreme crisis, to transport millions of tons of supplies and thousands upon thousands of men around the globe with sustainable losses.

5

1918: Crisis and Decision

Western Front 1918

The war was finely balanced as 1918 began. Although Russia was out of the war, the Allies now included (as an Associated Power) the United States of America. While the USA had huge potential, its small peacetime army was undergoing massive expansion and would not be ready for combat until well into 1918. Although France and Britain had survived the gruelling year of 1917, the inconclusive and bloody Western offensives had led to war weariness on both the home and fighting fronts. The defeat of Russia by the Central Powers handed Germany the strategic initiative. It soon became obvious that the Germans were sending troops from the Eastern to the Western Front and preparing for a large-scale offensive that would complete their victory by forcing France and Great Britain to come to terms before thousands of American reinforcements could tip the balance in the Allies' favour. Franco-British forces were thus compelled to go on the defensive and await the storm.

At the end of 1917, Imperial Germany held the trump cards. One option would have been to open serious negotiations with the Allies, offer to restore territory captured in the west and then use the peace to exploit the vast empire Germany had carved out of the moribund Russian empire. Given the serious crisis on the home front and the problems being endured by its tottering allies, this would have been a sensible approach. However, Ludendorff and Hindenburg, effectively running the German government, decided in favour of the military option, a decision taken on, of all dates, 11 November: exactly one year later, the Armistice that ended the fighting on the Western Front would come into effect. The primary target of Operation *Michael* would be the BEF. With Britain defeated, it was hoped that the French would be forced to make peace. Nineteen-eighteen would become a race against time: could the German army win a truly decisive victory before the pendulum swung against the Kaiser's regime?

A manpower crisis forced Haig to reduce the size of British divisions. Taken in by German deception operations and realising he could not be strong everywhere, Haig chose to keep most of his forces defending the critical areas that led to the Channel ports. This was undoubtedly the correct decision, but it left Gough's Fifth Army, which unknown to Haig was to be *Michael's* main target, dangerously weak. Gough had a mere twelve infantry divisions to hold a front of 42 miles. At 4:40a.m. on 21 March 1918, nearly 10,000 guns and trench mortars began to pound Fifth and part of Third Army's position. Five hours later, German stormtroopers from Second and Eighteenth Armies went on to the attack, with overwhelming superiority: fifty-two divisions faced just twenty-six. The British, inexperienced in defensive operations, were using defence-in-depth for the first time but often men were crammed into the forward positions that were intended to be lightly held. Aided by fog, and by poor morale in some British units, the Germans succeeded in reopening mobile warfare, capturing 500 guns and 38,000 prisoners. The attackers did not have it all their own way: some Fifth Army units put up fierce resistance and the Germans did not reach all their objectives. On Gough's left flank, the Germans had much less success against Byng's Third Army.

MORALE AND DISCIPLINE[1]

From the vantage point of the twenty-first century, it seems difficult to understand how soldiers were able to cope with the appalling conditions of the First World War, when the chances of being killed or wounded were so high. In fact, there was nothing unique about the ghastliness of this war. All modern industrial wars are terrible for front-line combatants and it should not be forgotten that large numbers of rear-area troops were not regularly exposed to the rigours of the trenches and combat.

One of the key factors that kept soldiers in the ranks during the First World War was discipline. Military discipline, at its simplest, makes the difference between a mob and an army. It can be defined as a form of behaviour that is the consequence of training and indoctrination, designed to ensure compliance with orders among individuals and groups that creates and maintains cohesion in military units. Discipline is the reason why senior officers can issue orders for a unit to attack an objective and expect those orders to be carried out. The undermining of officers' authority in Russia after the March 1917 Revolution was a factor in the mass desertions that followed. Discipline is created and enforced by a mixture of the carrot and stick: rewards are given for correct behaviour while infractions are punished. Since ancient times, discipline has been the ingredient that has enabled soldiers to defeat often larger numbers of warriors, who may have courage and skill but lack the glue that holds groups together and makes them act as one in response to orders.[2]

Armies in the First World War drew upon a pool of recruits, some of whom were already accustomed to a form of discipline. Germany and Britain, for example, were highly industrialised and urban societies in 1914. The nineteenth-century industrial revolution radically changed work patterns: factory employees had to submit to 'industrial discipline', to be subordinate to the equivalent of Non-Commissioned Officers who gave their orders. They had to remain at their place of work for the entire shift and accept 'regularity, routine and monotony quite unlike pre-industrial rhythms of work'.[3] All working-class soldiers (and the vast majority of all armies consisted of men from the lower reaches of society) would have been used to being at the bottom of society, with all that implied. There were positive aspects of military life, such as regular food and comradeship, and these helped to outweigh the negatives for some soldiers. Even so, all armies subjected new recruits to basic training, which ranged from the unpleasant to the brutal, the aim being to break down the individuality of the new soldiers and mould them into a group that would carry out orders unquestioningly. Middle-class, educated men who found themselves in the ranks rather than in the officers' mess tended to resent this process more than working-class men, who found it to be an intensified version of their civilian existence.

Punishments differed from army to army. Most were fairly minor: withdrawal of privileges or giving offenders unpleasant or dangerous duties. British Empire forces used Field Punishment. The most severe form involved tying a malefactor to a fixed object for a period of time. Although much resented, this was more humane than the traditional punishment of flogging (which was still used on Indian troops). As an emergency measure, the Russian army reintroduced flogging in 1915. Imprisonment was a possibility, although as it offered a way out of the trenches, it was used sparingly in the British army.

Mutiny was the gravest military crime, for it struck at the very heart of military discipline and for similar reasons desertion was not far behind. Nearly all armies executed malefactors. Sometimes the purpose was *pour encourager les autres* (to encourage others). The strict justice of sentences passed on individuals was sometimes regarded as being less important than the disciplinary needs of the army. There were certainly cases, perhaps numerous ones, of psychiatric casualties being shot. Civilian justice and military discipline served two different purposes. Germany used the ultimate penalty sparingly: only 48 out of 150 death sentences were carried out. The number shot by the French army is unknown, as it included some summary executions, but the shooting of 600 men (of 2,000 condemned) is documented. However, in the aftermath of the mutinies of 1917, while 554 men were sentenced to death, far fewer were actually executed.[4] The British executed 346 men under the Army Act, plus an unknown number of Indian soldiers. The Australian government refused to allow death sentences to be carried out on their men, who were otherwise subject to British military law. Punishments were particularly savage in the Italian army. It included 'decimation', choosing soldiers by lot from a unit that had failed in some way and executing them. A favoured policy of General Luigi Cardona, decimation was discontinued by his successor as de facto Commander-in-Chief, General Armando Diaz, who sought to restore the discipline of the army after the disaster at Caporetto in 1917. Overall, some 750 Italian soldiers were shot.

Discipline was an important factor in holding armies together but it was not the only one. Morale, by definition, was critical. The nineteenth-century military philosopher Carl von Clausewitz differentiated between 'mood', which could change rapidly, depending on whether an individual was hungry or well-fed, cold or warm, and 'spirit', the willingness to endure and to fight. It is perfectly possible for soldiers or entire units to grumble but their spirit to be intact. When their spirit is broken, as happened to large parts of the Russian army in 1917 and the German army in October–November 1918, it can spell the end of an army as a fighting unit. Depending on the army and the individual, belief in the cause, loyalty to unit and/or comrades, leadership and other issues were also significant. So were very basic things such as letters from home, opportunities for leisure, home leave, tobacco, alcohol, hot drinks and, not least, food. In 1918,

Austrian soldiers were deterred from deserting because the army's meagre rations were preferable to facing famine at home. In some armies, notably the British and, to some extent, the German, paternal officers who saw looking after their men as a duty were critical to maintaining morale. One of the factors in the serious French mutinies of 1917 was the failure of many French army officers to take paternalism seriously.[5]

Over the next few days the attack began to lose impetus. Ludendorff shuffled his pack. General Oskar von Hutier's Eighteenth Army, which originally had been a flank-guard, had advanced the furthest and was designated the primary effort in an attempt to drive a wedge between the southernmost British and northernmost French formations. This new plan dissipated the strength of the German attack and, remarkably, Ludendorff failed to concentrate on capturing critical communications centres. If these had fallen into German hands, the BEF's ability to fight would have been compromised, perhaps fatally.[6] Facing the nightmare of the Allies being divided and defeated separately, the British agreed to a long-standing French objective: unity of command under a French officer. On 26 March, General Ferdinand Foch became 'Generalissimo'.

The German tactics of using hurricane artillery bombardments and stormtroops were not infallible. That became clear when Operation *Mars*, a new phase of the offensive aimed at Arras, was decisively defeated by British Third Army on 28 March. Moreover, *Michael* was faltering as British resistance stiffened and French divisions arrived. The Germans could not maintain their momentum as the infantry moved beyond the range of supporting artillery and the attackers' supply problems increased as those of the defenders eased. A lunge at the vital railway centre at Amiens was halted on 4–5 April at Villers Bretonneux by Australian and British troops. It was *Michael's* last gasp. German losses killed, wounded and missing were an estimated 239,800; combined Allied losses amounted to 254,816. The offensive had made impressive gains – on paper: but

Figure 11   Marshal Ferdinand Foch, French commander and Allied Generalissimo in 1918.

the forty-mile-deep salient was to be difficult to defend. The BEF had recovered well from its initial setbacks. Crucially, Ludendorff had failed to interpose his forces between the French and British armies. *Michael* had failed and the battle ended in a defensive victory for the Allies.

Ludendorff next switched his attention to Flanders. Another hammer blow (code-named Operation *Georgette,* known as the Battle of the Lys to the British) fell on the Allied lines, on the old 1915 Neuve Chapelle battleground, on 9 April. Once again the initial attack seemed extremely dangerous from the perspective of Allied headquarters. Portugal, an ancient ally of England's, had entered the war in 1916 and a Portuguese division was directly in the way of the German advance. It broke and fled, forcing the British formations on the flanks slowly to give ground. If the prospect of the French and British armies being divided was a nightmare for the Allies, so was the threat posed to the Channel ports and hence the BEF's supply lines to the UK. The situation appeared so dire on 11 April that Haig issued his famous order: 'Every position must be held to the last man: there must be no retirement. With our backs to the wall and believing in the justice of our cause each one of us must fight on to the end'.[7] Hard fighting by British Empire forces held the Germans before Hazebrouck, the key communications hub in Flanders. Foch was parsimonious in sending French reinforcements, correctly judging that the BEF could hold on. In the end, although the BEF had to abandon much territory, including the gains of the Passchendaele offensive, the Germans could not break through. A subsidiary drive on Amiens was launched on 24 April and again stopped at Villers Bretonneux, in an action famous for including the first tank versus tank battle in history. By the end of April, when operations were halted, the Germans had suffered 110,000 casualties, the Allies 147,000.

Then followed a lull until 27 May, when Operation *Blücher* was launched on the Aisne. French Sixth Army, which included a British corps, ignored the principles of defence-in-depth and fell victim to the combination of a shattering bombardment followed by stormtroopers. The advance of forty miles netted 50,000 Allied prisoners and the city of Soissons before it ran out of steam. The offensive signally failed to break the French army. Ominously for the Germans, among the forces that were committed to contain the advance was the US 1st Division, which had its first taste of action at Cantigny on 28 May and 3rd Division, which fought at Château Thierry on 31 May. US 2nd Division blocked the German advance at Belleau Wood in early June. The presence of small numbers of

Figure 12   General Erich Ludendorff, German First Quartermaster-General 1916–18.

American forces in the field indicated that Ludendorff was running out of time before they arrived in overwhelming strength.

Ludendorff planned a wearing-out offensive against General Georges Humbert's French Third Army in the River Matz sector as a preliminary to Operation *Hagen*, the climactic battle in Flanders. Launched on 9 June by Hutier's Eighteenth Army, Operation *Gneisenau* gained six miles on the first day, but on the 11th a French counter-offensive under General Charles Mangin, who had been side-lined after the Nivelle Offensive but was now restored to favour, blunted the attack. Four days of fighting, which included the 1st and 2nd US Divisions, continued before the battle petered out. *Gneisenau's* relative failure led OHL to seek another offensive to wear down French strength before *Hagen* was unleashed against the BEF in Flanders.

The turning points: the Second Battle of the Marne and the Battle of Amiens

'Second Marne' was to be one of the most significant battles of the war. On 15 July 1918, German Third and First Armies attacked to the east of Reims, supported by Seventh and Ninth Armies to the west. The defenders consisted of two French army groups, commanded by Generals Paul Maistre and Marie-Émile Fayolle, which included nine American, two Italian and two British divisions. By that stage, German tactics had lost their novelty and unlike on the Aisne in May, defence-in-depth was used effectively by the Allies. On the front of French Fourth Army, the attackers were delayed and disrupted in the outpost zone before being defeated in the battle zone. The Germans had forfeited the element of surprise; the Allies learned the timing of the offensive from interrogation of prisoners and started a disruptive counter-bombardment ninety minutes before the German attack was due to begin. However, German Seventh Army succeeded in crossing the Marne and advanced four miles. Foch held his nerve. He launched French Tenth Army, under the ever-aggressive Mangin, against the western flank of the bridgehead and pinned the six German divisions on the far bank of the Marne into a constricted salient out of which they could not advance.

Then, on 18 July, the Allied counter-offensive began. General Jean-Marie Degoutte's French Sixth Army achieved surprise, which was multiplied when Mangin's attack went in. French and

US artillery, infantry and tanks pushed the Germans back four miles. Tenth Army's haul amounted to 15,000 prisoners and 400 guns. This was not the end of the battle. The German salient came under remorseless pressure as two fresh Armies, French Fifth and Ninth, were committed to battle. Ludendorff had no choice but to sanction the evacuation of the Marne bridgehead. By 6 August, the day that Foch was created a Marshal of France, the battle was over. The Flanders offensive was postponed indefinitely, for the Allies had wrested the strategic initiative from the Germans. Ludendorff described Second Marne as the 'first great setback for Germany'.[8] German casualties for the period 9 April to 18 July amounted to 448,000. The stubborn Allied resistance to the series of offensives had resulted in the drastic weakening of the German army. Ludendorff had failed to achieve his decisive victory. It remained to see whether the Allies could do any better.

In response to Foch's orders for an Allied offensive, Haig prepared to attack around Amiens. Rawlinson's British Fourth Army and Debeney's French First Army were the striking forces. Rawlinson fielded British III Corps (Lieutenant-General Sir Richard Butler), Lieutenant-General Sir John Monash's Australian Corps and, brought down from the north in great secrecy, Currie's Canadian Corps. The Canadians were among the most effective, strongest and freshest formations at Haig's disposal; had the Germans detected their presence in the Amiens sector it would have put them on the alert to expect an attack. But the security and deception measures worked very well. The excellence of British artillery by this stage in the war also helped to maintain surprise. Adept at 'shooting off the map', no longer needing to signal an intention to attack by firing preliminary rounds, the Allied attack achieved complete surprise.

A divisional-sized operation on 4 July at Hamel, involving an Australian formation with some US troops attached, had demonstrated the effectiveness of the BEF's assault methods. Applied on a larger scale, these were to prove highly effective in the Battle of

Amiens. The objective of the operation was to reduce the enemy salient east of the important railway centre of Amiens. Fourth Army had seventeen divisions and 400 tanks; French First Army seven divisions and ninety tanks. Critically, the Allies had a substantial advantage in guns and aircraft. Facing it were twenty worn-out divisions of the German Second and Eighteenth Armies, whose rifle strength was as low as 4,000 per division.

The attack began at 4:20a.m. on 8 August 1918. The successful use of artillery was critical to the success of the attack. Of 530 German guns, 504 had been identified by the BEF before the battle began. From zero hour, these guns were subjected to relentless and accurate shelling.[9] With German artillery largely neutralised, the attacking infantry and tanks, supported by a creeping barrage and ground attack aircraft, breached the German defences on a ten-mile front. Demoralised defenders surrendered in droves; approximately 16,000 were brought in during the first two hours. A maximum penetration of eight miles was achieved before nightfall. The Germans had suffered over 27,000 casualties; Fourth Army 8,800. Ludendorff later referred to 8 August 1918 as 'the black day of the German Army in the history of the war'.[10] On the right, Debeney's French First Army also made steady progress. Fighting continued over the next few days but advances were far less significant. However, on 10 August General Georges Humbert's French Third Army joined the battle and captured Montdidier. If Second Marne saw the seizure of the strategic initiative by the Allies, Amiens, the beginning of the 'Hundred Days' offensive, marked the point at which they began to exercise it.

The Hundred Days

Amiens came as a brutal shock to German High Command. Although decisive victory had slipped out of Germany's grasp, OHL clung to the hope that a moderate peace might be offered by the Allies if they could make advances prohibitively expensive in casualties. The twin defeats on the Marne and at Amiens also damaged the morale of the ordinary German soldier, which became increasingly fragile over the coming months. Out of the aftermath of the battle a war-winning operational formula emerged for the Allies. Foch wanted to continue attacking in the Amiens sector but Haig was persuaded by his subordinates to argue against this. Haig won the argument and the battle was closed down and a major new offensive was planned. This was to be launched by Third Army about ten miles to the north, across the 1916 Somme battlefield. The speed and efficiency of the staff work involved in planning and organising such an immense operation is noteworthy. So are the facts that the British logistic infrastructure was highly effective and that the BEF now had such a large number of guns and an abundance of ammunition that there was no need to transfer a vast quantity of artillery between Armies; the mobilisation of industry was bearing fruit. Unlike in the wake of Messines in June 1917, it was now possible rapidly to switch offensives from sector to sector.

Between Amiens and the Armistice, the Allies fought a series of limited operations, ending battles when attacks began to lose momentum and rapidly mounting fresh offensives on a different part of the front. This approach put the defenders under enormous pressure, ensuring that their troops were thinly spread, constantly struggling to react to attacks and desperately juggling with diminishing resources to prevent the line collapsing. Allied advances were shallow, so that infantry did not outrun their artillery support and were logistically sustainable. This avoided the problems encountered by the Germans in their offensives earlier in the year. By the end of August, Foch, urged on by Haig, was expanding the scope of the Allied offensive, moving beyond a rather limited approach to think in terms of co-ordinated and decisive operations. Foch's battle cry of '*Toute le monde à la bataille*' ('everyone into battle') sums up this new campaign philosophy.[11]

After Amiens, Foch's forces rained blow after blow on the Germans. On 20 August, Fayolle's French Army Group attacked the southern part of the Montdidier-Amiens salient. Mangin's Tenth Army advanced eight miles between the rivers Oise and Aisne. The operation planned by the BEF as the successor to Amiens was begun by Third Army on 21 August, with Fourth and First Armies soon joining in to extend the battlefront to some forty miles. The cumulative effect was too much for the Germans and on the night of 26–27 August they retreated, in the process giving up ground that had been captured in the spring battles. French First and Third Armies attacked on 27–29 August and Noyon fell into their hands. German hopes of stabilising their defences along the River Somme were ended by a fine all-arms attack by the Australians, who seized Péronne.[12] Similarly, another key German defensive position, the Drocourt-Quéant Switch Line near Arras, failed to hold up the Allies: the Canadians broke through it on 1 September and forced a further withdrawal to the Canal du Nord and the Hindenburg Line. Fayolle's French Army Group contributed to the battle by attacking the Germans as they fell back.

To the north, a combination of the impact of the withdrawal to the Hindenburg Line and the offensive launched on 23 August by British Fifth Army, now commanded by General Sir William Birdwood, compelled the Germans to abandon the territory won at great cost during the fighting in April. On 6 September, they retreated. The Allies closed up to the Germans as they fell back. Between 12 and 26 September they followed the retreating Germans; the BEF fighting the battles of Havrincourt and Epéhy to capture positions from which it could launch an assault on the Hindenburg Line itself. Since the beginning of the Hundred Days, Haig's forces had sustained heavy losses – some 180,000 casualties – but unlike in 1916 and 1917 there were tangible gains to show for them; an advance of some twenty-five miles on a front of forty miles. Expectations began to rise as it was becoming clear that the German army of autumn 1918 was not of the same quality as its predecessors of earlier campaigns.

WHY WAS FIGHTING ON THE WESTERN FRONT DIFFERENT IN 1918?

As the British assault and German riposte at Cambrai in late 1917 indicated, by that stage, under the right conditions, attacks could succeed. The swing of the tactical pendulum meant that the defender no longer automatically had the upper hand. The fighting in 1918 was largely mobile, with advances of up to forty miles being achieved. The reasons for this remarkable change in conditions lay in the evolution of effective modern tactics that harnessed the various advanced military technologies available by the last year of the war. At roughly the same time, with some interchange of ideas between the Allies, and with influences crossing No Man's Land, the German, French and British armies developed 'all arms' methods that combined infantry with artillery, tanks, aircraft and engineers into a 'weapons system'. No longer, as had happened too often in earlier years of the war, did foot soldiers and gunners fight effectively separate battles. In place of lines of infantry armed with rifles and bayonets, infantry evolved into small groups – called 'blobs' by the British – based around light machine guns. Crucially, artillery had also become more accurate. Primitive radio technology helped to bind these weapons systems together. These changes, and doctrines of devolved command, helped to ameliorate (although not completely solve) problems of command and control. In addition, the Allies' logistic infrastructure had improved greatly, with, for example, increasing use of motor transport. Conversely, German logistics had deteriorated, with increasing reliance on under-strength teams of under-fed horses. Combined with other local factors, such as positions held by weak units, low morale, defensive maldeployment and fog, these new tactics on occasions allowed troops not merely to break into but to break through defended positions. This tactical unlocking of the battlefront allowed the higher military arts of operations and strategy, largely in abeyance on the Western Front since late 1914, to come back into play.

The cumulative effects of attrition on the German army also played their part. The impact of the casualties of the campaigns of 1915–17 was magnified by the heavy losses sustained by the Germans in their 1918 offensives. Civilian sufferings on the German home front, the collapse of support for the Kaiser's regime and political subversion severely eroded the morale of individual soldiers and the cohesion of army units. Moreover, the operational methods of the Allies and the battlefield skills and will-to-win of British Empire forces were, by the second half of 1918, clearly superior to those of the Germans.

The arrival of large numbers of enthusiastic American forces raised Allied morale and depressed that of the Germans. All these factors contributed to the German army suffering a series of cataclysmic defeats between July and November 1918, which only ended when the German government sued for peace.[13]

The Grand Offensive

The British advance to the Hindenburg Line was part of Foch's concept, influenced by Haig, of a Grand Offensive that would bring maximum pressure to bear on the Germans. Over four days, a series of sequential offensives would ripple along the front. First, on 26 September, there would be a combined French and American push in the Meuse-Argonne area. On the following day, British First and Third Armies would strike towards Cambrai. The next operation would begin on 28 September, when an Army Group commanded by King Albert of the Belgians, which included French divisions

Figure 13   Logistics, old and new: a French truck is dragged out of mud by a team of horses.

and Plumer's British Second Army, would attempt to break out of the Ypres Salient. Finally, British Fourth and French First Armies would attack in the St Quentin sector.

While the timely reinforcement of American manpower was extremely welcome to the Allies, the arrival of sizeable US forces in France complicated the conduct of strategy. General John J. Pershing, the senior American commander in Europe, had the firm conviction that it was in the US national interest to, as far as possible, keep his formations together and fight as a unitary American Army. He was prepared to allow US troops to be attached to Allied forces for training and to gain experience but resisted the pleas of the French and British that they should come permanently under their command. This caused considerable tensions in the higher echelons of the coalition. In early September, Pershing was determined to command First American Army in an attack on the St Mihiel Salient near Verdun as a preliminary to an advance on Metz. Foch and Haig were, rightly, opposed to this, as it made far more sense for the Americans to attack northwest as part of a series of concentric offensives. Nevertheless, the St Mihiel operation was launched on 12 September, when the Americans, reinforced by French divisions, caught the Germans pulling out of the sector. With this victory under Pershing's belt, as a result of the compromise previously agreed with Foch, the US Army was transferred to the Meuse-Argonne area. This sixty-mile move presented the American logisticians with a severe challenge but allowed the Americans to take part in the Grand Offensive.

When on 26 September 1918 American First Army and French Fourth Army attacked on a front that extended from the River Meuse to the Argonne Forest, they came up against a very tough defensive zone some twelve miles deep. It was defended by German Army Groups commanded by General Max von Gallwitz and the German Crown Prince. The French were halted after a four-day general advance of nine miles. Pershing's forces pushed on five miles to the Meuse heights but advanced only two miles in the dense and tangled vegetation of the Argonne. The inexperience of

Figure 14   General John J. Pershing, Commander-in-Chief of the American Expeditionary Forces, 1917–19.

the Americans told against them, as did Pershing's neglect of the lessons learned so painfully over previous years by the French and British. His belief that the infantryman's rifle, rather than quick-firing artillery, was the key to success on the battlefield cost the lives of many of his soldiers. On the ground, the Americans learned quickly and by the end of the fighting had become a much more combat-capable force. The formation of US Second Army on 12 October, under General Robert L. Bullard, meant that Pershing stepped up to be a de facto Army Group commander. His replacement at US First Army, General Hunter Liggett, was a distinct improvement.[14] Liggett reorganised his force, conducting operations more in accordance with established Anglo-French methods and with greater success.

The second phase of the American attack began on 4 October. Four weeks of costly frontal attacks followed before the tenacious defenders gradually gave way. By 31 October, the pursuing American and French divisions had advanced ten and twenty miles, respectively. The offensive resumed on 1 November. By the time of the Armistice, American and French forces had pressed on a further twenty-one miles to threaten the vital railway hub at Sedan. American losses in what was their greatest military effort of the war amounted to 117,000 killed, wounded and missing. French casualties were approximately 70,000; German between 90,000 and 120,000. Pershing had failed to win the clear-cut decisive victory he wanted but the effect of attrition of Meuse-Argonne was important in bringing about the German collapse. Probably just as important was the psychological impact on German High Command and soldiers on the front line of their enemies receiving such a huge and apparently inexhaustible boost in manpower: to many the war was already lost.[15]

While this grinding attrition was taking place on the southern flank, on 27 September the BEF drove towards Cambrai. The Canadian Corps of First Army broke through the formidable defences of the Canal du Nord, which included three trench systems, with Third Army acting as First Army's flank guard. Having suffered blows in the south and centre, the Germans were next hit in the north. On 28 September, King Albert's Flanders Army Group (GAF) crossed the 1917 battlefield east of Ypres in a single day. By 30 September the Passchendaele and Messines ridges were once more in Allied hands. Shortly afterwards, a logistic snarl-up forced operations to be halted for two weeks but the GAF's success soon prompted the Germans to abandon the Belgian coast – thus fulfilling one of Britain's primary war aims.

The final act of the Grand Offensive began on 29 September 1918. Monash's Australian Corps (Fourth Army), with II American

Corps under command, attacked the sector of the Hindenburg Line at Bellicourt, near St Quentin. Here, the St Quentin Canal passed into a tunnel, which was heavily defended but Rawlinson and Monash reasoned that it was easier than attacking across the open canal. A methodical bombardment attempted to prepare the way for the attack. However, a little way to the south, 46th (North Midland) Division, a hitherto undistinguished formation of Lieutenant-General Sir Walter Braithwaite's British IX Corps, achieved surprise by employing a mass of guns in a brief, violent bombardment and attacked across the open canal. The turning point was the capture of a small bridge at Ricqueval in a *coup de main* by an infantry patrol from 137 Brigade, a Territorial Force formation of Staffordshire battalions. Other men crossed the canal wearing lifebelts from Channel ferries; 46th Division smashed through the Hindenburg Line and broke the deadlock on the Australian Corps' front. The Germans had lost their last major defensive position and with it any chance of retarding the relentless enemy advance. Across most of the BEF's front, the Germans began to retreat.

Some tough fighting remained to be done but the end of the war was near. Cambrai was captured by the BEF on 9 October and Rawlinson's Fourth Army, which included II American Corps, won an important victory on the Selle on 17 October. French Fifth and Tenth Armies drove forward as the German forces fell back to another defensive position. While in some places, for example in the British Fifth Army sector, German units were retreating so quickly that the Allies struggled to keep pace with them, in others they fought hard. In October, an advance of about twenty miles cost the BEF 120,000 casualties. The Canadians seized Valenciennes on 1–2 November and the BEF's last major offensive of the war, the Battle of the Sambre, was launched on 4 November. For British Third and Fourth Armies and French First Army, the Sambre was a hard but successful fight that ended in mass surrender of the Germans and the defenders being turned out of yet another strong position. Any illusions that German High Command may have had about the outcome of the war were dispelled. With the home front collapsing behind them, Germany's allies Austria–Hungary, Turkey and Bulgaria dropping out of the war, and German soldiers in the front lines surrendering in droves, the end had come. The Allies debated among themselves whether to fight on to inflict more damage on the Germans, or even to advance into Germany. Faced with mounting logistic problems, the fear of, in Haig's words, 'a life and death struggle', stiffening resistance if the Allies pushed on and even a Bolshevik revolution that would spread beyond Germany's borders, the Allies accepted Germany's request for an armistice.[16]

Allied casualties in this final advance to victory were approximately 1,070,000, almost all killed, wounded or missing. German losses amounted to 785,833 killed and wounded and the huge number of 386,342 prisoners. The Armistice came into effect at 11a.m. on 11 November 1918. Germany, having suffered a catastrophic series of defeats in the field, was forced to capitulate.

KEY COMMANDERS IN THE LATER YEARS OF THE WAR

Field-Marshal Sir Douglas Haig (1861–1928)

Commander-in- Chief of the BEF in France and Flanders from December 1915 to April 1919, Field-Marshal Sir Douglas Haig is one of the most controversial figures in British history. His attritional battles of 1916–17 have cast him as a callous 'butcher', although modern scholarship has largely debunked this unflattering portrait.[17] Born to a prominent Scottish distiller's family, he was the top student in his year at Sandhurst and spotted as an exceptionally promising officer from early in his career. He saw active service in the Sudan (1898) and made his name in the Second Boer War (1899–1902). The next decade was largely spent in demanding administrative posts, in which he had a major influence on the reform of the army. This included overseeing the writing of *Field Service Regulations,* the doctrine that was to be used in 1914–18, and acting as the military right-hand man of the great reforming Liberal Secretary of State for War, Richard Burdon (later Lord) Haldane, in the creation of the British Expeditionary Force and the Territorial Force.

Haig commanded the BEF's I Corps in France and Belgium during 1914, making his name at the First Battle of Ypres, and First Army throughout 1915. Succeeding Field-Marshal Sir John French, following political fallout engendered by the Battle of Loos, he took command of the BEF on 17 December 1915. During July–November 1916, he committed the bulk of available forces to the long, drawn-out Anglo-French offensive on the Somme. The mixed strategy of attempted breakthrough and consequent attrition continued with enormous losses in men and material into 1917, with the Arras and Third Ypres (Passchendaele) campaigns. His finest hour came in the immediate aftermath of the great German spring offensives with the advance to victory during the 'Hundred Days' offensives (August–November 1918). As C-in-C, Haig was far more than just a battle-field commander: he was, among other things, closely involved in training the army and had a lively appreciation of the importance of logistics. Created an Earl in 1919, he finished his active military career in 1921 and spent the remainder of his life as the unofficial leader of British war veterans, including acting as a very popular President of the British Legion. He died in 1928, mourned as a hero across the Empire.

Marshal Ferdinand Foch (1851–1929)

Born in the Hautes-Pyrénées commune of Tarbes, Foch first rose to prominence as an artillery specialist after service in the Franco-Prussian War. Foch was commandant of the *Ecole de Guerre* from 1907–11 and his lectures and publications were influential in promot-ing the French army's cult of the offensive. He was commander of XX Corps at the outbreak of war and succeeded in halting the German advance on Nancy during the Battle of the Frontiers (August–Septem-ber 1914). Foch was then appointed to command Ninth Army, which played a key role in the decisive First Battle of the Marne. He also co-ordinated Allied forces during the First Battle of Ypres in Octo-ber–November 1914. Foch commanded the French Northern Army Group during the 1915 offensives and had a prominent role in the 1916 Somme offensive. He was removed at the end of 1916 and had, in effect, a sabbatical, during which he had leisure to think through his military ideas.

Foch was recalled to service as Chief of the General Staff in May 1917 by the new French Commander-in-Chief, Pétain. In March 1918, Foch was the obvious choice as Supreme Allied Commander (or Generalissimo), not least because he was trusted by Haig. Foch was not made commander of the French army as Pétain remained in that post. Foch refused to act in the partisan interests of his country. It was this fact, allied to his remarkable diplomatic and military skills, which made him an outstandingly effective co-ordinator of the Allied armies on the Western Front during 1918. Widely regarded as the man who, in a military sense, won the war in 1918, Foch's reputation later fell into the doldrums in the Anglophone world as he became forgotten, but it has undergone a deserved revival among historians in recent years.

Field-Marshal Paul von Hindenburg (1847–1934) and General Erich Ludendorff (1865–1937)

The German commanders Hindenburg and Ludendorff achieved remarkable national fame as a consequence of their operations against the Russians in the early years of the war. The failure of Falkenhayn's strategy in 1916 led to Hindenburg being appointed Chief of the General Staff and Ludendorff as First Quartermaster-General respectively. Hindenburg had retired in 1911 but was recalled to service in 1914. Ludendorff, a relatively obscure staff officer, came to prominence for his role during the capture of the Belgian fortress of Liège in August 1914. Sent to the Eastern Front following the crisis engendered by the Russian invasion of East Prussia, their victories (Tannenberg, Masurian Lakes, the Gorlice-Tarnow Offensive) during 1914–15 made their names. Hindenburg, who was immensely popular with the public (his nearest contemporary equivalent in this regard was Kitchener in Britain), acted as titular commander, while Ludendorff devised plans and made command decisions. In 1916, the two men took over supreme military command in Germany, replacing Falkenhayn, and became the government of Germany in all but name, establishing a 'Silent Dictatorship'. However, the 'Hindenburg Programme' of mobilising German economy and society proved to be disastrous for the cohesion of Wilhelmine Germany. A further failure occurred in 1917, when the gamble to resume unrestricted submarine warfare backfired and the attempt to win a decisive victory on the Western Front turned Germany's position of great strength into one of cataclysmic defeat. Ludendorff suffered a nervous breakdown in the autumn of 1918, as the German armies were being defeated before his eyes and he resigned on 26 October, falling out with Hindenburg in the process. He was replaced by General Wilhelm Gröner. Any sober consideration of the evidence must come to the conclusion that the command team of Hindenburg and Ludendorff was a disaster for the country they served.

Hindenburg's reputation survived the loss of the war and, although a firm monarchist, he served as President of the new German Republic. He died in office in 1934, which allowed his Chancellor, Adolf Hitler, to unite the two posts under the title *Führer* (leader). Ludendorff's extreme nationalism and ideas of total war were proto-Nazi and it is no surprise to find him associated with Hitler; he took part in the failed Beer Hall Putsch in Munich in 1923.

Italian and Balkan Fronts 1918

Austria-Hungary, its armed forces torn by ethnic divisions, managed to launch one more major offensive on 15 June. The first stages went well and put the Italian defenders on the Piave under some pressure, with Austrian troops advancing up to five miles. Diaz, supported by British and French troops, counter-attacked and retook the ground, inflicting 143,000 casualties on the Austrians. The failure dealt a severe psychological blow to the Hapsburg army and, not before time, Conrad paid for the failure with his job. Influenced by his allies and by the need to improve Italy's position in future negotiations about the post-war settlement, Diaz, with his armies re-organised and re-equipped since the Caporetto disaster of the previous year, prepared a final offensive against Austro-Hungarian positions north of the Piave River in autumn of 1918.

The Battle of Vittorio Venito was the climactic battle of the war in Italy. On the right, five armies, including French, British and American units, were committed to storming the defences of Borojević's Fifth and Sixth Austro-Hungarian Armies. On the left, First and Sixth Italian Armies were tasked with holding the Trentino front forces of Archduke Charles in place. By mid-October, Diaz had assembled fifty-six divisions and 7,700 guns opposite fifty-five comparatively weak divisions supported by 6,000 guns. The great offensive opened – one year to the day after the Caporetto rout – on 24 October. Striking the hinge of the enemy army groups, Italian Fourth Army forced the Austrians to commit reserves from the lower Piave. With the enemy's central front denuded, Diaz opened his main attack three days later on 27 October. The slow advance developed into a major breakthrough on the 28th, as three separate bridgeheads across the Piave were conjoined, followed by a determined forward thrust all along the line. British and French troops played a prominent role: indeed, Italian Tenth Army was commanded by a British general, Lord Cavan and Twelfth Army by a Frenchman, General Jean Graziani. The blow proved fatal for the Dual Monarchy and resistance collapsed from the Trentino front to the Adriatic. Italian cavalry and armoured cars pursued a fleeing enemy that surrendered en masse. Approximately 500,000 prisoners were taken. Italian losses killed, wounded and missing were 38,000. On 3 November a truce was signed at Villa Giusti. The bitter war on the Italian front was over.

On the Salonika front, on 15 September 1918, the deadlock was finally broken in dramatic fashion. The Allied Salonika Army, under the dynamic leadership of a new French commander, General Franchet d'Esperey ('Desperate Franktie' to the British) began the Vardar offensive, broke through the Bulgarian defences in the mountains, advancing up to forty miles. Serbian units that excelled at mountain warfare and were grimly determined to regain their homeland and French forces played a central role. The defeat forced Bulgaria, which was suffering from considerable discontent on the home front, to surrender on 30 September. Allied forces pushed on through the Macedonian hinterland to reconquer Serbia and cross the Danube as a preliminary to the invasion of Hungary before armistice negotiations terminated further hostilities.

Ottoman Fronts 1918

The Mesopotamian campaign resumed with a major British offensive in October 1918. With a final objective of seizing the Ottoman-held northern provinces, especially the oil-rich area around Mosul, military operations progressed with a series of frontal assaults and flanking manoeuvres until the demoralised defenders surrendered on 29 October. There was also, in the aftermath of the collapse of Russia, competition between the British and Central Powers for Persia and the oil fields around Baku.

A simmering revolt among the Arab tribes in the Hejaz proved a significant distraction to the Ottoman army in the Middle East and thus indirectly aided the offensive operations of the British forces in Palestine. Arab guerrilla forces carried out classic 'hit and run' operations, especially against railways, which disrupted Ottoman lines of supply and tied down sizeable numbers of troops. One of the principal leaders was Prince Feisal ibn Hussein, the son of the Sherif of Mecca. Feisal proved to be an effective guerrilla leader and had an essential role in uniting the various tribes. He was assisted by Colonel T.E. Lawrence. Before the war Lawrence had done some work as an archaeologist in the Middle East. Becoming a temporary officer in 1914, he was posted as an Intelligence Officer to Cairo and in October 1916 began work as liaison officer with Feisal. An enigmatic figure, Lawrence identified strongly with Arab culture and political aspirations.

'Lawrence of Arabia's' image, fostered by the American journalist Lowell Thomas, was of a glamorous figure in an unglamorous war. In his post-war writings Lawrence created the image of himself as a master of guerrilla warfare who used his understanding and sympathy for Arabs and their culture to build a highly effective irregular army. Some believe Lawrence exaggerated his role, taking credit that rightly belonged to Feisal.[18]

THE AIR WAR AWAY FROM THE WESTERN FRONT

Strategic bombing – attacks on targets not directly related to the battlefield – began very early in the war. In September 1914, British Royal Naval Air Service (RNAS) aeroplanes attacked Zeppelin sheds in Germany. However, it was the Germans who initiated the bombing of civilian targets. Two naval Zeppelins crossed the North Sea on 19 January 1915 and bombed Great Yarmouth and King's Lynn. Five people were killed and a number of buildings damaged. The raid caused outrage in Britain. This was followed by a raid on London in May 1915. Zeppelin raids on Britain continued intermittently until August 1918, killing 556 people. Using Zeppelins was expensive: thirty-four German aeroplanes at 1914 prices could have been constructed for the price of an airship and they were really only effective when opposition was minimal. As anti-aircraft defences improved, they became vulnerable. In September 1916, Captain William Leefe Robinson of the Royal Flying Corps (RFC) became the first British pilot to shoot down a Zeppelin and was rewarded with the Victoria Cross.

In the latter part of the war 'heavier-than-air' aeroplanes, rather than Zeppelins, became the mainstay of the German offensive against targets in Britain. In 1917, the German resumption of unrestricted warfare was accompanied by an intensification of the bombing campaign. German High Command's plan aimed for nothing less than 'to crush the island's [i.e. Britain's] will to fight by disrupting war industry, communications and supply in southeastern England'.[19] This plan, which began in May 1917, was wildly over-ambitious and far beyond the capabilities of the aircraft available, the Zeppelins and Gotha IV and giant Staaken R6 aeroplanes, impressive as the latter were by 1917 standards. It failed in its objectives and the attacking aircraft suffered heavy losses as British defences improved.

Nevertheless, this campaign is highly significant. First, it was a use of air power to achieve high-level strategic, not merely tactical (battlefield) objectives. Second, it did achieve a measure of success. On 13 June, 162 people were killed in London in a daylight raid by fourteen Gothas. Although these numbers were small by the standards of the Second World War, they did cause alarm on the British home front and forced a rethink of Britain's use of air power. It was a factor in the creation by the British in April 1918 of the Royal Air Force, the world's first air service that was independent of either an army and navy. Inter-war memories of the 'Gotha summer' also stoked fears about what would happen in a future war, epitomised by the statement made in 1932 by Stanley Baldwin, a senior British politician: 'the bomber would always get through'. Fear of the bomber – as it turned out, exaggerated fear – had an important influence on British policy, strategy and indeed popular culture during the approach to the Second World War.

The British responded to the 1917 raids by bombing German airbases and in the following year the Royal Air Force attempted a strategic campaign of its own.[20] The curiously-named 'Independent Air Force' was formed in 1918. Like the German operations, the ambitious goals of this campaign paid scant regard to what was possible and prefigured the bombing of the Second World War by its attack on non-military targets. While Sir William Weir, the civilian President of the Air Council, called in September 1918 for 'a really big fire in one of the German towns' because 'the German is susceptible to bloodiness', historian George Williams has commented that 'sustained long-range day bombardment was manifestly an unrealisable goal'.[21] No nation possessed an air force of sufficient potency to do real damage to the infrastructure of an enemy state or to the morale of its population.

Aircraft also had a vital role at sea. Airships, with greater endurance than aeroplanes, proved particularly effective in the maritime reconnaissance role when outside the range of fighter aircraft. Just like the Zeppelins used against land targets, airships were at the mercy of the weather to an even greater degree than aeroplanes. Poor conditions, for example, meant that during the Jutland battle of 1916 the German High Seas Fleet was denied potentially vital intelligence from Zeppelins deployed in a scouting role. Both airships and aeroplanes were used with some success by the British in an anti-submarine role. Although the chance of a U-boat successfully being attacked from the air was vanishingly small, if a convoy had an air escort it was highly likely to deter submarines from getting within torpedo range for fear of being spotted. Aircraft might have been ineffective submarine killers but they could alert naval escorts to their presence.[22]

The main arena of air activity was Western Europe but aircraft were used extensively in other theatres. On the Eastern Front, Germany had a significant advantage, as Russia suffered from shortages of aircraft and trained aircrew. Russia's problems were shared by Austria-Hungary. Italy mounted a sustained strategic bombing offensive against Austria-Hungary in 1918, but it was on too small a scale and too late in the war to make much difference. This experience fed into the ideas of an Italian airman, Guilio Douhet, who was a very influential advocate of strategic bombing in the inter-war period: 'every time that an air attack was carried out vigorously in 1915–18', he argued, 'it reached its goal'.[23]

The Palestine theatre demonstrated what could happen when an air force dominated the skies. In the summer of 1918, British and Australian airmen fought and won a battle for air superiority over their Ottoman and German counterparts. Deprived of air reconnaissance, the Central Powers High Command under Liman von Sanders was effectively blinded. Having achieved command of the air, in the course of the Battle of Megiddo (September 1918) Allenby's forces proceeded to exercise it. As Ottoman troops retreated before the Allied attacks, Bristol Fighters, S.E.5as and D.H. 9s bombed and machined-gunned them with devastating effectiveness. Liman recorded that 'The low-flying British bombing formations, relieved every half hour, littered the road with dead troops, horses and shattered vehicles'. British and Australian aircraft struck deep into the Ottoman rear, ensuring that a defeat was converted into a decisive victory. [24]

The main blows against the Ottoman forces in the Middle East were delivered by Allenby's army. At the end of 1917, the British hoped to make a major effort against Turkey but the German spring offensive forced Allenby to send 60,000 British troops to France. He received Indian troops as replacements but they were not ready to take the field in a major offensive until September. Allenby's campaign was masterly. A deception plan (which included dummy horses and horse lines) persuaded Liman, the commander of the Ottoman force, that the weight of the British attack would be inland, but instead Allenby struck along the coast. Employing similar techniques to those that were proving successful on the Western Front, an effective artillery bombardment heralded the assault of two infantry corps. The impact of the attack was multiplied by the effect of the surprise achieved and Allenby's troops broke through the Ottoman defences. Cavalry and armoured cars poured through the gap in pursuit and the Royal Air Force aircraft attacked the retreating Turks from the skies. Arab irregulars harried the flanks of the routing defenders. The battle of Megiddo destroyed the Ottoman army in Palestine. In conjunction with the Arab guerrillas led by Feisal and Lawrence, the subsequent advance took Damascus on 1 October and Beirut on the 2nd and ended some 200 miles further up the coast at Aleppo, where on 25 October the Ottomans under Mustapha Kemal succeeded in checking the British. Five days later the Ottoman war came to an end when the Turks agreed to an armistice.

6

Total War

The First World War was the most 'total' war the world had yet seen. While there are various ways of understanding the term, here total war is defined as a conflict in which all the resources of a state – human, economic and technological – are devoted to waging war, the conduct of which is marked by extreme ruthlessness and the pursuit of far-reaching aims. The First World War was 'a struggle that became the definition of, and template for, total war'.[1] No state, however, entered the conflict with a clear concept of total war or indeed knowledge of the term. Both practice and terminology were to emerge during 1914–18.

Casualties

Overall losses in the First World War are to some degree a matter of guesswork. In many cases, record keeping was sketchy and hence figures for casualties, including fatalities, are imprecise. However, an authoritative source gives the figures in Table 1. Table 2 breaks the figures for the British Empire down further.

Including some minor states not included in Table 1, the Allies mobilised 46 million men, of which 5.39 million died, 12.8 million were wounded and 4 million were missing or became prisoners of war. Total Allied military casualties thus amounted to the huge figure of 22.2 million men or 46 percent of those mobilised. The equivalent figures for the Central Powers was 26 million men mobilised, 4 million dead, 8.5 million wounded, 3.6 million

State & population in millions	Mobilised	Dead	Wounded	Missing/ POW	Total	% casualties of all who served
Entente & Allies						
Russia (167)	15.8m	1.8m	4.9m	2.5m	9.2m	59
French Empire (39.5)	7.8m	1.3m	4.2m	500,000	6m	78
British Empire (400)	8.9m	900,000	2m	190,000	3.1m	36
Italy (35)	5.6m	580,000	950,000	600,000	2.1m	38
USA (92)	4.3m	114,000	235,000	4,500	352,500	8
Romania (7.5)	1m	250,000	120,000	80,000	450,000	45
Serbia (5)	750,000	280,000	135,000	16,000	431,000	57
Belgium (7.5)	365,000	39,000	45,000	35,000	119,000	32
Central Powers						
Germany (67)	13.2m	2m	4.2m	1.1m	7.3m	56
Austria-Hungary (50)	9m	1.1m	3.6m	2.2m	7m	77
Ottoman Empire (21)	3m	800,000	400,000	250,000	1.5m	50
Bulgaria (5.5)	400,00	87,500	152,000	27,000	267,000	67

Table 1 Military casualties of the First World War[2]

missing or prisoners of war for a total of 16 million military casualties. The grand total for all belligerents amounted to 71.5 million mobilised, 9.5 million dead, 21.2 million wounded, 7.6 million missing or POW, a total of 38.2 million, 53 percent of those mobilised. Twelve percent of British and Irish soldiers[3] died, while the figures for Germany and France were fifteen and sixteen percent respectively.[4]

Civilians as well as service personnel could become victims of the war. Figures for civilian fatalities are even more difficult to estimate than military deaths. Excluding deaths from Spanish influenza,

Country & population in millions	Mobilised	Casualties	Total Dead	Total Dead per 1,000 population	Total dead per 1,000 mobilised
United Kingdom of Great Britain & Ireland (46.5)*	6,147,000	2,535,400	723,000	16	118
Canada (7.5)	629,000	210,100	61,000	8	97
Australia (5)	413,000	215, 600	60,000	12	145
New Zealand (1)	129,000	58,526	16,697	15	124
South Africa (6)**	136,000	21,000***	7,000****	1	51
India (316)	953,000	140,000	54,000	0	57

Table 2:   British Empire Military Casualties of the First World War[5]
*An estimated 210,000 Irishmen joined the British forces, of which approximately 35,000 were killed. Keith Jeffery, *Ireland and the Great* War (Cambridge: Cambridge University Press, 2000), p.35.
**White population only.
***An unsourced figure that is often quoted is 18,000.
****Another source gives 'almost 12,500' South African dead – this seems to include losses among non-white personnel. Bill Nasson, *Springboks on the Somme: South Africa in the Great War 1914–1918* (Johannesburg: Penguin, 2007), p.244.

the generally accepted figure is around 6.5 million civilian dead.[6] These include fatalities due to enemy action and deaths in excess of those that would have been expected in peacetime. Civilians in Russia (2 million dead), Germany (c.478,500), Serbia (c.600,000), Austria–Hungary (467,000), Italy (600,000), Romania (c.400,000), Bulgaria (275,000), suffered particularly badly.[7]

These figures, horrendous as they are, cannot reflect the depth of human suffering caused by the war. They do not reflect the often brutal treatment of prisoners of war, especially away from the Western Front, or individuals who died of war-related causes after the formal end of the war, or men and women who suffered from what would now be called Post-Traumatic Stress Disorder. Children who were orphaned, parents and wives who were bereaved and women who lost their chance to marry also fall outside the bald statistics. Digging deeper into the figures, it is clear that two small nations suffered particularly heavy losses when compared to the size of their populations. Serbia, with a population of five million, suffered 427,000 casualties, 57 percent of all who served. Just over one million New Zealanders sustained 58,526 casualties. Including military deaths on the New Zealand home front and those who died 'of war-related conditions up to 1923', the number of fatalities given in Table 2 would rise to 18,166.[8] These caveats to the figures for New Zealand suggest how the number of deaths given for other belligerents might not reflect the true picture.

The heavy loss of life on fronts other than the Western gives pause for thought. The historian Jay Winter has argued that, generally speaking, 'the further east you went in the European and Ottoman' theatres, 'the higher the casualty rates', in part because 'the longer the war and its related conflicts dragged on'. Across all armies, seventy percent or so of casualties were aged twenty–twenty-four. A sizeable majority had a rural/peasant background (Britain was an exception). However, officers, predominantly drawn from the higher social classes, had a greater chance of becoming casualties. In Britain, losses from the social elite were extremely high. About twelve percent of men mobilised in Britain became fatalities but the figure for peers and their sons aged fifty or younger in 1914 was nearly nineteen percent.[9] This reflects the high level of commitment to the armed forces among this social group, overwhelmingly as officers, and the fact that on the battlefield regimental officers led their men in the literal sense.

Battles in earlier wars could be bloody: an extreme case is Albuera (16 May 1811), where the British suffered thirty-nine percent casualties and the French twenty-six percent, but the First World War saw 'mass killing'. This was the product of the unprecedented levels of mobilisation, which put more men than ever before on the battlefields, the fearsome weapons produced by highly industrialised societies, the expansion of the battlefield, the sheer length of battles, which lasted months rather than days, and the length of the war.[10] But in some respects, 1914–18 was a mere essay in total war. Civilian losses were far lower than those of the Second World War, which amounted to perhaps thirty million. Several reasons stand out. First, in Western Europe, armies fought over a relatively restricted area, which spared most large conurbations from becoming battlefields (which was not the case in the 1939–45 war). Second, the primitive state of aircraft meant that bombing raids on cities were by later standards ineffective, although the death and destruction delivered from the air were shocking at the time. In 1914–18, 1,239 people were killed on British soil by German air raids. The figure for German deaths through Allied bombing was 746. Between 1939 and 1945 the comparable figures for air raid victims were 60,595 British and 353,000 Germans.[11] For all that, the willingness to target civilians, also shown in the German fleet's shelling of English coastal towns and the German shelling of Paris in 1918 by a super-heavy gun, was a facet of total war that pointed the way to the even more brutal and extreme total conflict of 1939–45. So was the genocide committed by the Ottomans from April 1915 onwards against its Armenian population, which killed roughly one million people.[12]

On top of everything else, an influenza pandemic began in 1918 that lasted until 1920. This highly infectious disease may have originated in China. Early cases occurred in military camps in the USA but it was detected in February 1918 in Spain – hence the nickname 'Spanish flu' – and rapidly spread across the world. The first strain, while unpleasant, was only rarely fatal but the second, which began in early autumn, killed far more people than died on the battlefields (there was a third strain in 1919). An estimated thirty million people died from the influenza pandemic but in reality they might number as many as one hundred million. Most deaths were in Asia, especially in India. Nearly 730,000 influenza cases were recorded in the United States Army and Navy, with the death rate running at 7.2 percent.[13]

The war did not 'cause' the pandemic. Poor nutrition was not responsible for the virulence of the second strain of Spanish flu (wealthier, better-fed people died just as readily as those from the poorer classes), although undoubtedly the sudden onset of the disease exacerbated the strains of war. Spanish flu killed young and old, fit and unfit alike. Adults between twenty–forty years old were particularly vulnerable and the impact of Spanish flu was magnified by the fact that large numbers of young men were cooped up together in military units, making transmission easier. Influenza affected all armies but it seems that the Germans were particularly badly affected. At the Battle of Amiens, 8 August 1918, their divisions were already understrength because of the heavy losses sustained in the severe fighting in the spring and summer, which could not be fully replaced. The effects of influenza made a bad situation far worse for the Germans during the Hundred Days.

Refugees and atrocities

Among the first victims of total war were the civilians who fled before advancing enemy armies. Folk memories of Cossack barbarity during the Russian invasion of East Prussia in the Napoleonic Wars helped stoke panic when the Russians once again crossed the frontier in August 1914. The behaviour of the Russians in 1914, when perhaps 100 civilians were killed, was mild compared to that of their successors of the Red Army, who in 1945 visited mass death and rape on a colossal scale on the civilians of East Prussia. In 1914, an estimated 684,000 French and one million Belgian refugees fled from the Germans. While most French refugees were temporarily settled in non–occupied parts of the country, 250,000 Belgians came to the British Isles, the greatest influx of refugees in British history; it is suggestive that Agatha Christie's fictional Belgian detective, Hercule Poirot, is depicted as having originally come to Britain as a refugee.[14] A group of Belgians de-training in Northampton were met by 'Kind-hearted ladies [who] were ready at the station with steaming coffee, buns and sweets'. Such refugees arriving in the English Midlands 'brought home to us the tragedy of their martyred country'.[15] All too often, with the passage of time, tensions grew between the newcomers and the host communities. The Austro-Hungarian invasion of Serbia created a refugee crisis but a far greater one came with the Central Powers' conquest of the country in 1915. Serbians, military and civilian, together with 20,000 Austro-Hungarian prisoners, retreated over the Albanian Alps, in winter, to the Adriatic Sea, from where they were evacuated to Corfu. As many as 140,000 people perished during the journey.[16]

The Austro-Hungarian invasion of Serbia in 1914 was accompanied by atrocities against civilians, some 3,500 to 4,000 being killed. It is likely that the Serbs, too, committed war crimes.[17] The situation was, however, worse on the Western Front. Stories of German atrocities during the invasion of France and Belgium rapidly circulated, often in an exaggerated form. After the war, tales of priests being used as human clappers in bells and the like served to discredit allegations of atrocities, making it more difficult to believe stories of Nazi crimes. However, it is now firmly established that in 1914 German troops murdered French and Belgian civilian hostages, carried out summary executions of civilians and used them as human shields. In August to October 1914, 5,521 Belgian and 906 French civilians were 'intentionally killed' by the German army. Two hundred and forty-eight Belgians died in Louvain (today, Leuven) when, along with a sixth of the city's buildings, the university library was burned down, an act of cultural vandalism that caused international outrage and added to the German reputation for barbarism.[18]

The German policy of *Schrecklichkeit,* which the British translated as 'frightfulness', was in keeping with their colonial methods of counter-insurgency, albeit in a watered-down form. The methods of European armies in colonial warfare were in general ruthless and bloody (the British campaign in South Africa in 1900–02 is an example) but Germany carried this tendency to extremes. In a campaign against the Herero people in South-West Africa (modern-day Namibia) in 1904–08, the Germans employed a strategy of genocide, with probably sixty-six–seventy-five percent of the Herero dying. This has been seen as part of a continuum of German military culture that involved extreme violence; this culture lasted until the end of Nazi Germany in 1945.[19] In 1914 the Germans were outraged that armed civilians (*franc tireurs*) should oppose their invading armies, although the vast majority of civilian victims did nothing of the sort. While a few incidents probably originated with nervous or over-zealous soldiers, most were carrying out orders. At Dinant, German troops were told to 'kill all civilians shooting at us' but a soldier stated that 'in reality... [we] fired at all civilians we found in the houses from which we suspected there had been shots fired; in that way we killed women and even children. We did not do it light-heartedly but we had received orders from our superior officers...'.[20] The use of terror was a deliberate policy intended to cow the population. It was a foretaste of German rule in occupied territory.

As two modern French historians have commented, French and Belgian citizens in occupied territories had to cope with 'a genuine reign of terror' and 'a kind of siege', enduring privations greater than those endured by their fellow citizens on the other side of the front line. There was the ever-present heavy hand of the occupier, imposing restrictions and dealing out all manner of humiliations.[21] Germany imported forced labour from Belgium and France (100,000 in the case of the latter). The Bishop of Lille, in April 1916, responded to German deportation of girls and young women from the occupied zone of France by writing to a German general in terms of fear of 'the promiscuity which inevitably accompanies removals en masse' and the impact on already divided families: 'Their mothers, who ... had no other joy than that of keeping their daughters beside them, in the absence of father and sons fighting or killed at the front – these mothers are now alone'.[22]

German policies grew even harsher when Ludendorff and Hindenburg established their 'silent dictatorship' in 1916. Drawing on a deliberate twisting of the ideas of Clausewitz, Ludendorff believed that 'the war cannot be regarded as ended so long as the will of the enemy has not been broken, i.e. its government and its allies have been compelled to sign the peace or the people compelled to subjection'. In Alan Kramer's words, 'This would have been the fate of France, Italy or Poland, if Germany and its allies had won the war: "annihilation" of the armed forces, occupation and subjection of the people'.[23] Sixty thousand Belgians were deported to Germany between October 1916 and February 1917, in terrible conditions, and a minimum of 900 died. A difference between the Second and Third Reichs is that protests, from within Germany and without, halted the deportations.

The conscription of hunger was a more subtle means of getting people from the occupied territories to work for Germany: the harshness of life at home was intensified by the Germans stripping Belgium of industrial plants, thus throwing many out of work, while offering financial and other inducements. By November 1918, 160,000 Belgians had worked for the German war effort. Similar policies were in place on the Eastern Front.[24] Just as in 1944, when in the period from August to November 1918 Allied forces drove the German army back, they were greeted as liberators by French and Belgian civilians who had endured four years of brutally harsh alien rule.[25]

The 'Spirit of 1914'?

One of the most enduring images of the First World War is of wildly cheering crowds in cities across Europe enthusiastically greeting the coming of war – crowds which, in retrospect, were rushing, lemming-like, to destruction. This is the picture presented, for example, in the 1960s' play and film *Oh! What a Lovely War*. The fact that for the British, the coming of war coincided with an August Bank Holiday, a traditional time for the working-classes to let their hair down, allegedly added to the carnival atmosphere. Likewise, a photograph of a crowd in Munich supposedly captured the young Adolf Hitler celebrating the outbreak of war. In recent years historians have largely dismantled this view of widespread jubilation at the destruction of peace and a much more nuanced approach has replaced it. An individual's reaction to the outbreak of war depended on a number of factors, including age, gender, class, political views and where they lived. There was no uniform reaction. At one extreme were the deep forebodings of mothers fearful at seeing their sons go off to fight; at the other were young men just out of school, caught up in the mood of the moment and patriotically determined to test their manhood. The myth of naïve enthusiasm for war serves the agendas of those who wish to portray the masses as having been duped into the war, or the war as futile, but it does not accurately depict the complexity of emotions in July–August 1914.

The crowds in Berlin in late July and early August 1914 were predominately quiet, simply curious to find out what was going on, waiting for special editions of newspapers (a primary source of information in that pre-broadcasting era). The left-wing opposition SPD (Social Democrats) held sizeable anti-war demonstrations. However, it was the activities of pro-war youths, who paraded through the '"sacred" national sites of Berlin' that came to be seen as representing Germany in its entirety. Far more representative was the report in late July from a journalist in Frankfurt:

> A powerful excitement has taken hold of our whole city. Everything is changed... Over everything lies an enormous seriousness, a frightening peace and quiet... Inside their quiet rooms wives and young women sit with their serious thoughts concerning the near future. Separation, a great fear of the horrible, a fear of what might come.[26]

One can imagine similar scenes occurring all over Europe. Once war was declared, it suited the temporary mood of national unity in Germany for the fiction of enthusiasm and unity to be upheld, even if the SPD interpreted the 'Spirit of 1914' in a rather different way from right-wing nationalists, as signifying the need for democratic reform, rather than unity behind the Imperial government's foreign and domestic policy.[27]

Doubt has been cast on the traditional narrative of Britain in 1914 for many years. The 'rush to the colours' really got into its stride after the 'Amiens Dispatch' was published in the press on 30 August, which gave news of the heavy casualties incurred by the British army in the Mons campaign. Between the first day of the war, 4 August 1914, and 12 September, 478,893 men volunteered for the army, of whom 301,971 enlisted after 30 August.[28] This suggests that the idea of mass enthusiasm for war in early August 1914 has been exaggerated. As in the example of Germany, activities in the capital city have frequently been taken as representative of Britain as a whole, which is a dubious proposition. But even there, contemporary reports speak of subdued rather than cheering crowds. A big anti-war rally held by the Labour Party on 2 August in Trafalgar Square – the symbolic heart of London – passed off without a major 'counter-demonstration'. The notion that Britain's leaders were influenced by jingoistic mobs while deliberating over the awesome issues of war and peace, as implied after the war by David Lloyd George, does not hold water. A recent study of the reaction of the United Kingdom (which then included the whole of the island of Ireland) to the outbreak of war argues that 'war fever' was absent – as many contemporary observers commented.[29] Thus the 'lemming' analogy is wholly inappropriate; rather, the evidence suggests that there was clear recognition of the issues at stake and the threat posed by Germany.

The sea interposed a barrier between Britain and Germany but German troops posed an immediate threat to French soil, which was rapidly brought home to many by the floods of refugees arriving from the war zone. There was one major anti-war protest in Paris in late July but thereafter the German threat concentrated French minds. Rallies in Paris on 1 August demonstrated national resolution and unity rather than enthusiasm for war as such. In the countryside, 'shock and consternation' was a common reaction. A contemporary report said only five percent of the population in one rural area showed keenness for war. But, as in the capital, the general mood was determined that German aggression had to be opposed.[30]

It had been the fond hope of some socialists before 1914 that if a major conflict looked likely, a pan-European general strike by workers would bring preparations for war grinding to a halt. That hope was dashed. The vast majority of people fell in behind their governments. In Germany, as we saw in Chapter 1, Russian mobilisation allowed the war to be presented as a defensive one. A *Burgfrieden* (Fortress Truce) temporarily united all factions, including the SPD. The French version was the *Union Sacrée* (Sacred Union) that, for the moment, brought together left and right. The fierce partisan battle in Britain over the future of Ireland was put on the back burner. Even in Russia there was a superficial unity, although behind the façade lay anti-mobilisation riots and resignation rather than enthusiasm. In Austria-Hungary, there was some surface froth of jubilation, with contrived rallies in favour of the war, but the mood of the masses was similar to that of those in Russia.[31] The 'Spirit of 1914' had some substance. All the major states went into the war with their populations more or less united. The next few years were to place that unity under severe strain.

Adjusting to war

The coming of war took the populations of the belligerent states by surprise and the latter part of 1914 saw a difficult and uncomfortable period of adjustment. Train journeys were disrupted, with the military taking over much or all of the railways. Both France and Germany handed the section of their railways in the war zone over to the military.[32] The streets of European towns and cities were filled with men wearing uniforms, as reservists reported for duty, exchanging the day job at the plough or work bench for, in some cases, half-forgotten military life. Railway stations became scenes of patriotic demonstrations and tearful farewells. Soon, railway stations hosted hospital trains bringing back wounded men from the battlefronts, before they were distributed to various hospitals. Many large buildings were turned into temporary hospitals and medical centres. Glamis Castle, home of a Scottish aristocrat, the Earl of Strathmore, became a convalescent home. Here, a future British queen, the 14-year-old Lady Elizabeth Bowes-Lyon, helped tend to the wounded. Existing medical facilities were turned over to the military: this was the fate of Beelitz-Heilstätten, a pre-war sanatorium in Berlin, which became a military hospital.

The sudden departure of men from farm, office and factory meant that older men, boys below military age and women had to take over their jobs. Businesses of all sizes had to cope as best they could, albeit often believing that the war, and hence the disruption, would be short. The effect on local economies varied greatly. One comparison must stand for all the belligerent states. In England, Leicester, a centre of boot-making, thrived on government contracts. Not many miles away, the city of Nottingham provided many more recruits for the army than did Leicester.[33] This was related to Nottingham's status as the home of lacemaking. Such peacetime frivolities fell victim to an economy gearing up for war. Many families of newly-mobilised soldiers and sailors had to adjust to a drop in income, as separation allowances and the like were often inadequate.

John Keegan's view that women 'with the most insignificant exceptions, have always and everywhere stood apart' from warfare could not be more wrong.[34] In the First World War, women played a crucial role. With their menfolk very often away from home in uniform, they took on many roles traditionally performed by males, as well as the usual tasks of bringing up a family and keeping a home together, made far more difficult by wartime conditions and without the support of their partners. In Germany and Austria-Hungary in particular, simply ensuring that their families had enough to eat was an appallingly difficult job. One should not under-rate the psychological burden of worrying about husbands, sons, fathers and brothers in the armed forces, longing for a letter from a loved one but dreading the arrival of a telegram bringing news of his death or wounding. Increasingly, women were called upon to take up the 'double burden' of employment and domestic work by replacing men in the workforce. The Vienna Tramway Company, for example, had 287 female employees in June 1914 but 7,490 four years later. Perhaps seventy-eight percent of the workforce in some Austro-Hungarian munitions factories consisted of women.[35] To some degree, the participation of women in national war efforts brought political, social and economic advances. The example of women in Britain is a case in point. New, more liberating fashions, such as wearing trousers and smoking cigarettes, came into vogue. Thanks to war work, some women had a measure of financial independence for the first time. The vigorous and sometimes violent pre-war Suffragette campaign had failed to achieve votes for women. Women over thirty were enfranchised in 1918, albeit as part of a broadening of democracy primarily aimed at giving more men the vote.[36] But in general it was a case of at best two steps forward, one step back. Many women lost their jobs when men were demobilised and re-entered the labour market, although female employment in many clerical jobs was much higher after the war than it had been before 1914. Societies still regarded the role of women primarily in traditional terms, as wives and mothers who lacked even formal equality with men.[37] The Great War marked only the beginning of the revolution in women's place in western societies, which was to encompass another world war and the decades of change afterwards.

From very early in the war, governments began a process that was to escalate as the war went on, becoming more centralising and interventionist, controlling or taking over activities that had previously been the domain of the private sector, including key sections of the economy, and generally playing a more intrusive role in people's lives. This tendency was known as 'war socialism' in Germany, a state with a government that ideologically was not remotely socialist: it, and parallel developments in other states, were pragmatic responses to the demands of total war. Under the 1851

Prussian Law of Siege, the military were given 'extensive… powers of arrest, search, censorship, opening mail, forbidding the sale of particular goods and closing businesses'.[38] Similarly, Britain passed the Defence of the Realm Act (DORA), which gave the government sweeping, if less draconian, powers.

Voluntarism

In every belligerent, the apparatus of the state was paralleled, from earliest days of the war, by voluntarism. Indeed, it would not have been possible to mobilise societies for total war were it not for voluntary commitment by individuals and organisations. Civil voluntarism took many forms, from knitting socks for troops to working in canteens on railway stations and fund-raising for war charities. In many cases, women played an important role. A British woman, Miss Hope Clarke, raised the enormous sum of £60,000 to support the work of the Red Cross and other bodies. Like other German towns and cities, Freiburg had many voluntary associations: one organised summer holidays for poor children, a venture which became even more important in wartime.[39] Voluntarism also formed a key part of war finance. Although taxation increased in some states, such as Britain, New Zealand and Canada, fighting the war could not be financed in that way, partly for practical reasons but also because of the need to maintain public support. Taxation in the USA and Britain covered only about twenty-five percent of the day-to-day costs of the war, while in the case of Austria-Hungary, Russia and France taxation accounted for none at all.[40] Instead, governments borrowed money, from foreign sources, banks and, through war bonds (or loans), their own people.

War bonds were a financial mechanism to encourage citizens to lend to the state, thus becoming stakeholders with a powerful interest in ensuring victory. The entry of the USA into the war in 1917 prompted posters advertising 'Liberty Loans' stressing that buying a Liberty bond was a way of serving one's country. Germany issued, at half-yearly intervals, nine war loans. The most enthusiastic response came in March 1916, when 5.2 million people subscribed. The much more muted response to the September 1916 loan perhaps reflected that the confidence of the German middle-class had begun to waver at a time of heavy losses at Verdun and on the Somme. In all, the German war loans raised '100,000,000,000 marks or two-thirds of war costs'. In David Stevenson's words, 'The European middle classes proved willing to gamble with their own prosperity as well as with their children's lives'.[41]

All major continental European states in 1914 maintained large conscript armies. As a consequence, when war came, volunteering for the armed forces was of relatively minor importance. The German student volunteers who went into action in the First Battle of Ypres in 1914, supposedly singing patriotic songs, are the most famous continental volunteers. The heavy losses they sustained attacking British Regulars became mythologised as the *Kindermörder* – the massacre of the innocents – and proved a mainstay of later nationalist and Nazi propaganda.[42]

The British Empire lacked conscript armies. In August 1914, Lord Kitchener appealed for volunteers for the army. By the end of 1915, 2,466,719 million men had volunteered, with conscription being introduced in the following January. The numbers were so vast that to prevent the army being overwhelmed, a number of units were raised by local authorities, private organisations and even individuals before eventually being handed over to the War Office, although 'officially' raised battalions were in the majority. Many of the new units had a strongly local character, epitomised by the 'Pals' battalions such as the four raised in Hull: the Hull Commercials, Hull Tradesmen, Hull Sportsmen and Athletes and the wonderfully named 'T' Others' (formally, 10th, 11th, 12th and 13th Battalions of the East Yorkshire Regiment). The pre-war part-time volunteer army, the Territorial Force, also underwent significant expansion.[43]

Figure 15   Field-Marshal Earl Kitchener of Khartoum, British Secretary of State for War, 1914–16.

This pattern of recruitment was repeated across the Empire. The Labor Leader of the Opposition in Australia, Andrew Fisher, famously said that the old country would be supported to the 'last man and last shilling'. Men poured into recruiting stations. Net enlistments in the Australian Imperial Force (AIF) for 1915 amounted to 52,561. One man, it was reported in September 1914, rode twenty-five miles across Queensland on a borrowed horse and then walked another fifty miles to the enlistment station.[44] Across the Tasman Sea, 14,000 men enlisted in New

Zealand in the first week of the war.[45] In Canada, 'more than two-thirds of Toronto's eligible men volunteered for duty' between the beginning of the war and May 1917 when conscription was announced.[46] Two groups in the Empire, however, proved largely resistant to the appeals: Boers (Afrikaners) in South Africa, many of whom were not reconciled to the incorporation of their countries into the Union of South Africa, and French Canadians. The latter were generally suspicious of the British Empire and many felt little allegiance to France. Only five percent of the Canadian Expeditionary Force came from a community that amounted to thirty-five percent of Canada's population.[47]

IRELAND'S DECADE OF REVOLUTION

Ireland in 1914 was part of the United Kingdom, and when the First World War began it was on the brink of civil war. Two years before, Asquith's Liberal government, supported by the constitutional moderate nationalist Irish Parliamentary Party (IPP) led by John Redmond, had sought to bring Home Rule to Ireland. This would have devolved some powers to an executive in Dublin. Supported by the main opposition party at Westminster, the Unionists (Tories), the Protestants in Ulster were determined to resist Home Rule as the thin end of the wedge. With both the (Protestant) Ulster Volunteer Force (UVF) and the (Catholic) Irish Volunteers armed and drilling, sectarian conflict seemed imminent. The officers of the British army, which included a sizeable number of Irish Protestants, were split. In March 1914, a crisis was provoked by a number of officers based at the Curragh camp near Dublin, led by Brigadier-General Hubert Gough, declaring that they would resign rather than be used to coerce Ulster into accepting Home Rule.

War with Germany averted the immediate prospect of civil war. Home Rule was put on to the statute books but immediately suspended for the duration of the war. Ulster Protestants enthusiastically joined the war effort, with the UVF forming part of 36th (Ulster) Division. After some hesitation, in his Woodenbridge speech of 20 September, Redmond pledged whole-hearted support for British involvement in the war 'in defence of right, of freedom and of religion...'.[48] Undoubtedly there was political calculation behind this move; the belief that loyalty to Britain during the war would help

Ireland achieve something like dominion status. But Catholic Irish opinion was genuinely outraged by German behaviour towards their co-religionists in Belgium, another small country dominated by a powerful neighbour. Catholic nationalists joined 10th (Irish) and, especially, 16th (Irish) Divisions. Redmond's brother, Willie, a leading figure in the IPP, joined the British army and was killed, at the age of 56, while serving on the Western Front. While there was a fragile consensus in Ireland in favour of the war, some more radical nationalist groups, such as the Irish Republican Brotherhood (IRB), stood outside it. At Easter 1916, the IRB staged an insurrection in Dublin supported by elements of the Irish Volunteers and the Irish Citizens' Army.

Among the buildings seized was the General Post Office in O'Connell Street, where Patrick Pearse proclaimed the formation of an Irish republic. Appealing to 'Irishmen and Irish women' in 'the name of God and the dead generations', the Provisional Government announced the establishment of a 'sovereign independent state'.[49] In the face of indifference and even hostility from the population, the Easter Rising was militarily doomed and it was rapidly crushed by British forces. Fatalities amounted to 64 insurgents, 254 civilians, 116 military and 16 police. However, the clumsy reaction of the British authorities helped to bring about popular support for the insurgents. Rebel leaders were executed over a prolonged period. The outraged response of public opinion to the 'policy of dribbling executions' of leaders of the uprising, as the Home Ruler John Dillon termed it, between 3 and 12 May played into the hands of the separatists.[50] The number of Irish volunteers for the army declined dramatically and men from the mainland had to be drafted into Irish regiments to keep them up to strength. By failing to reach a settlement acceptable to nationalists, the British government fatally undermined Redmond, their best ally in keeping Ireland within the UK. In 1918 the government brought in a bill that applied military conscription to Ireland, linked to Home Rule. Although it was never enforced, the threat of conscription in Ireland perhaps did even more than the memory of the Easter Rising to radicalise nationalists. The IPP's inability to prevent conscription made it look weak and the radical nationalist party, Sinn Féin, was the beneficiary.

Sinn Féin won seventy-three seats to the IPP's seven at the December 1918 British General Election; in the north of Ireland, Unionists took twenty-two seats. Refusing to go to Westminster, Sinn Féin met in a new parliament in Dublin, the Dáil Éireann. The conflict variously known as the Anglo-Irish War and the Irish War of Independence began in earnest in the following year when British attempts to use military force to reassert authority in Ireland were resisted by a guerrilla campaign. A ceasefire came about in 1921, which was followed by negotiations that ended the war. The island of Ireland was partitioned between the Irish Free State and Northern Ireland, which remained within the UK. This compromise was rejected by bitter-enders in the South and an eleven-month civil war within the Free State ensued. The victory of the Free State in 1923 ended a decade of revolution in Ireland, which had begun with the Third Home Rule Bill and ended with most of Ireland effectively independent from Britain.

The emergence of total war economies

At the heart of total wars are competitions between economies. In this respect the Western Allies had three priceless assets. They were 'Britain's place at the heart of the global economic web'; the vast economic power of the USA; and the supremacy on the world's oceans of the Royal Navy. Theo Balderston sums up Britain's advantage as giving it 'critical leverage in moving resources towards the Allies and away from the Central Powers'.[51] The Royal Navy ensured that the Entente powers had access to North America, which just as in the Second World War supplied vast quantities of war material and food. Simultaneously, the naval blockade of Germany denied German shipping access to the markets of the neutral USA and prevented neutral shipping with goods for Germany from reaching European ports. Thus Moltke's idea of leaving the Netherlands alone to allow Rotterdam to act as a windpipe for German commerce, built into the Schlieffen Plan, proved to be a chimera.

Austria-Hungary's mobilisation for total war was haphazard and half-hearted. It did not help that the state was relatively under-industrialised. Moreover, the delicate political balance that had to be maintained within this multi-national, multi-ethnic and multi-lingual state (particularly given the rivalries between the authorities in Vienna and Budapest), meant that before the war the numbers of men called up for military service were limited, as was the money raised through tax for military purposes. The same political calculations underpinned the Austro-Hungarian leadership's response to the challenges posed by the war. It feared that thoroughgoing mobilisation was likely to trigger unrest among the minorities that might bring about the collapse of the rickety Empire. Thus the army was modernised cautiously and increases in munitions production were painfully slow. An expansion plan for war industries that was begun in November 1916 as a sort of pale imitation of the Hindenburg Programme failed because, in the words of one historian, of 'lack of capital, labour, raw materials and transport': in other words, lack of just about everything.[52]

In some ways, Russia's mobilisation for total war was impressive. From early 1915, Russian authorities took steps to put the country's industries on a proper war footing, so that, for instance, production of shells increased by 100 percent over the coming months, to which were added substantial imports. Government and private industry co-operated to reorganise production and allocate resources. This was achieved in spite of extreme difficulty: the Central Powers' offensives of 1915 resulted in the capture of some of Russia's most productive agricultural land and industrial plant regions home to some twenty million people. Moreover, unlike her allies, Russia was only able to take limited advantage of access to the global market, not least because of lack of unblockaded ports. In spite of rapid pre-war industrialisation, there were inefficiencies within the system. In the spring of 1916, 3.5 million tons of coal sat at pitheads because of problems of transporting them to where they were needed by rail. Key industrial workers were conscripted into the army; as one industrialist complained in 1916, if this problem was not sorted out 'then there is little point in our buying machinery'. The problem of achieving a balance between the demands of the labour force and the demands of the armed services was by no means confined to Russia. New workers, including women, refugees from the border lands and prisoners of war entered the labour force. Productivity went up sharply in 1915 but slumped in 1916 and, with Russia in turmoil and revolution, plummeted in the remaining years of the war. [53]

The story of French mobilisation for total war is a remarkable one of overcoming handicaps to build an impressive war economy. Pre-war, eighty percent of French steel and fifty-five percent of its coal came from territory that was lost to the Germans in the initial stages of the war. Imports helped to offset this problem: fifty per cent of steel used in French factories in 1915–18 came from the USA and Britain, and Britain also supplied some weapons and ammunition. Rational organisation of the French economy for war was critical. The French co-operated with the British in purchasing in the US market and a productive partnership between the government, industrialists and organised labour emerged, with firms co-operating to reduce overlap and inefficiencies. The socially reforming activities of Albert Thomas, a Socialist who became Minister of Munitions in France in 1916, helped to keep trade unions within the national consensus. The labour force was topped up by large numbers of women, prisoners of war and foreign workers, including many from the French colonial empire. The French war economy developed to such an extent, with 261,000 shells being produced per day by 1918, that US troops arriving on the Western Front in 1918 were largely equipped by French industry.[54] With good reason, France has been called the 'arsenal of democracy' of the First World War.[55]

During the course of the First World War, the British built an impressive war economy from a very low base. The initial approach of 'business as usual' soon collided with the urgent need for government intervention as it became clear that the war would be long and Britain would need to develop a mass army.[56] Nineteen-fifteen saw the creation of the Ministry of Munitions, partly as a result of the 'shell scandal' in that spring, when newspapers attacked Lord Kitchener's handling of the war effort. The emergence of the dynamic David Lloyd George at the head of the new ministry was symbolic of the government's grasp of this new reality.[57] Government expenditure as a percentage of Gross Domestic Product grew from 8.1 in 1913 to 38.7 in 1917. By the Armistice of November 1918, the economy had grown to support a continental-scale army and a huge air force. Half a million shells were produced in 1914, 69.8 million in 1918; 99 aero engines (units) in 1914, 22,088 in 1918.[58] Whereas the British army's operations in the first part of the war had been hampered by lack of materiel, in the Hundred Days Haig's forces were able to fight a 'rich man's war' with effectively unlimited supplies.[59]

Germany's economy was transformed after the outbreak of war as a consequence of the government, especially the army, entering into partnership with big business. Walther Rathenau, a leading industrialist, emerged as a vital figure in the creation of the 'War Materials Section (KRA)' of the War Ministry. This brought about central control via 'a remarkable marriage of public and private power'. Eventually some 200 'war corporations' were created, the first, War Metals, Inc., on 2 September 1914. The War Committee for German Industry was set up in 1914, giving big business huge influence over the German war economy.[60]

By mid-August 1916, with the German army struggling to contain Allied attacks on the Somme and having gone on the defensive at Verdun, the failure of Falkenhayn's strategy on the Western Front was clear. Kaiser Wilhelm was reluctantly forced to replace him with the partnership of Hindenburg and Ludendorff. Their arrival from the Eastern Front marked not just a change of army command but also the ascendency of the military in the government of Germany. A civilian chancellor remained nominally in charge of the government but this concealed the real power that rested with Hindenburg and Ludendorff. Wilhelm II was largely sidelined in decision-making and Hindenburg took his place in public affection as *Ersatz* (substitute) *Kaiser:* a calm, apparently wise, father-figure of the nation. The two generals were now the most important people in the land and they attempted to gear the entire economy and society to wage total war. The Hindenburg Programme set wildly overambitious targets for munitions production. In a few months, by spring 1917, production of shells was to double and manufacture of machine guns and artillery was to increase three-fold, with armaments factories receiving three million extra workers. Using

Figure 16   British machine-gunners on the Western Front, c.1917.

the vehicle of the *Kriegsamt* (War Office), Ludendorff set out to 'centralize and streamline the economy... transforming Germany into a garrison state with a command economy'. The Auxiliary Service Law of December 1916 made all men from seventeen to sixty liable to industrial conscription and severely restricted the ability of workers to change their employer.[61]

The consequences of the Hindenburg Programme were far-reaching. Predictably, industry failed to achieve production targets and the expedients employed damaged the economy. The cohesion of German society was another casualty of this full-blooded attempt to create a total war state. There was little attempt to gain the consent of the masses. People already suffering were placed under further strain, causing large sections of the population to be increasingly alienated. The Hindenburg Programme contributed mightily towards the eventual collapse of respect for, and loyalty towards, the Kaiser's regime.[62] The democratically elected but ineffectual Reichstag, a body elbowed aside by the militarists in government since the outbreak of war, aided by the SPD's decision to collude with the regime, belatedly began to show some independence. In July 1917, the 'Peace Resolution' that demanded 'a peace without annexations or indemnities' was passed. This had no effect on foreign policy but was deeply embarrassing for the government and very publicly demonstrated that fissures were starting to appear in the facade of national unity. The working class became increasingly radicalised, with a section of the SPD, committed to ending the war, breaking away from the majority Socialists that stood by the regime. There were many strikes, including a huge one in January 1918, against the war. Then, about a million workers included calls for more democracy among their demands. Strikers risked being put into uniform and sent to the front. Reflecting the increasing polarisation of German society, the 'German Fatherland Party' was created in September 1917. It gained 1.25 million members, thus becoming larger than the SDP. Its supporters were attracted by its uncompromising message of victory with annexations abroad, and opposition to democratic reform and the Peace Resolution at home. 'Patriotic instruction' was introduced into the army.[63] The *Burgfriede* of 1914 was dead and the conditions for the revolution and near-civil war that was to break out just over a year later were in place, conditions that were to cost the lives of thousands of Germans between the Armistice and the signature of the Treaty of Versailles.

Food supply

Supplying enough food to feed the military and civilian population was a central concern for belligerents in the First World War. In Russia, a mixture of incompetent governmental policies, loss of productive agricultural land to enemy occupation, a chaotic transportation system, speculators, and peasants choosing to send less produce to the market created a food crisis. The failure of the authorities to ensure that the people had enough to eat undermined the war effort and contributed to bringing down the Czarist government.[64] Austria-Hungary, too, faced severe shortages of food. In the Hapsburg lands grain production collapsed: the 9.2 million tons grown in 1914 had fallen by 3 million tons by 1917 and were down to 5.3 million in 1918. Hungary reduced the amount of food that it would sell to the Austrian part of the Empire, preferring to sell to Germany, and problems in areas occupied by Slavs, as well as the Allied naval blockade, hit many people hard. Late in life a man who had been a small child in Vienna during the war recalled:

> [W]e got half a loaf of [maize] bread a day [between a mother and six children]... one of us went to get the bread and put it in Mother's apron – since it fell apart – and everyone got a handful of crumbs. Well, we were often hungry, very hungry.

In 1915, bread and flour rationing was introduced. The ration card of a worker in heavy industry entitled him to 1297.2 calories per day. However, such a worker usually consumed a minimum of 3900 calories. The squeeze on working-class living standards led to protests. Forty-one percent of all strikes in Austria in 1916 were about food. In 1917 the figure rose to 70.2 percent. Many families began to keep goats for their milk and in June 1918 the 'War Kitchens Campaign' began. These kitchens served low-priced food, with one in Vienna serving 100,000 people.[65]

There were similar problems in Germany. A police report of October 1915 stated:

> It should certainly come as no surprise if enormous butter riots [arise] again very soon... The bad humor [sic] among the people ... grows from day to day. The view is frequently voiced that the war will not be decided on the front but, rather, through Germany's economic defeat.[66]

Things grew worse later in the war. During the 'Turnip Winter' of 1916–17, the German civilian diet was reduced to black bread, fatless sausage, potatoes (three pounds per person per week) and 'Prussian pineapples' – turnips. [67] Substitute – *Ersatz* – and adulterated food became commonplace. In March 1917, a woman joked that she didn't mind sausages being made of rat 'but I have a real horror of rat *substitute!*'[68] Some indication of the desperation prompted by sheer hunger among the German working classes can be gauged from this eyewitness account of an emaciated horse falling dead in the street, probably through overwork:

> In an instant, as though they had been lying in ambush, women armed with kitchen knives stormed out of the apartment build-ings and fell upon the cadaver. They screamed and hit one another to get the best pieces, as the steaming blood sprayed their faces.[69]

Horse meat had been unpopular before the war. Class and income helped to decide what was available to eat. The better-off had access to the black market. The Director of Public Health in Freiburg wrote in late 1916 that 'Meat is scarce' and eggs were even harder to come by, 'but both are so expensive that poor and even middle-income families cannot afford this luxury, even if it were avail-able in sufficient quantity'.[70] Farmers and their families, for obvious reasons, tended to eat well. Large cities, dependent on food being sent from a distance, fared worse than smaller towns that could make use of farms in the hinterland.[71]

This crisis in food supply was due in large part to the Allied blockade. Before the war Germany had imported roughly a quarter of the food it needed. In addition, much of the fodder needed for its livestock was brought in from the New World, and Russia and Chilean nitrates were heavily used in fertilisers. The blockade rapidly caused German agriculture to lose about twenty-five percent of its production. This problem was exacerbated by various factors. Chief among them was bureaucratic maladministration. The Prussian Law of Siege devolved control of food to the Army, which had twenty-four relevant departments, leading to confusion and inefficiency in supply and distribution.[72] Corporations – initially for grain and later for forty different foodstuffs – attempted to control the supply of food. The creation of a toothless War Food Office failed to sort out the mess. Rationing 'fail[ed] to acknowledge inequalities of wealth… [and] took very little account of physical inequalities'.[73]

In the first part of the war, the German home front, like its French and British counterparts, just about coped with the demands of the war. From 1916, the situation worsened and Germany was plunged into what Jay Winter has called 'a demographic crisis of major proportions'. Civilians – and the adults were overwhelmingly women and men who were beyond the age for military service – were short not just of food but of clothing (*Ersatz* garments were made of inferior paper fibre), coal for cooking and heating, and soap for washing. They were worn out by long hours spent queuing for rations and working to meet the demands of the Hindenburg Programme. They worried about their relations at the front or in war hospitals, or grieving for those that had been killed. They worried about how they were going to feed their children. All this contributed to a rise in death rates. An estimated 478,500 German civilians 'died as a result of conditions attributable to the war'. What is particularly significant is that no similar rises in civilian mortality occurred in Britain and France.[74]

Rationing was introduced in France and Britain in 1917. Although some foods were in short supply, queuing was an everyday occurrence and civilians had to endure meatless days and posters urging them to 'Eat Less Bread', for the western Entente countries there was nothing like the crisis in food supply that occurred in Germany. This was true in spite of the fact that France lost twenty percent of cereal production and half of sugar beet production thanks to the German occupation of part of the country, and that in general French agriculture was less productive than in peacetime. France was, however, able to prevent a crisis in the production and distribution of food. Male farm workers called into the army were replaced by women, youngsters and men too old for military service.[75] Absolutely critical to food supply in Britain and France was Britain's place at the core of the global economy and the Royal Navy's maritime superiority, which meant that in spite of the best efforts of German submarines, the flow of merchant ships bringing food across the oceans to feed the population at home was never seriously disrupted – although the situation appeared dire on occasions.

Moreover, in Britain, some factors actually led to improvements in civilian health. The total war economy temporarily abolished unemployment and labour shortages drove real wages up. Health insurance became more common and welfare provision for infants and expectant mothers improved. Thus there was a reduction in poverty and malnutrition, which were major factors in premature deaths. There were, however, some negative factors: for a variety of reasons respiratory diseases increased, but overall the war saw 'an increase in the life expectancy of the working class [which amounted to about eighty percent of the entire population] and in particular of the worst-off sectors within it'.[76] In this sense, the British population benefited from the First World War, as did, to a lesser extent, the French.

Total war, at its core, is about outlasting the enemy. From 1916 onwards, the British and French home fronts exhibited more resilience and cohesion than those of Germany and Austria-Hungary. By 1918 the internal market in Germany was breaking down. Farmers stopped sending their produce to cities, exacerbating the problems. As the Kaiser's government had failed in some of its most basic duties, those of keeping the German population fed, warm and healthy, people ceased to support it or actively turned against it. The loss of the regime's legitimacy was a major factor in the collapse of the German home base in the second half of 1918. Similar points could be made about Austria-Hungary.

THE UNITED STATES OF AMERICA AND THE WAR

One of the most important actors in the conflict was neutral for most of it. Unlike his pro-Allied predecessor, Theodore Roosevelt, President Woodrow Wilson, a high-minded former academic, was determined to keep the USA out of the war. His decision was based on a mixture of pragmatism (the polyglot American population included large numbers of people hostile to the Allies, including Germans and

Irish) and idealism: he believed the USA was simply above the sordid power politics of Europe. Wilson, austere, moral and, to his critics, self-righteous, aspired to be the New World mediator who brought peace to the Old World.

The USA did extremely well out of the war. One newspaper, the *New York American*, did not attempt to disguise its relish at the prospect that was opened up. 'Europe's tragic extremity', it wrote in August 1914, was 'America's golden opportunity – the opportunity not of a lifetime but of a century of national life'. The war meant that the British and French imports of war-related and other goods from America increased from $750 million to $2.75 billion in the period 1914–16. Thanks to the Royal Navy's domination of the seas, exports to Germany effectively collapsed.[77] The American economy received a huge boost but access to the US market was a distinctly two-edged sword for the British. It certainly enabled Britain (and its allies, which London was also bankrolling) to fight a war of materiel, and thus was a critical factor in the eventual Allied victory. Contrary to those who claim that the British waged the First World War for profit, the reality is that it brought about what Kathleen Burk describes as 'financial catastrophe' for the British. London was engaged in heedless spending in the USA, raising loans with US banks and using up London's gold reserves to buy dollars to purchase American goods. Gloomily surveying the situation, Reginald McKenna, the Chancellor of the Exchequer, told the Cabinet on 24 October 1916:

> If things go on as present, I venture to say with certainty that by next June or earlier, the President of the American Republic will be in a position, if he so wishes, to dictate his own terms to us.[78]

Just over a month later, on 28 November 1916, it seemed that moment had come. In support of his attempt to force the belligerents to the conference table, Wilson intervened in the financial market. 'British credit was devastated and the pound was in dire straits... [plunging Britain into] a desperate financial crisis'.[79] Various expedients kept the British war effort afloat. Britain had become a client state, reliant on US goodwill; only when America entered the war in April 1917 as result of the German resumption of unrestricted submarine warfare did it become certain that Britain would be able to remain in the war. Financial crisis and American pressure came close to achieving what the German army and navy failed to do – forcing Britain to make peace. As it was, the USA replaced Britain as the world's greatest financial power, an important step on the road to supplant completely Britain's global position.

The fact that Britain and France came shopping across the Atlantic for war goods helped ready the still-neutral USA for involvement in the war in the sense that it developed an industrial base for war materiel. In the event, much equipment of the wartime US army was supplied by its European allies, as American factories were committed to orders from Britain and France. A Council of National Defense, set up in 1916, helped to commence mobilising of national resources. Psychologically, the nation was readied for war by apostles of 'preparedness' – prominent individuals allied to elements of the Wilson administration and the armed forces.

Once at war, American society had to adjust to the demands of the conflict. Like Britain's in 1914, the peacetime US army was small (128,000 regulars and 164,000 National Guard). It had rapidly to expand, through accepting volunteers, enacting Selective Service (a form of conscription) and embodying the National Guard. The army grew to almost 3.9 million men.[80] On the home front, the Wilson Administration went some way down the path taken by European governments of increased intervention into everyday life. The Food Administration, under a future President, Herbert Hoover, sought to control food consumption: 'Meatless Tuesdays' became a feature of American life. So did rabid anti-Germanism, despite (or because of) the large number of German-Americans. The 'One Hundred Per Cent Americanism' campaign demonstrated how intolerant a democratic society can be in time of war. A Socialist politician, Eugene V. Debs, who ran for President in 1912, was jailed for encouraging young men to dodge the draft. The war triggered the move of 400,000 Black Americans from the southern to northern states to work in war factories. This was a social phenomenon that had great importance for the USA in the long term. In some ways, America's experience of total war in 1917–18 was a dress rehearsal for the even greater effort, which resulted in even more profound changes, of 1941–45.

1917–18: revolution in Russia, re-mobilisation in Britain and France

The causes of the Russian Revolution of March 1917 were the product of long-term alienation of groups from the state and an immediate crisis. Initially, the success of the Brusilov Offensive, launched in June 1916, promised to give the Russian war effort a new lease of life but even a victorious campaign took a heavy toll.

Figure 17   Nicholas II, Czar of Russia (reigned 1894 to 1917), among his troops.

The losses and the failure to capitalise fully on the initial successes added to the increasing disillusionment with the Czarist regime and the growth of opposition. Alongside shortages of fuel and food, from late 1915, Czar Nicholas II alienated many by turning his back on some of the modest political reforms that had helped rally opinion behind the government during the crisis of the Great Retreat of earlier that year. The *Zemgor*, for instance, was a comparatively broadly-based committee that ran parallel to the government in supplying munitions, uniforms and other equipment and carried out many other tasks such as caring for the wounded. Nicholas' appointment of reactionaries to key government posts and the supposedly malign influence of the German-born Czarina and her favourite, the sinister monk Grigorii Rasputin, contributed to the situation where 'he managed to lose the confidence of everyone'. Socialist agitators in factories and military units were finding increasingly sympathetic audiences. A police report in January 1917 warned that mothers, exhausted by constant queuing in shops and 'worn out by the suffering of seeing their children half-starved and sick' were growing dangerously disaffected. In

March 1917 serious strikes in Petrograd escalated into a rebellion, which troops refused to crush. A clique of generals forced Nicholas' hand and he abdicated on 15 March. The new rulers of Russia were the members of a liberal Provisional Government.[81] The new regime attempted to continue with the war. The July 1917 'Kerensky Offensive' was a failure that sacrificed much support. A rival to the Provisional Government was at hand. In April 1917, Vladimir Illych Ulyanov (1870–1924), a prominent Marxist revolutionary better known by his *nom de guerre,* Lenin, had arrived in a sealed railway train, thanks to Germany. The German calculation that Lenin would destabilise the Provisional Government proved accurate. Seizing power in November (October by the Russian calendar), by March 1918 Lenin's Bolsheviks had taken Russia out of the war.

In Britain, 1916 saw an intensification of the totality of war in many ways. The replacement in December 1916 of H.H. Asquith as British Prime Minister by David Lloyd George, his fellow Liberal, marked an escalation of the war effort. In May 1915, with disquiet growing about the Liberal government's supposedly lackadaisical approach to prosecuting the war, Asquith had formed a coalition with the Unionist (Conservative) opposition. An event of great symbolic as well as practical consequence was the gradual introduction of conscription in Britain, beginning with the call-up of single men in January 1916. Voluntary enlistment had been in decline during 1915. The Derby Scheme, a halfway house between the voluntary principle and compulsion launched in 1915, had clearly failed by the end of the year. However, it would be perverse to argue that voluntarism was an overall failure: around half of all soldiers who served in the British army in the First World War were volunteers. In the dominions, New Zealand and Canada also introduced conscription. Two bitterly divisive referenda were fought in Australia over the issue with conscription being rejected and many soldiers voting against it.[82] The advent of conscription brought a new word into the English language: 'conchie' or conscientious objector. Men who refused to fight for religious or political reasons amounted to barely two percent of those who sought to avoid or defer military service (other motives included supporting a family or being a key worker in a small firm). All had their cases heard by a tribunal; at least 1.25 million cases were assessed.[83] Some conscientious objectors settled for a non-combatant role and a few were imprisoned. While there were pockets of anti-war sentiment and activity, such as 'Red Clydeside', the vast majority of the British (as opposed to the Irish) population supported the war.

Industrial strikes were generally aimed at taking advantage of the need for labour and achieving better pay and conditions. They were very different in character from the revolutionary strikes in Russia. The main working-class political party was the Labour Party. This was a reformist, social democratic body, rather than a Marxist revolutionary movement, and it served as a junior partner in the wartime government. Trade Unions were similarly part of the wartime consensus. The gains made by Labour in the 1918 General Election further signalled that the British working-classes did not pose a threat to the state.

Georges Clemenceau was, in many ways, the French equivalent of Lloyd George. The seventy-six-year-old 'Tiger' became Prime Minister in November 1917 and his appointment similarly meant an intensification of the struggle. A charismatic, populist human dynamo, his manifesto was simple: 'I make war'. Clemenceau, in Jeremy Black's words, 'added a powerful strand of authoritarianism to the French war economy and this helped focus industrial production on the war effort'.[84] Clemenceau balanced this robust approach to opposition with conciliation of organised labour, an important factor in the maintenance of national unity.[85]

War-weariness reached such a peak in France and Britain in 1917–18 that both countries needed to remobilise to see the war through. Remobilisation was a mixture of repression and persuasion. Both governments had exaggerated fears of pacifism and sought to censor pacifist journals and make examples of individuals. E.D. Morel, a pacifist leader of the Union of Democratic Control in Britain, was sentenced to six months in jail in 1917. But such

Figure 18   Georges Clemenceau, Prime Minster of France 1917–20.

an approach risked backfiring, as when a French feminist, Hélène Brion, was court-martialled in 1918, accused of being a defeatist. Not only did she merely receive a suspended sentence, but the trial enabled her to put her views before a wider audience. Labour unrest also posed a potentially very serious threat. There were many strikes in both countries as the workers sought to take advantage of their strong position to gain better pay and conditions but these could have been politicised and turned against the war. Arrests of individuals perceived as troublemakers and the banning of strikes were accompanied by pragmatic negotiations to bring industrial action to an end. Clemenceau, for example, balanced this robust approach to opposition with conciliation of organised labour, an important factor in the maintenance of national unity in France.[86]

Persuasion was thus the counterpart of coercion. The third full year of the war, 1917, saw the espousal of democratic war aims and social, democratic and industrial reform at home. Notably, the British 'Representation of the People Act' passed in June 1917, and which came into force in January 1918, tripled the elector ate by bringing about universal male suffrage and giving the vote to women over thirty years old. The alliance of state and organ- ised labour meant that French and British trade unions had more influence in bargaining over pay and conditions for their members than ever before.[87] Propaganda also played an important role. Both France and Britain set up organisations at arm's length from the state to conduct campaigns, the *Union des Grandes Associations contre la Propagande Ennemie* (UGACPE, Union of Associations Against Enemy Propaganda) and the National War Aims Committee (NWAC). Posters, tracts, and public meetings, traditional means of persuasion familiar from electoral campaigns, were used alongside the new medium of film: both organisations used mobile cinemas to spread their message.

The First World War saw the birth of modern propaganda and did much to give it its unsavoury reputation. In the inter-war years there was a widespread belief that British propaganda had been highly effective in bringing the neutral USA into the war and had played a role in the defeat of the Central Powers. While there is some truth in this, the accompanying view that British propaganda had been based on outright lies was wrong. Under Charles Master- man, the principal British propaganda organisation, Wellington House, worked on the principle of 'present[ing] facts and argu- ments based on these facts'.[88] The audience at which propaganda was directed (originally, primarily opinion in the USA), was given 'selected facts and arguments and invited to make up their own minds… Only very rarely and with reluctance did British official propagandists disseminate what they knew or suspected to be a lie'.[89] There was a difference, however, between lying and allowing the unvarnished truth into the public domain. Thus France, which had a similar policy to Britain, censored reports of the army mutinies of 1917.

The Great War was the first in which belligerent states founded bodies specifically to disseminate propaganda and also the first in which propaganda was woven into the very warp and weft of a state's war effort. By no means was all propaganda generated directly by governments. Newspapers and other private organisations and individuals enthusiastically joined in the effort. One striking example appeared in a 1915 children's book, which claimed that at the Battle of Loos 'the British were to use gas – not poisonous gas, which caused terrible agony and death, such as the Germans had used, but a gas which would at least make those who breathed it unconscious'.[90]

Propaganda directed at home fronts had been a feature of the war from the very beginning, often in attempts to modify behaviour. A Canadian poster was fairly typical: an elderly woman is shown in a kitchen instructing a younger woman, with the caption 'Waste not – Want Not – Prepare for Winter. Save Perishable Foods by preserving them *Now*'. A common type of poster advertised war loans. Perhaps ten million posters were issued in 1918 for the US Fourth Liberty Loan. One of the most powerful propaganda images is of the massive, square head of Hindenburg (a cult of personality developed around him, in part deliberately manufactured) above a caption: 'The man who subscribes to the War Loan is giving me the best birthday present: von Hindenburg'. Posters from 1917–18 illustrate the remobilisation process in action. A French poster of 1917 shows a mother putting a little girl to bed; a photograph of a soldier, by implication the child's father, hangs on the wall. The caption is 'So that your children will no longer know the horrors of war'. A British poster of the same period has an older workman telling a younger colleague, of an age to be conscripted: 'It's worthwhile − that's why'. [91]

Remobilisation was successful. In both Britain and France, the commitment to the war effort, which had wavered, recovered in 1918 and remained strong until victory was achieved. The French Ministry of the Interior reported in March 1918 that 'the labouring and thinking mass… understands clearly that a peace without victory would be for France an irreparable disaster'.[92] British sentiments were identical. The juxtaposition of the punitive peace imposed in March 1918 by victorious Germany on vanquished Bolshevik Russia, and the dramatic military success achieved by the Germans on the Western Front just a few weeks later, helped to stiffen public opinion. As ghastly as the war was, a German victory was regarded as being worse than continuing the fight.

Battlefronts and home fronts were inextricably linked. In a total war fought in an age of mass armies consisting largely of civilians in uniform it could not be otherwise. Bad news from home about the sufferings of their families undoubtedly undermined German soldiers' morale in 1918. If the population at home remained resolute, it gave the armies a platform for success. If the home front crumbled, it placed the entire war effort in jeopardy. In a war of materiel, industrial workers were as important as soldiers.

Strategically, it was thus completely logical deliberately to target civilian populations. In Europe, the Allied blockade was by far the most significant outcome of this strategy. There was some bombing of civilians but this made little difference to the outcome. In the much greater and more total conflict that began a generation later, the weight of bombs dropped on civilians was altogether more significant. It ended with two Japanese cities being destroyed by nuclear weapons, in a further extension of the logic of total war. In an assessment of the reasons for the outcome of the First World War, the Allied victories on the battlefield in 1918 were clearly of critical importance. But the resilience of the French and British home fronts, which contrasted sharply with the way that their German equivalent buckled under the strain of total war, exacerbated by the Allied naval blockade, was also hugely significant.

The failed search for a compromise peace

An integral part of total war is the mobilisation of people's attitudes. In spite of the deadlock, no government was faced by strong demands for a compromise peace until 1917. This meant that states could wage exceptionally bloody campaigns and pursue far-reaching war aims that made a negotiated settlement impossible. Popular hatred of the enemy developed very quickly after the outbreak of war. The French described Germans as *sale Boche* (dirty rascals). English-speakers adopted the term 'Hun', after the barbarian invaders of the Roman Empire, for Germans. In Britain, there were examples of German-owned businesses being attacked and looted. For Germans, Britain – or 'England' – rapidly became the main enemy, ahead of France and Russia. 'It has become a matter of common belief', a Centre Party newspaper stated when the war was barely two weeks old:

> that the English declaration of war is the result of a policy of encirclement, whose origins lie in the fear of Germany's economic development and whose ultimate goal is to keep Germany weak. For this reason a feeling of relief is evident... that finally the true aims of English policy have been revealed for all to see.[93]

Such sentiments, allied to the belief that to settle for anything less than victory would be a betrayal of those who had already sacrificed their lives, made it extremely difficult for any belligerent to contemplate a compromise peace. There were those on the left who wanted one, and indeed some on the right. A senior British politician, Lord Landsdowne, who was horrified by the destruction of the social elite on the battlefield, publicly advocated a compromise peace at the end of 1917, but his views jarred with the popular mood.

The primary barrier to a negotiated peace was the simple fact that Germany and the Allies had utterly irreconcilable aims. Germany was waging a war of conquest to achieve hegemony, while its enemies fought to thwart this ambition. During the campaign of 1914 in the West, the Germans seized important territory in Belgium and France and then for the most part remained on the defensive, defying the French and British to dislodge them while turning their attention to Russia. With the Western Front deadlocked and its army achieving successes in the East, the Germans saw no reason to compromise. France and Britain could have of course agreed to a peace in which Germany retained its conquests in the West; but this would have amounted to accepting a defeat that left both French and British security gravely weakened. Bethmann Hollweg, the German Chancellor, put forward in September 1914 a programme that laid out how ambitious German objectives were. Belgium would become a 'vassal state'. France would be reduced to a third class power, its strength crushed by being forced to pay an enormous indemnity. A strip of the Channel coast would be German. The Imperial German Navy would have ports on, and therefore access to, the Atlantic and Indian Oceans and the Mediterranean. A customs union, *Mitteleuropa* (Middle Europe), would 'stabilize Germany's economic dominance over Central Europe', while *Mittelafrika* (Middle Africa) would be established, a vast band of territory across Africa.[94]

In the East, Germany's appetite grew, fed by military victory over Russia. The September Programme envisaged forcing Russia's borders to the east and the non-Russians in the marcher lands removed from the Czar's control. By 1917, plans had evolved to include the creation of German puppet states in Poland, the Baltic region and Ukraine. From Berlin's point of view, this was a mistake. Some highly placed individuals in the Central Powers certainly understood the importance of achieving a compromise settlement with Russia. In July 1915, in the aftermath of the great victory of

Gorlice–Tarnow, Conrad wrote of the need to 'build golden bridges for separate peace with Russia… [W]e must above all firmly avoid any humiliation of Russia and in the first place renounce without question any substantial territorial concessions on Russia's part'.[95] This wise suggestion, of breaking up the anti-German coalition by offering Petrograd peace terms it could accept, went unheeded. Instead, the terms were too stiff for the Russians, who had been offered Constantinople and the Dardanelles by their allies (which of course closed off the option of the Entente making a separate peace with the Ottoman Empire) and the tentative proposals were rejected.[96]

The war aims of France were, at a minimum, to recover the territory it had lost in 1914. Although France did not go to war to accomplish the return of Alsace-Lorraine, it nevertheless soon became a war aim. Like the British, the French sought to expand their empire. Again, this was not why France went to war but was a facet of policy that developed as the war went on. British war aims were at one level fairly limited – the Germans had to be expelled from Belgium – but also very wide-ranging, if less tangible: the balance of power in Europe had to be restored and Prussian militarism destroyed, so a contrite post-war Germany would no longer be a threat to world peace. As part of the campaign of remobilisation in 1917–18, British war aims were reframed in terms of defending and spreading democracy and self-determination for the national groups within the Austro-Hungarian Empire.

At the end of 1916, there appeared to be a fleeting chance of a compromise settlement. Germany issued a 'Peace Note' on 12 December, albeit one that gave few hints of flexibility in its position. Later that month, President Wilson publicly asked the belligerents to put forward their war aims. Britain and France responded on 10 January 1917 with democratic war aims that cleverly highlighted the difference between what the two alliances were trying to achieve. Wilson's response was to articulate his view of 'peace without victory'. Rather inconsistently, the French and British also hoped to split up the Central Powers. In March 1917

Figure 19   Woodrow Wilson, 28th President of the United States of America, 1913–21.

the Emperor Karl, who had succeeded to the Hapsburg throne on the death of Franz Josef in 1916, cautiously sounded out the possibility of a separate peace using an intermediary, his brother-in-law, Prince Sixtus of Bourbon-Parma, a Belgian army officer. When the Germans discovered this initiative, Karl was immediately reined in. Another attempt to bring about a compromise peace was launched by Pope Benedict XV, who issued a Peace Note on 1 August 1917 but it had little impact. Lloyd George, in his Caxton Hall speech of January 1918, explicitly stated that Britain was not 'fighting to destroy Austria-Hungary'. He also sought to drive a wedge between the Kaiser's government and the German people by calling for 'a really democratic constitution' in Germany that would be a step towards a 'broad democratic peace'.[97]

Shortly after Lloyd George's Caxton Hall speech, Wilson publicly announced his Fourteen Points. This was an idealistic and far-reaching programme of liberal internationalism. Point I called for the abolition of secret diplomacy; point II for 'freedom of navigation upon the seas'; point IV for reductions of 'national armaments' to the 'lowest point consistent with domestic safety'. These proposals, together with others for collective security and self-determination of nationalities, were intended to overturn the way international relations were conducted. Behind the scenes, they immediately brought Wilson into conflict with France and Britain. Clemenceau, the French prime minister, sarcastically commented that while Wilson had set out Fourteen Points, God had confined himself to ten.[98]

Wilson's initial pronouncement had no impact on the plans of the militarists running Germany. In early October 1918, with the German army suffering defeat after defeat, the Fourteen Points took on new importance. Facing the stark reality of military catastrophe, Ludendorff advised the Kaiser to 'bring ... into the government [those Social Democrats and Liberals] whom we can mainly thank that we have come to this ... They should make the peace that must now be made. They made their bed, now they must lie in it!'[99] This was a deliberate attempt to exculpate German High Command from their catastrophic failure by manufacturing the 'stab in the back' myth; that the German army had not been defeated but betrayed by traitors at home. The liberal Prince Max of Baden became Chancellor and appealed to Wilson for peace founded on the Fourteen Points. This attempt to divide and rule annoyed the British and French but Germany's playing of the Fourteen Points card was a failure.

A series of changes in Germany occurred at bewildering speed. The state became (in theory, at any rate) a constitutional monarchy, Ludendorff was replaced by his rival General Wilhelm Gröner and mutiny broke out in the High Seas fleet. The option of a *Levée en masse*, the rousing of the German population to fight to the bitter end, was debated but rejected.[100] With the home front convulsed by revolution and mutinies breaking out in the army, on 9 November 1918 Gröner told the Kaiser to his face that it was the end: 'Sire, you no longer have an army. The army will march home in peace and order under its leaders and commanding generals but not under the command of Your Majesty, for it no longer stands behind Your Majesty'.[101] Forced to abdicate, Wilhelm fled to the Netherlands. A Social Democrat, Friedrich Ebert, became Chancellor of the new German Republic. The Germans asked for an armistice; two days later, the Armistice was signed at Compiègne. The fighting in the West was over.

Epilogue: The Aftermath of the War

The Treaty of Versailles and its consequences

The peace settlements that formally ended the First World War were some of the most radical and ambitious in history. By the time the statesmen of the world convened in Paris in January 1919, old Europe was in ruins. The new German republic was struggling to survive amidst revolutionary turmoil. The Russian Empire was no more and the new Bolshevik regime (which, like Germany, was not represented at the peace conference) was fighting a bitter civil war. Austria–Hungary had ceased to exist as, in the last days of the war, constituent nationalities such as the Czechs had simply broken away. The Ottoman Empire was falling apart. Now was the chance to remake Europe. Although representatives of many states attended, proceedings were dominated by the 'Big Three', the leaders of France (Georges Clemenceau), Britain (David Lloyd George) and the USA (Woodrow Wilson). Wilson and Clemenceau in particular were eager to seize the moment and had rather different ambitions. What followed was a clash between idealism, hard-headed realpolitik and the practicalities of an enormously complex situation.

Clemenceau was determined to achieve security for France by crippling German power. He was only partially successful. Alsace and Lorraine, seized by Germany in 1871, once again became French. Clemenceau's demand that a separate Rhineland state be detached from Germany was blocked by Lloyd George, for the British had no wish to see France become too powerful. The compromise was an agreement that the Rhineland would be demilitarised, with Allied forces in temporary occupation of the area. Germany was to be forced to pay huge reparations (£6,600 million) to recompense the Allies for the enormous cost of the war. Article 231 of the 1919 Treaty of Versailles, stated:

> Germany accepts the responsibility of Germany and her allies for causing all the damage to which the allied and Associated Governments and their nationals have been subjected as a consequence of the war imposed upon them by the aggression of Germany and her allies.[1]

Germany's army was limited to 100,000 men and forbidden to have tanks, there were to be no military aircraft, and the navy was restricted in size and banned from deploying modern battleships or U-boats. Separate treaties were concluded with Austria, Hungary, Bulgaria and Turkey. They resulted in the German-speaking rump of Austria being banned from uniting with Germany, the creation of Yugoslavia – the state that Serbia had aspired to create in 1914 – from Serbia, Montenegro and former Hapsburg lands, and the former Ottoman territories in the Middle East being given to the British and French empires in the guise of the 'mandates' from the newly-created League of Nations.

Woodrow Wilson sought to re-mould the world along principled lines of 'justice and generosity'.[2] Such an ambition was bound to be disappointed. Wilson's tenet was the self-determination of peoples. This often collided with the less lofty principle of security. The German-speaking population of the Sudetenland was included in Czechoslovakia, to give the new state a defensible frontier. Germany was forced to give the 'Danzig corridor' of land to the newly re-created Poland, allowing it access to the sea. Democracy, another of Wilson's cherished principles, failed to take root in much of the new Central and Eastern Europe. A third, the idea that collective security should replace the old ways that he believed had led to war, was also soon shown to be a dead letter. Wilson's own country refused to join the League of Nations and no state was prepared to risk its security by relying on collective action to punish aggressors. Nonetheless, Wilson was a hero in many of the newly-formed states, which saw him as their midwife.

Versailles left Germany shrunk in size and bitter at the 'War Guilt clause' but it was not as harsh as the settlement that a victorious Germany had forced upon the Bolshevik government in 1918. If looking for a truly Carthaginian peace imposed on Germany, one should look to 1945, not 1918. At the end of the Second World War Germany was occupied and divided into two states by its enemies. Direct rule by the victors was imposed and the social system remodelled, with the West becoming a capitalist democracy and the East a Marxist-Leninist state. The territorial losses of 1945, with the consequent ethnic cleansing, were vastly greater than those of 1919. In retrospect, the ideal solution in 1918–19 would have been to treat the post-imperial German government as representing a successor state, and to have blamed the *Kaiserreich* for the sins of the recent past, wiping the slate clean and welcoming the young Weimar Republic into the international family. This would have given Weimar Germany a fighting chance of establishing itself. While such a broad-minded vision might have been realisable in an environment that allowed disinterested consideration of what would be best for European security in the long term, it was impossible in the febrile atmosphere at the end of the First World War. Millions of casualties suffered in a war that was firmly believed to have been launched by Germany, a war that involved entire populations, led to demands to 'hang the *Kaiser*' and make Germany pay. Under the circumstances, a mild, conciliatory peace was out of the question. In fact, the Versailles settlement brought about the worst of all worlds: an embittered Germany that was left strong enough to take revenge. A harsher peace, on the lines of 1945, would have been wiser but, having failed to take the war on German soil and ensure military occupation of the entire country, the Allies would have been unable to enforce it, even if the political will had been there.

It is a commonplace that the Versailles Treaty, by imposing a punitive settlement on Germany, made a second round of hostilities inevitable. Marshal Foch stated flatly: 'This is not Peace. It is an Armistice for twenty years'.[3] He was to be proved right but could easily have been wrong. Within a decade significant alterations had been made to the Versailles settlement, in Germany's favour. A major problem with the 1919 settlement was that the victorious powers failed to enforce it. When the French army entered the Ruhr in 1923, in response to the German failure to pay reparations, the British and Americans refused to support them. John Maynard Keynes's scathing criticisms in *The Economic Consequences of the Peace* began to undermine the credibility and even the legitimacy of the Versailles settlement in the very year in which it was signed. By the end of the 1920s, there was a widespread belief among Anglo-American intellectuals that Germany had been treated unfairly, and sympathy for German attempts to revise Versailles gained ground.

It is not impossible, to play the counterfactual game, to imagine a German government in the 1930s revising its eastern borders, perhaps even by means of a local, limited war with Poland, without triggering a general conflict. Thus, to argue that the Treaty of Versailles 'caused' the Second World War is too simplistic. Versailles might have led to a lasting peace if the Wall Street Crash of 1929 and the Great Depression that followed had not diverted world history in a new direction. The economic crisis fatally undermined the Weimar Republic and aided the electoral growth of the Nazis, the National Socialist Democratic Workers Party. Even then the Nazi attainment of power in 1933 was the consequence of a peculiar set of circumstances, including miscalculations by opponents who hoped to draw the party's fangs by bringing it into government. Once in government, the Nazi leader, a charismatic Great War veteran, Adolf Hitler, acted swiftly to seize power, establishing a single-party dictatorship and crushing his enemies. Hitler was no ordinary dictator. An ideologically driven racist zealot with a hatred of both democracy and Marxism, from the very beginning he dreamed of waging a brutal war of conquest against his enemies, especially the Jews and the Soviet Union. In the event, Hitler got his global war, a conflict of a nature and scale that was very different to a putative local German–Polish war fought to revise the international frontier imposed by the Versailles settlement.[4]

The short twentieth century

Although it should not be assumed that it is possible to trace a straight line between the Versailles settlement and the outbreak of the Second World War, 1914 was of course the beginning of a long period of war, ideological struggle and instability. In the 1990s, the British Marxist historian Eric Hobsbawm termed this era the 'short twentieth century'. Beginning at Sarajevo in 1914, it endured until the collapse of the Soviet Union in 1991.[5]

The short twentieth century was an era distinctly different to that which came before and that which came afterwards. The First World War reduced the power of the European states. Particularly significant was the arrival of the United States of America as a first class power. For a brief moment in 1918, the USA's military might matched its vast economic strength. Although there was a return to isolationism after 1919, the Second World War saw the USA, however reluctantly, once again pick up the sword. This time, after the defeat of Germany and Japan, it did not lay it aside. Instead, America emerged as the undisputed leader of a power bloc, the ideological heirs of Woodrow Wilson. The USA and its allies engaged in the Cold War with the Soviet Union, the state founded by V.I. Lenin, Wilson's competitor in the battle for ideas. The Cold War reached its climax in the 1980s. Actions taken after a period of extreme international tension by a new Soviet leader, Mikhail Gorbachev, to reduce the threat of war, were carried out in tandem with his attempts to reform the USSR's system to make it work more efficiently, so it could better compete with the USA and the West. These rapidly span out of control. After seven decades of austerity and often brutal dictatorship, the opportunity to have a more open society, with goods to buy in shops, proved irresistible.

The final triumph of the democratic-capitalist model over Marxist-Leninism occurred more than seventy years after the clash of ideologies began during the First World War. Long after both their deaths, Wilson finally defeated Lenin.

The thawing of world politics after the end of the Cold War saw the unstable Yugoslav state disintegrate. It had been held together by the Communist strongman, Josip Tito, from the 1940s until his death in 1980. In the 1990s the state fell apart in a bloody series of inter-related civil wars. Just as in 1914, external powers were dragged into the fighting in the Balkans, this time in the shape of NATO, and Russia also played a critical diplomatic role. As the twentieth century drew to a close, European politicians and militaries, along with the Americans, found themselves grappling with one of the most intractable legacies of the First World War.

One of the great paradoxes of the First World War was that one of the key victor states, France, found itself relatively weaker in terms of the European balance of power in 1919. Defeated Germany, although beaten in the short term, could see a time when things would move in its favour. In 1914 France had had a strong eastern ally, in the form of Imperial Russia. Until 1921 revolutionary Russia was in the throes of a vicious and destabilising civil war and thereafter had the position of a pariah state, with an ideology obnoxious to the West and whose military capability was viewed as highly suspect. In 1939, the British and French in effect decided that Poland was a more credible ally than the USSR, a judgement that, within a few short years, was shown to be ludicrous. In 1919 the victorious coalition rapidly disintegrated. The USA returned to isolationism and the British showed no interest in continuing the wartime alliance. Thus France found itself without a major continental ally. As a substitute for Czarist Russia, France tried to box in Germany with a 'Little Entente' of Yugoslavia, Czechoslovakia and Romania and an alliance with Poland, which amounted to a pale imitation of the pre-war alliance. The break-up of Austria-Hungary left Germany the largest power in Central Europe; it did not need much foresight to see that if and when it regained its military strength, it would be able to dominate the smaller successor states to the Hapsburg Empire.

Democracy survives and fails: Britain, Germany, Italy

Britain, too, had to come to terms with a changed strategic situation. Superficially, Britain seemed stronger than ever but the reality was different. The 1921 Washington Naval Treaty, which ceded parity between the British and United States navies, reflected the shifting balance of power at sea. British wealth had been severely depleted by the war. Some of the newly acquired territories proved difficult and expensive to govern and garrison. The dominions were on the path to full independent nationhood and the governance of India was beginning to emerge as a problem that needed to be addressed. British troops were soon committed to fighting a major insurgency in Mesopotamia (Iraq). There was also trouble in some territories that had been parts of the Empire in 1914. There was major unrest in Egypt, and the Anglo-Irish War (1919–21) resulted in Ireland being partitioned between the Irish Free State in the south and the six-county Northern Ireland that remained part of the United Kingdom. At home, demobilised troops rapidly discovered that, contrary to the promises of the politicians, Britain in the immediate post-war period was not a land fit for heroes. After the wartime boom, unemployment levels started to climb and remained high throughout the inter-war period. There was a good deal of industrial militancy as trade unions sought better conditions for their members. The return of millions of demobilised soldiers, sailors and airmen inevitably brought about some unrest. There were demonstrations, riots and mutinies. There were fears that Bolshevism would come to Britain. In some deprived areas with a radical tradition, such as South Wales and Clydeside, there were some tense moments. But the demobilisation disturbances were transitory. The breakdown of discipline in the army after the Armistice owed much to a widespread feeling among the troops that they had enlisted to do a job, the task was completed – Germany was defeated – and their part of the contract was fulfilled.

Alongside the demobilisation disturbances, Field-Marshal Haig was fêted as a national hero and went on a triumphant tour of the country in 1919. Just as significantly, the Labour Party – as noted above, a moderate semi-socialist body firmly committed to parliamentary democracy – made sweeping gains in the 1918 General Election, becoming the main opposition party. Labour went on to form minority governments in 1924 and 1929–31. These were not the signs of a state on the verge of a proletarian communist revolution. Remarkably swiftly and peacefully, Britain adjusted to the new situation presented by the post-war world, a more democratic country in which politics was dominated by the Conservatives and their allies. In some ways, the British people made social gains as a result of the war. Whereas in other countries, such as France, Italy and Germany, radicalised war veterans' groups became politically powerful, in Britain they mainly acted as welfare organisations and drinking clubs. Haig became President of the largest ex-servicemen's group, the British Legion, a conservative body. Such was his prestige that, had Haig chosen to take the Legion in a radical direction, inter-war British politics would have looked very different. British governments in the 1920s and 1930s were parsimonious towards war veterans, particularly the wounded. The opposite was the case in Weimar Germany. Yet German war veterans turned against the state that had, especially when measured against other European countries, treated them generously.[6] Germany at the end of the war, and in the months that immediately followed, was wracked by disorder, and fighting between left and right. In January 1919 the leftist so-called 'Spartacist Uprising', a large-scale strike accompanied by heavy fighting, took place in Berlin. Just over a year later, the right-wing Kapp Putsch attempted to seize power in the German capital. The Weimar Republic survived but was riven with crises, including hyper-inflation in 1923. It was clear even before the Nazis came to power in 1933 that democracy in Germany was failing.

Italy's liberal state was a victim of the war. The huge losses and economic damage wreaked by the war had undermined the cohesion of Italian society and weakened the standing of the quasi-democratic regime. Although Italy had made some territorial gains, her allies had denied some others, such as the city of Fiume, which became a free state, and the coast of Dalmatia, which was awarded to the newly-created state of Yugoslavia. From this atmosphere of disappointed aspirations and disillusionment emerged an extreme right-wing nationalist 'strong man', Benito Mussolini, at the head of a new political party, the Fascists. He became Prime Minister in 1922 amidst political turmoil and in 1925 he became *Duce* (Leader) of a totalitarian regime. A former socialist, Mussolini had served in the army during the war. He pioneered a new sort of mass, totalitarian political party: Mussolini's followers wore a uniform of black shirts. This innovation was admired and emulated by Adolf Hitler. In popular memory, Mussolini is now mostly remembered and ridiculed for his military failure during the Second World War but in the inter-war period he was much admired. Fascism seemed a bulwark against communism and Mussolini's apparent (actually much exaggerated) success in Italy contrasted with the failures and disappointments of democratic states. Many, such as Winston Churchill, said complimentary things about Mussolini that they lived to regret.

Legacies of war outside Europe

The dismantling of the Ottoman Empire had profound implications for world politics and we live with the consequences to this day. The Allies' fight against the Turks was a parallel war to the main conflict against Germany, intersecting at times but distinctly separate. Safeguarding the security of their respective empires and expanding at the Ottomans' expense were war aims of both France and Britain. In spite of the 1904 Entente Cordiale, the two states remained colonial rivals but, after intense negotiations from late 1915 onwards, in March 1916 they signed an agreement on the division of part of the Ottoman Empire. The third major member of the wartime alliance, Russia, went along with the agreement, which became known by the names of the principal negotiators, Sir Mark Sykes and François-George Picot. Broadly, the Sykes-Picot agreements gave Syria and Lebanon to France and Mesopotamia and Palestine to Britain. Matters were complicated by the 1917 Balfour Declaration which, in a bid for Jewish support for Britain, declared that 'His Majesty's Government views with favour the establishment in Palestine of a national home for the Jewish people'.[7] Balfour admitted that the 'clear-cut policy' was absent and, in David Reynolds' words, Britain found itself in 'a monumental mess in the Middle East'.[8] T.E. Lawrence and Prince Feisal, present at the Paris Peace Conference to represent the cause of independent Arab states, were left disappointed. Arab nationalism, the eventual creation of the state of Israel, and the rise of radical Islam are all at least partially rooted in the reshaping of the Middle East during and after the First World War.

In the early 1920s, a strong unitary Turkish core state emerged from the disintegrating Ottoman Empire under the leadership of Mustapha Kemal, who had distinguished himself as a commander at Gallipoli in 1915 and later came to prominence in the Graeco-Turkish War (1919–22). The secular state created by Atatürk ('Father of the Turks', as Kemel became known) was a success. It was more than able to hold its own in the international arena and thus the Dardanelles and the city of Constantinople (now known as Istanbul), remained in Turkish hands. Winston Churchill dearly wished to bring Turkey into the Second World War as an ally. Atatürk's successors (he had died in 1938) kept Turkey neutral but after the war Turkey became a bastion of NATO's southern flank.

In the USA, disillusionment with the recent past soon set in. Many Americans came to believe that the country had been inveigled into the war by cunning British propaganda and/or the machinations of arms manufacturers and bankers.[9] Moreover, many held as an article of faith that America had somehow been denied the rightful fruits of victory. In reality, the USA emerged from the war stronger than when it went in. Increasingly, the American elite looked uneasily at another rising power, Japan. The Japanese had played a minor role in the fighting during the war, as a British ally. The benefits gained far outweighed the commitments. Japan's trade and economy grew and it gained former German colonies in the Pacific. In 1915, Japan's Twenty-One Demands increased the grip of its informal empire in China. At the end of the First World War there was no doubt that Japan was now a Great Power. The next two decades were to see Japan build on the power it acquired during the First World War by embarking on an expansionist policy that would eventually bring war with China and the United States. It is not going too far to say that the atomic bombings of Hiroshima and Nagaski were legacies of the First World War.

The second great war[10]

The war that was to break out a generation after 1914–18 took totality to a new level. Many of the political and military leaders of the Second World War had served in a junior capacity in the First. Hitler had been an infantry NCO, as had Mussolini. The Soviet general Georgy Zhukov had been an NCO in a Czarist cavalry regiment. A few, such as Winston Churchill, had seen the First World War from a senior level. Another was Franklin D. Roosevelt, who had served as US Assistant Secretary of the Navy. All leaders and states, both in preparing for war and then fighting it in the 1930s and 1940s, looked back to their experiences of 1914–18 for guidance. The massive losses sustained on the Western Front left deep psychological scars on Britain and, in particular, France. The use of war as an instrument of state policy was largely discredited and the popular mood was one of 'never again'. Franco-British strategy in 1939 and early 1940 was based on the principle of avoiding offensive action directly against Germany. Instead, the Maginot Line, an updated and highly sophisticated version of the trenches of 1914–18, was relied upon to provide protection while the two states mobilised for total war.

After the catastrophic failure of this strategy, and Britain's expulsion from the continent at Dunkirk, Churchill and his generals showed a marked reluctance to engage in operations that risked Somme-scale casualties. Instead, Britain had the luxury, not available in 1914–18, of conducting a peripheral strategy of fighting in the Mediterranean, while carrying out strategic bombing and commando raids that kept military casualties fairly low. After June 1941, this British strategy was facilitated by the Soviet Red Army performing the role of the Anglo-French armies in 1914–18, taking on and wearing down the German forces in battles of attrition, albeit using Deep Battle, a highly effective form of mobile warfare. The British approach, based on experience of the First World War, brought about a series of sharp clashes with the USA, its primary ally after December 1941. American forces had seen relatively little action in 1918 and although their losses had been proportionately heavy, they had not changed US strategic culture, which was focused on the direct approach. Not until D-Day, the amphibious invasion of France in June 1944, did the American way of war prevail over the legacy of Passchendaele. Then, in the North-West Europe campaign (June 1944–May 1945) British fears were realised in part: proportionately, losses were often higher than on the Western Front but as the size of the British army was much smaller than in 1916–18, the absolute casualties were much lower.

Especially after Churchill became Prime Minister in May 1940, Britain applied the lessons it had learned about waging a total war with great effect. The allocation of man- (and woman-) power was centrally regulated from an early stage, avoiding the free-for-all of 1914–15. Churchill's alliance with organised labour was critical. It was personified by Ernest Bevin, a powerful trade union leader who acted as poacher-turned-gamekeeper as Minister of Labour and National Service, second only to Churchill himself as a key figure in the British war effort. In contrast to 1914–18, food rationing was introduced from early on. With the exception of the USSR, the British mobilised for total war more thoroughly than any other state. To keep, as the British did, the civilian population relatively well-fed, healthy and content while placing intense demands upon them as a command economy developed and they were subjected to aerial bombing, at times very heavy, was a formidable achievement.

Although the fighting in France and Flanders was halted in November 1918, conflict continued on what had been the Eastern Front. In Russia, the Civil War intermingled with the Russo-Polish War of 1919 to 1921. In 1920, Bolshevik troops reached the outskirts of Warsaw, only to be driven back by Polish forces. The war was a Polish victory, with Poland extending its borders to the east. Under Josef Stalin, the USSR's series of Five-Year Plans, which began in 1928, helped to prepare the state for total war by building its industrial base. These plans owed something to the bitter experiences of war between 1914 and 1921, as well as the threat that Stalin feared was posed by the USSR's ideological enemies. After the German invasion of 22 June 1941, the USSR mobilised for, and then conducted, total war with a ruthlessness that put all other examples in the shade. In 1945, the victorious Red Army imposed its social system on conquered enemy territory and 'liberated' lands alike. The territory taken by the Poles in 1920 was annexed, with Poland receiving territorial compensation in the west at the expense of Germany.

Perhaps surprisingly, Nazi Germany did not make good use of the lessons of fighting a total war between 1914 and 1918. By attacking the USSR when Britain was very much undefeated, it ensured that Germany once again had to fight a war on two fronts. The organisation of the economy for war was frequently chaotic, although this was in part related to the nature of the Nazi regime, which fostered competition and overlap between various power centres, a 'divide-and-rule' policy intended to prevent a challenge to the leadership. One distinct element of continuity between Germany's experiences of war in 1914–18 and 1939–45 was the carving out of a vast European empire. In both world wars, Germany carried out economic exploitation of its conquered territories. However, while the German treatment of its subject peoples in the First War had been very harsh, in the Second it was brutal and genocidal. Atrocities in the west, such as the destruction of the French village of Oradour-sur-Glane in August 1944, and the murder of its inhabitants, can be seen as taking the First World War policy of *Schrecklichkeit* to extremes. The mass murder of Jews, Slavs and other racial and political enemies was a terrible escalation in brutality. The Kaiser's Germany on occasions pursued genocidal policies in its colonies but its behaviour towards occupied people in Europe, while brutal and sometimes bloody, did not sink to these depths. Indeed, in the First World War Jews in eastern European territories captured by Germany could expect better treatment then they had received at the hands of the anti-Semitic Czarist regime.

Superficially, the military conduct of the Second World War seems very different from its predecessor. The popular image, at least in the UK, is of fast-moving *Blitzkrieg* (lightning war) campaigns rather than attritional trench fighting. This view contains some truth but it tends to mask the continuities between the two conflicts. Some continuities are easy to spot. Just as in 1914–18, the Western Allies' victory in 1939–45 was founded on sea power, especially the ability of merchant ships to convey supplies, troops and equipment across the globe. As in the First World War, Germany used its U-boats to try to disrupt this traffic. The struggle between the submarine and the merchant ship and its naval escort began at the beginning of the Second World War and went on to the end. This was part of a wider attritional struggle. Once again, in economic, social and political terms, the anti-German coalition proved able to outlast its enemies.

An aspect of the Second World War that on the surface appears very different from the First was the use of bomber aircraft to attack civilian targets. While this had occurred in the Great War, the scale was vastly different. The extent to which US and (especially) British strategy rested on bombing was also of a different order from the First World War. Carpet bombing was in fact a development of the methods of 1914–18, in both that the aircraft and weapons were much more sophisticated and that the deliberate physical attack on civilians was an escalation of the strategy of the hunger blockade, which targeted their stomachs.

Just as a peculiar set of circumstances produced deadlock on the battlefield in 1914–18, a different set produced a period of quick victories in the early years of the Second World War. Broadly speaking, on the Western Front in the First World War, the Germans on one side, and the British and French on the other, were comparable in terms of 'fighting power' (weapons, tactics, morale, doctrine and the like). This contributed towards the trench deadlock. In 1940, the Germans had a marked superiority over the Allies. Combined with a healthy slice of luck, this enabled France to be over-run in a six-week campaign. By 1942, however, Germany's enemies had substantially closed the gap and as a result battles tended to become long, drawn-out, attritional affairs. Some, unlike those in the west in 1915–18, were also mobile: the technology of 1939–45 made this possible. Yet the Second World War had its battles in which armies became deadlocked, sometimes for months at a time, in an updated version of the trench warfare of the Great War: Tobruk in 1941; Stalingrad in 1942–3; Monte Cassino, Normandy and Imphal in 1944; Iwo Jima in 1945. Many soldiers of the Second World War saw combat under circumstances remarkably similar to those endured by their fathers and uncles a generation before. Given that the battles of the Second World War were fought with weapons that were generally more powerful than those of 1914–18, and that the war lasted longer and was in some respects fought on an even larger scale, it is not surprising that the casualties were higher. For reasons explained above, this did not apply to Britain.

Although sometimes regarded as an aberration in the development of warfare, the First World War was actually a turning point. New weapons such as the tank and chemical agents were introduced and existing weapons such as the machine gun and submarine reached something approaching their true potential. The introduction of the trinity of artillery, aircraft and radio was a truly revolutionary step that produced, in embryo, the style of warfare that continues to be employed to the current day. In this respect, the First World War was the first truly modern conflict.

A world transformed

To imagine what the world would look like today if the First World War had not happened is next to impossible. Too many streams were abruptly diverted or dammed by the Great War and too many flowed anew. To change the metaphor, the Great War of 1914–18 was 'like a terrible volcanic eruption... there was little that was not marked in some way by this man-made catastrophe'.[11] It changed history, for good and ill. Whether it is the rituals of remembrance and mourning for the war dead of a century ago, the reshaping of landscapes, the way armed forces fight battles, the USA's position of global dominance or the troubles of the Middle East, the world we live in was shaped to a remarkable degree by the war triggered by the events of 28 June 1914, when an Austrian Archduke fell victim to an assassin's bullet.

Further Reading

The literature on the First World War is truly vast and its centenary has spurred the production of yet more works. Some are excellent, such as the three-volume *Cambridge History of the First World War,* edited by Jay Winter (Cambridge: Cambridge University Press, 2014), which unfortunately appeared too late to be consulted for this book. Others are unoriginal and derivative. Some are worthless. What follows is a selection of the most significant English-language books on the war. Many other books and articles are to be found in the reference notes.

General books

The best analytical single volume history of the war is David Stevenson, *1914–18: The History of the First World War* (London: Allen Lane, 2004). We await volume II of Hew Strachan's projected trilogy; volume I, published by Oxford University Press in 2001, *The First World War: To Arms*, is a tour de force. A much older book by a Great War veteran, Cyril Falls's *The First World War* (London: Longman, 1960) has a mixture of narrative and analysis that makes it worth reading more than half a century after its original publication. Michael Howard, *The First World War* (Oxford: Oxford University Press, 2002) is a fine study in miniature; Spencer C. Tucker, *The Great War 1914–18* (London: UCL Press, 1998) is a good, fairly short, narrative history. Lawrence Sondhaus, *World War One: The Global Revolution* (Cambridge: Cambridge University Press, 2011) is especially welcome for its expert coverage of the war away from the Western Front. John Horne (ed.), *A Companion to World War I*

(Chichester: Wiley-Blackwell, 2012) is an indispensable compendium of short articles that reflect up-to-date scholarship. Spencer C. Tucker, *The European Powers in the First World War: An Encyclopaedia* (New York: Garland, 1996) is also useful, as are the essays in Matthias Strohn (ed.), *World War I Companion* (Oxford: Osprey, 2013). Saul David, *100 Days to Victory: How the Great War was Fought and Won* (London: Hodder and Stoughton, 2013) takes the unusual and effective approach of analysing certain key days throughout the war. Gary Sheffield, *Forgotten Victory: The First World War – Myths and Realities* (London: Headline, 2001; Endeavour e-book, 2014) ranges widely but focuses on Britain and the British army.

Specialist studies

Although the 'Sleepwalkers' thesis proposed by Christopher Clark in *The Sleepwalkers: How Europe Went to War in 1914* (London: Allen Lane, 2012) has received much media applause, it has been less enthusiastically received by the academic mainstream, which continues to see Germany and Austria as bearing the primary responsibility for launching the war. Recent scholarship is well covered in Annika Mombauer, *The Origins of the First World War: Controversies and Consensus* (Harlow: Pearson, 2002); William Mulligan, *The Origins of the First World War* (Cambridge: Cambridge University Press, 2010); and Holger Afflerbach and David Stevenson (eds.), *An Improbable War? The Outbreak of World War I and European Political Culture Before 1914* (New York: Berghahn, 2007); the latter is one of the most stimulating books on the causes of the war published in a long time. Annika Mombauer, *The Origins of the First World War: Diplomatic and Military Documents* (Manchester: Manchester University Press, 2013) is an exceptionally useful collection of primary sources.

An impressive trans-national series of studies of home fronts is to be found in Jay Winter and Jean-Louis Robert, *Capital Cities at War: Paris, London, Berlin 1914–1919*, two volumes (Cambridge:

Cambridge University Press, 1997 and 2007). Two vital topics are covered in Stephen Broadberry and Mark Harrison, *The Economics of World War I* (Cambridge: Cambridge University Press, 2005) and Susan R. Grayzel, *Women and the First World War* (Harlow: Pearson, 2002). All aspects of Germany and Austria-Hungary's war are covered in Holger Herwig's indispensable *The First World War: Germany and Austria-Hungary, 1914–1918* (London: Edward Arnold, 1997). Roger Chickering, *Imperial Germany and the Great War, 1914–1918* (Cambridge: Cambridge University Press 1998, second edition 2004), is excellent on Germany. Leonard V. Smith, Stéphane Audoin-Rouzeau and Annette Becker, *France and the Great War 1914–1918* (Cambridge: Cambridge University Press, 2003) does a similarly sterling job for France. Jennifer D. Keene, *Doughboys, the Great War and the Remaking of America* (Baltimore: Johns Hopkins University Press, 2003) is a superb book on the USA and the war. We lack a comprehensive study of Russia's war, in English at least, but for some important aspects see Peter Gatrell, *Russia's First World War: A Social and Economic History* (Harlow: Pearson Longman, 2005).

Turning to Britain and its Empire, for the British home front Adrian Gregory, *The Last Great War: British Society and the First World War* (Cambridge: Cambridge University Press, 2008) is the gold standard. Australia is well covered in Joan Beaumont, *Broken Nation: Australians in the Great War* (St Leonards, NSW: Allen & Unwin, 2013). For Canada and New Zealand, see two collections of essays, respectively David Mackenzie (ed.), *Canada and the First World War* (Toronto: University of Toronto Press, 2005) and John Crawford and Ian MacGibbon (eds.), *New Zealand's Great War* (Auckland: Exisle, 2007). For South Africa, see Bill Nasson, *Springboks on the Somme: South Africa in the Great War 1914–1918* (Johannesburg: Penguin, 2007) and for India see the relevant sections of Kaushik Roy, *The Indian Army in the Two World Wars* (Leiden: Brill, 2012).

Max Hastings, *Catastrophe: Europe Goes To War 1914* (London: William Collins, 1913) is a compelling and provocative book on the first year of the war. David Stevenson, *With Our Backs to the*

Wall: Victory and Defeat in 1918 (London: Allen Lane, 2011) is an outstanding blend of military, political and many other sorts of history. Although dated, Norman Stone, *The Eastern Front 1914– 1917* (London: Hodder and Stoughton, 1975) has not yet been replaced. There is an excellent comprehensive study of the war at sea: Paul G. Halpern, *A Naval History of World War I* (London: UCL Press, 1994). Andrew Gordon, *The Rules of the Game: Jutland and British Naval Command* (London: John Murray, 1996) is a brilliant book that says much about the nature of command and leadership that is also applicable in a non-naval context. The relevant chapter in John Buckley, *Air Power in the Age of Total War* (London: UCL Press, 1999), forms an excellent introduction to the air war, while John H. Morrow, Jr, *The Great War in the Air: Military Aviation from 1909 to 1921* (Shrewsbury: Airlife, 1993) gives a detailed account. Richard F. Hamilton and Holger H. Herwig (eds.), *War Planning 1914* (Cambridge: Cambridge University Press, 2010) contains up-to-date assessments of a vital topic. Roger Chickering and Stig Förster (eds.), *Great War, Total War: Combat and Motivation on the Western Front, 1914–1918* (Cambridge: Cambridge University Press, 2000) contains some very important essays.

For the French Army, see the superb book by Robert A. Doughty: *Pyrrhic Victory: French Strategy and Operations in the Great War* (Cambridge, MA: Belknapp Press, 2005) and Elizabeth Green-halgh, *Foch in Command* (Cambridge: Cambridge University Press, 2011). The US army in Europe can be approached through Mark Ethan Grotelueschen, *The AEF Way of War: The American Army and Combat in World War I* (Cambridge: Cambridge University Press, 2007) and Donald Smyth, *Pershing: General of the Armies* (Bloomington, IN: Indiana University Press, 2007). Jack Sheldon's still growing and hugely useful series of books, e.g. *The Germans on Vimy Ridge, 1914–1917* (Barnsley: Pen & Sword, 2008) examines the German army through contemporary accounts. Douglas Haig continues to be immensely controversial. For two contrasting views see Gary Sheffield, *The Chief: Douglas Haig and the British Army* (London: Aurum, 2011) and J.P. Harris, *Douglas Haig and the First*

World War (Cambridge: Cambridge University Press, 2008). One of the most important books ever written on the war in the West is Robin Prior and Trevor Wilson, *Command on the Western Front* (Oxford: Blackwell, 1992), which played a major role in reshaping historians' views on British conduct of operations.

Key books on Western Front battles include William Philpott, *Bloody Victory: The Sacrifice on the Somme and the Making of the Twentieth Century* (London: Little, Brown, 2009); Alistair Horne, *The Price of Glory: Verdun 1916* (Harmondsworth: Penguin, 1993) – (dated but still a classic); Bryn Hammond, *Cambrai 1917: The Myth of the First Great Tank Battle* (London: Weidenfeld & Nicolson, 2008), David T. Zabecki, *The German 1918 Offensives: A case study in the operational level of war* (London: Routledge, 2006), Michael S. Neiberg, *The Second Battle of the Marne* (Bloomington, IN: Indiana University Press, 2008); John Terraine, *To Win a War: 1918, The Year of Victory* (London: Cassell, 2008). Beyond France and Flanders, despite its bizarre title, Charles Townshend, *When God Made Hell: The British Invasion of Mesopotamia and the Creation of Iraq, 1914–1921,* (London: Faber and Faber, 2011) is a superb study that supersedes all previous works on the subject. Robin Prior, *Gallipoli: The End of the Myth* (New Haven: Yale University Press, 2009) is a trenchant book that punctures any idea that Gallipoli was a potentially war-winning stroke. The Turkish perspective is given by Edward J. Erickson, *Gallipoli: The Ottoman Campaign* (Barnsley: Pen & Sword, 2010). The best source for the Italian Front is Mark Thompson's very readable *The White War: Life and Death on the Italian Front 1915–1919* (London: Faber and Faber, 2008). Recently some excellent studies on Eastern Front campaigns have appeared in English: Dennis E. Showalter, *Tannenberg: Clash of Empire, 1914* (Dulles, VA: Brassey's, 2004); Graydon A. Tunstall, *Blood on the Snow: The Carpathian Winter War of 1915* (Lawrence, KS: University Press of Kansas, 2010); Richard DiNardo, *Breakthrough: The Gorlice-Tarnow Campaign 1915* (Santa Barbara, CA: Praeger, 2010); Timothy C. Dowling, *The Brusilov Offensive* (Bloomington, IN: Indiana University Press, 2008).

The vast topic of the aftermath and legacy of the war can be approached through David Reynolds' fine study *The Long Shadow: The Great War and the Twentieth Century* (London: Simon and Schuster, 2013). On remembrance, Jay Winter, *Sites of Memory, Sites of Mourning: The Great War in European Cultural History* (Cambridge, Cambridge University Press, 1995) is seminal. The British dimension is ably assessed by Dan Todman in *The Great War: Myth and Memory* (London: Hambledon Continuum, 2005). This can be profitably paired with Catherine Switzer's important book *Ulster, Ireland and the Somme* (Dublin: History Press Ireland, 2013).

Endnotes

Preface

[1] Hew Strachan (2009), 'Into History', *Journal of the Royal United Services Institute [JRUSI]* Vol. 154, No.4, p.5.

[2] The views of Professor Niall Ferguson, actually first propounded in 1997–8 (!) were widely reported in January 2014: 'Britain entering First World War was "Biggest error in modern history"', *Guardian*, 30 Jan. 2014. For rebuttals of this view, see Gary Sheffield, 'It was a Great War. One that saved Europe', *The Times*, 1 Feb. 2014 and Sir Michael Howard, letter, *The Times*, 3 Feb. 2014.

[3] *Guardian*, 21 May 2013, accessed 22 Nov. 2013.

[4] Tweets from @_paullay, 22 May 2013.

Chapter 1

[1] David Lloyd George, *War Memoirs,* abridged edition, Vol. II (London: Odhams, *c.*1938), pp.33–34.

[2] Quoted in Annika Mombauer, *The Origins of the First World War: Controversies and Consensus* (Harlow: Pearson, 2002), p.85.

[3] Christopher Clark, *The Sleepwalkers: How Europe Went to War in 1914* (London: Penguin, 2013 [2012]), p.56; Richard J. Evans, 'Michael Gove's History Wars', *Guardian,* Review section, 13 July 2013, pp.3–4; Margaret MacMillan, *The War that Ended Peace* (London: Profile, 2013), p.605, but see also p.xxxi.

[4] Simon Griffith, review of *The Sleepwalkers*, *Daily Mail,* 12 Nov. 2012.

[5]Holger Herwig, review, http://www.historynet.com/mhq-reviews-was-there-a-crime-in-the-tragedy-of-the-great-war.htm, 7 May 2013, accessed 22 Nov. 2013.

[6]Quoted in Gary Sheffield, *Forgotten Victory: The First World War – Myths and Realities* (London: Headline, 2001), p.26.

[7]Quoted in C.J. Lowe and M.L. Dockrill, *The Mirage of Power* Vol. I: *British Foreign Policy 1902–14* (London: Routledge & Kegan Paul, 1972), p.59.

[8]John Keiger, 'Crossed Wires, 1904–14', in Robert Tombs and Emile Chabal (eds.), *Britain and France in Two World Wars* (London: Bloomsbury, 2013), pp.39–41.

[9]Vernon Bogdanor, 'Diplomacy: Sir Edward Grey and the Crisis of July 1914', lecture screened on BBC Parliament channel, 5 Oct. 2013.

[10]Bogdanor, 'Diplomacy'; William Mulligan, *The Origins of the First World War* (Cambridge: Cambridge University Press, 2010), pp.81–82.

[11]Bogdanor, 'Diplomacy'.

[12]Richard C. Hall, 'Serbia', in Richard F. Hamilton and Herger H. Herwig, *The Origins of World War I* (Cambridge: Cambridge University Press, 2003), p.102.

[13]D.C.B. Lieven, *Russia and the Origins of the First World War* (London: Macmillan, 1983), pp.46, 49.

[14]Paul W. Schroeder, 'Stealing Horses to Great Applause: Austria-Hungary's Decision in 1914 in Systemic Perspective' in Holger Afflerbach and David Stevenson, (eds.), *An Improbable War? The Outbreak of World War I and European Political Culture Before 1914* (New York: Berghahn, 2007), pp.28–32.

[15]Frank McDonough, *The Origins of the First and Second World Wars* (Cambridge: Cambridge University Press, 1997), p.33.

[16]McDonough, *Origins,* p.36.

[17]Holger Afflerbach, 'The Topos of Improbable War in Europe Before 1914', in Afflerbach and Stevenson, *Improbable War?,* pp.161–82.

[18]Norman Angell, *The Great Illusion*, quoted in J.D.B. Miller, 'Norman Angell and Rationality in International Relations', in David Long and Peter Wilson, *Thinkers of the Twenty Years Crisis: Inter-War Idealism Reassessed* (Oxford: Clarendon Press, 1995), pp. 104–05; I.S. Bloch, *Is War Now Impossible?* (London: Grant Richards, 1899).

[19]Hall, 'Serbia', pp.106–8.

[20]Clark, *Sleepwalkers*, pp.56–58. I am grateful to Dr Sean Lang for allowing me to see an unpublished paper that has informed my ideas on this subject. See also Lieven, *Russia,* pp.139–40.

[21]Luigi Albertini, *The Origins of the War of 1914,* Vol. II (New York: Enigma Books, 2005 [1952]), p.82.

[22]This paragraph draws upon the work of Günther Kronenbitter, quoted in Annika Mombauer, 'The First World War: Inevitable, Avoidable, Improbable or Desirable? Recent Interpretations on War Guilt and the War's Origins', *German History* Vol.25 No.1 (2007), pp.83–84.

[23]Gordon Martel, *The Origins of the First World War* (London: Longman, 1996), p.79.

[24]Richard F. Hamilton and Herger H. Herwig, *Decisions for War, 1914-1917* (Cambridge: Cambridge University Press, 2004), p.62.

[25]Quoted in Martel, *Origins,* p.100.

[26]Quoted in Mombauer, 'The First World War', p.84.

[27]Albertini, *Origins,* II, pp.193, 290–91.

[28]Mombauer, 'The First World War', p.94.

[29]The English title was the more mundane *Germany's Aims in the First World War* (New York: Norton, 1967).

[30]Fritz Fischer, *War of Illusions: German Policies from 1911 to 1914* (New York: Norton, 1975).

[31]Fritz Fischer, *World Power or Decline: The Controversy over Germany's Aims in the First World War* (New York: Norton, 1974), p.84.

[32]This was the view of Fischer's great adversary Gerhard Ritter, quoted in Mombauer, *Origins,* p.144.

[33]James Joll, 'The 1914 Debate Continues: Fritz Fischer and his Critics', in H.W. Koch, *The Origins of the First World War* (London: Macmillan, 1984 [1972]), p.35.

[34]Fischer, *World Power or Decline*, p.viii.

[35]See however John Röhl's magisterial *Wilhelm II: Into the Abyss of War and Exile, 1900-1941* (Cambridge: Cambridge University Press, 2014), p.911, which makes a powerful case that 'the military-political-discussions' of 8 December 1912 'finally led to Armageddon in the summer of 1914'.

[36]Mark Hewitson, *Germany and the Causes of the First World War* (Oxford: Berg, 2004), pp.3–4, 228–89. Hewitson sees the German leadership as acting from a sense of confidence rather than 'weakness and despair' (p.228).

[37]My ideas in this paragraph have been particularly informed by Hewitson, *Germany,* Herwig, 'Germany' and Strachan, *The First World War* Vol. I, *To Arms* (Oxford: Oxford University Press, 2001), pp.86-91.

[38]Herwig, 'Germany', pp.178–85.

[39]Herwig, 'Germany', p.187; Niall Ferguson, *The Pity of War* (London: Allen Lane, 1998) pp.98–101.

[40]For details, see Rich, 'Russia', pp. 212–14.

[41]Quoted in Martel, *Origins,* p.101.

[42]For the view that Russian aggression was a major factor in launching the war, see Sean McMeekin, *The Russian Origins of the First World War* (Cambridge, MA: Belknapp Press, 2011). For a convincing counterview that stresses Russia's deterrent stance, see Ronald P. Bobroff, 'War accepted but unsought: Russia's growing militancy and the July Crisis, 1914' in Jack S. Levy and John A. Vasquez, *The Outbreak of the First World War* (Cambridge: Cambridge University Press, 2014).

[43]Lieven, *Russia,* pp.142–44.

[44]Quoted in Albertini, *Origins,* Vol. I, p.413.

[45]John F.V. Keiger, *France and the Origins of the First World War* (New York: St Martin's Press, 1983), pp.165–86; Eugenia C. Kiesling, 'France', in Hamilton and Herwig, *Origins,* p.234.

[46]Martel, *Origins,* pp.80–1, 106.

[47]For Britain's entry into the War, see Keith Wilson, 'Britain', in Keith Wilson (ed.), *Decisions for War* (New York: St Martin's Press, 1995).

[48]These arguments are summarised in Mombauer, *Origins,* pp.191–6; Mombauer is moderately sympathetic to Grey.

[49]Nigel Biggar, 'Was Britain Right to Go to War in 1914'? *Standpoint,* Sept. 2013, http://standpointmag.co.uk/node/5143

[50]Sheffield, *Forgotten Victory,* pp.33–40.

[51]David Stevenson, *Armaments and the Coming of War: Europe 1904–1914* (Oxford: Oxford University Press, 1996), p.40; in general, James Joll and Gordon Martel, *The Origins of the First World War* (Harlow: Pearson, 2007).

[52]Holger H. Herwig, 'Germany', in Hamilton and Herwig *Origins,* p.168.

[53]David Stevenson, *1914–18: The History of the First World War* (London: Allen Lane, 2004), p.41.

Chapter 2

[1]In Chapters 2 to 5, unless otherwise stated, details of operations and statistics are drawn from: Spencer C. Tucker, *The Great War 1914–18* (London: UCL Press, 1998); Cyril Falls, *The First World War* (London: Longmans, 1960); Michael Howard, *The First World War* (Oxford: Oxford University Press, 2002); John Ellis and Michael Cox, *The World War I Data Book* (London: Aurum Press, 2001); Lawrence Sondhaus, *World War One: The Global Revolution* (Cambridge: Cambridge University Press, 2011); and John Horne (ed.), *A Companion to World War I* (Chichester: Wiley-Blackwell, 2012).

[2]Hew Strachan, *European Armies and the Conduct of War* (London: Allen and Unwin, 1983), pp.108–11.

[3]Robert A. Doughty, 'France', in Richard F. Hamilton and Holger H. Herwig, *War Planning 1914* (Cambridge: Cambridge University Press, 2010), p.159.

[4]Quoted in Annika Mombauer, 'German War Plans', in Hamilton and Herwig, *War Planning*, p.57.

[5]Annika Mombauer, *Helmuth von Moltke and the Origins of the First World War* (Cambridge: Cambridge University Press, 2001).

[6]Holger Afflerbach, 'Planning Total War? Falkenhayn and the Battle of Verdun, 1916', in Roger Chickering and Stig Förster, (eds), *Great War, Total War: Combat and Motivation on the Western Front, 1914–1918* (Cambridge: Cambridge University Press, 2000), pp. 118–9.

[7]For important background see Robert T. Foley (editor and translator), *Alfred von Schlieffen's Military Writings* (London: Cass, 2003), pp. xv–12.

[8]See Terence Zuber, *The Real German War Plan: 1904-14* (Stroud: History Press, 2011).

[9]Robert A. Doughty, *Pyrrhic Victory: French Strategy and Operations in the Great War* (Cambridge, MA: Belknapp Press, 2005), p.67.

[10]Gary Sheffield and Stephen Badsey, 'Strategic Command', in Jay Winter (ed.), *The Cambridge History of the First World War* Vol. I (Cambridge: Cambridge University Press, 2014), pp.390-91.

[11]Dennis E. Showalter, 'War in the East and Balkans, 1914–18' in Horne, *Companion,* p. 66.

[12]Dennis E. Showalter, *Tannenberg: Clash of Empire, 1914* (Dulles, VA: Brassey's, 2004 [1991]), pp. 229–30. To be fair to the Russians, this was a besetting sin of all armies at this period of the conflict.

[13]Dennis E. Showalter, 'The East Gives Nothing Back: The Great War and the German Army in Russia', *Journal of the Historical Society,* II, 1, (2002), p.5.

[14]The best source on the war at sea is Paul G. Halpern, *A Naval History of World War I* (London: UCL Press, 1994).

[15]Jonathan Reed Winkler, *Nexus: Strategic Communications and American Security in World War I* (Cambridge, MA: Harvard University Press, 2008) pp. 5–6.

[16]Paul G. Halpern, 'The War at Sea', in Horne, *Companion,* pp. 142, 145.

[17]John Buckley, *Air Power in the Age of Total War* (London: UCL Press, 1999), p.50.

[18]Walter J. Boyne, *The Influence of Air Power Upon History* (Gretna, LA: Pelican, 2003) pp.80–81.

[19]Buckley, *Air Power,* p.53.

[20]Jonathan Krause, *Early Trench Tactics in the French Army: The Second Battle of Artois May–June 1915* (Farnham: Ashgate, 2013) p.4.

[21]Gary Sheffield, *Forgotten Victory: The First World War – Myths and Realities* (London: Headline, 2001) pp.101–2, 106–7.

[22]Albert Palazzo, *Seeking Victory on the Western Front: The British Army and Chemical Warfare in World War I* (Lincoln, NE: University of Nebraska Press, 2000), pp.76–77.

[23]J.E. Edmonds, *Military Operations: France and Belgium, 1915* Vol. II (London: Macmillan, 1928), pp.115–18.

[24]Jehuda L. Wallach, *The Dogma of the Battle of Annihilation: The Theories of Clausewitz and Schlieffen and Their Impact on the German Conduct of Two World Wars* (Westport, CT: Greenwood, 1986).

[25]Gary Sheffield, *The Chief: Douglas Haig and the British Army* (London: Aurum, 2011) pp.118–22.

[26]William Philpott, *Bloody Victory: The Sacrifice on the Somme and the Making of the Twentieth Century* (London: Little, Brown, 2009), p.555.

[27]Graydon A. Tunstall, *Blood on the Snow: The Carpathian Winter War of 1915* (Lawrence, KS: University Press of Kansas, 2010), pp.210–11.

[28]Richard DiNardo, *Breakthrough: The Gorlice-Tarnow Campaign 1915* (Santa Barbara, CA: Praeger, 2010), pp.138–42.

[29]Robin Prior, *Gallipoli: The End of the Myth* (New Haven: Yale University Press, 2010 [2009]), pp.249–52.

[30]The best source for the Italian Front is Mark Thompson, *The White War: Life and Death on the Italian Front 1915–1919* (London: Faber and Faber, 2008).

[31]Lawrence Sondhaus, *World War One: The Global Revolution* (Cambridge: Cambridge University Press, 2011), p.158.

Chapter 3

[1] Robert T. Foley, *German Strategy and the Path to Verdun* (Cambridge: Cambridge University Press, 2011) pp.187–208, 212.

[2] Sheffield, *The Chief,* pp.167–68, 171–73.

[3] Falls, *First World War,* p. 196.

[4] Timothy C. Dowling, *The Brusilov Offensive* (Bloomington, IN: Indiana University Press, 2008), pp.90–91.

[5] T.J. Mitchell and G.M. Smith, *Medical Services: Casualties and Medical Statistics of the Great War* (London: HMSO, 1931) pp.252–55.

[6] See Andrew Gordon, *The Rules of the Game: Jutland and British Naval Command* (London: John Murray, 1996).

[7] Stevenson, *1914–1918,* p.223.

Chapter 4

[1] Quoted in Sheffield, *The Chief,* p.216.

[2] See Paul Strong and Sanders Marble, *Artillery in the Great War* (Pen and Sword: Barnsley, 2011).

[3] Jonathan Bailey, *The First World War and the Birth of the Modern Style of Warfare* (Camberley: Strategic and Combat Studies Institute Occasional Paper No.22, 1996).

[4] Anthony Clayton, 'Robert Nivelle and the French Spring Offensive of 1917' in Brian Bond (ed.), *Fallen Stars: Eleven Studies of Twentieth-Century Military Disasters* (London: Brassey's, 1991), p.56.

[5] Elizabeth Greenhalgh, *Victory Through Coalition* (Cambridge: Cambridge University Press, 2005), pp.146–47.

[6] Robert Doughty, *Pyrrhic Victory: French Strategy and Operations in the Great War* (Cambridge, MA: Belknapp Press, 2005), pp.324–26, 335–52; Clayton, 'Robert Nivelle', pp.57–62.

[7] Doughty, *Pyrrhic Victory,* pp.361–64; Leonard V. Smith, *Between Mutiny and Obedience: The case of the French Fifth Infantry Division*

During World War I (Princeton, NJ: Princeton University Press, 1994), pp.175–214 (quote from soldier's letter is from p.188).

[8]Andrew A. Wiest, 'Haig, Gough and Passchendaele' in G.D. Sheffield (ed.), *Leadership and Command: The Anglo-American Military Experience since 1861* (Brassey's, 1997), pp.77–86.

[9]Sheffield, *Forgotten Victory*, pp.208–13.

[10]Richard Holmes, *The Western Front* (London: BBC, 1999), p.174.

[11]Dennis Showalter, 'Passchendaele' in Dennis Showalter (ed.), *History in Dispute,* Vol. 8 *World War I* (Detroit: St James Press, 2004), p.224.

[12]Quoted in Jack Sheldon, *The German Army at Passchendaele* (Barnsley: Pen & Sword, 2007), pp.315–16.

[13]Charles Harington, *Tim Harington Looks Back* (John Murray, 1940), pp.63–64.

[14]Charles Carrington, *Soldier From the Wars Returning* (London: Arrow Books, 1970), p. 101.

[15]Ernst Jünger, *The Storm of Steel* (London: Constable, 1994), p. 51.

[16]H.A. Foley, Somerset Light Infantry, quoted in Tom Donovan (ed.), *The Hazy Red Hell: Fighting Experiences on the Western Front 1914–18* (Staplehurst: Spellmount, 1999), p. 58.

[17]Peter Simkins, *World War I: The Western Front* (London: Tiger Books, 1991), pp. 82–85.

[18]J.M. Bourne and Bob Bushaway (eds.), *Joffrey's War: A Sherwood Forester in the Great War* (Beeston: Salient Books, 2011), pp. 191–92.

[19]Simkins, *World War I*, pp. 82–85.

[20]Bryn Hammond, *Cambrai 1917: The Myth of the First Great Tank Battle* (London: Weidenfeld & Nicolson, 2008), pp.31–39, 113.

[21]Quoted in Sondhaus, *World War One*, p.250.

[22]Mark Thompson, *The White War: Life and Death on the Italian Front 1915–1919* (London: Faber and Faber, 2008), pp. 294–324 (quote from p.313).

[23]Matthew Hughes, *Allenby and British Strategy in the Middle East* (London: Frank Cass, 1999), pp.27–30.

[24]John H. Morrow, Jr., *The Great War in the Air: Military Aviation from 1909 to 1921* (Shrewsbury: Airlife, 1993), p.367.

[25]Richard Hallion, *Strike from the Sky: The History of Battlefield Air Attack, 1911–1945* (Washington, DC: Smithsonian Institute Press, 1989), pp.19–21.

[26]Halpern, 'War at Sea', pp.150–52.

[27]V.E. Tarrant, *The U-Boat Offensive 1914–1945* (London: Arms & Armour Press, 1989) p.49.

[28]Sondhaus, *World War One*, p.287.

Chapter 5

[1]This section is a revised version of a piece that first appeared on the British Library website: http://www.bl.uk/world-war-one/articles/military-discipline

[2]This definition is informed by Gary Sheffield, *Leadership in the Trenches: Officer-Man Relations, Morale and Discipline in the British Army in the Era of the First World War* (Basingstoke: Macmillan, 2000) and Andrew Houghton and Richard Holmes, 'Discipline', in Richard Holmes (ed.), *The Oxford Companion to Military History* (Oxford: Oxford University Press, 2001), p.261.

[3]Eric Hobsbawm, quoted in Sheffield, *Leadership in the Trenches*, p.70.

[4]Gerard Christopher Oram, *Military Executions During World War I* (Basingstoke: Palgrave, 2003), p.18.

[5]Sheffield, *Leadership in the Trenches;* Alexander Watson, *Enduring the Great War: Combat, Morale and Collapse in the British and German Armies, 1914-1918* (Cambridge: Cambridge University Press), pp.108–39.

[6]David T. Zabecki, *The German 1918 Offensives: A case study in the operational level of war* (London: Routledge, 2006), pp.172–73.

[7]Quoted in Sheffield, *The Chief*, p.283.

[8]Quoted in Michael S. Neiberg, *The Second Battle of the Marne* (Bloomington, IN: Indiana University Press, 2008), p. 185.

[9]Robin Prior and Trevor Wilson, *Command on the Western Front* (Oxford: Blackwell, 1992), p.314.

[10]Quoted in Sheffield, *Forgotten Victory*, p.239.

[11]Sheffield, *The Chief*, p.323; Elizabeth Greenhalgh, *Foch in Command* (Cambridge: Cambridge University Press, 2011), pp.441–442.

[12]Michele Bomford, *Beaten Down By Blood: The Battle of Mont Quentin-Péronne 1918* (Newport, NSW: Big Sky Publishing, 2012), p.228.

[13]See Jonathan Boff, *Winning and Losing on the Western Front: The British Third Army and the Defeat of Germany in 1918* (Cambridge: Cambridge University Press, 2012) for an excellent analysis of the experiences of the British and German armies in 1918.

[14]David F. Trask, *The AEF and Coalition Warmaking 1917–18* (Lawrence, KS: University Press of Kansas, 1993), pp.161–62.

[15]For a sophisticated recent assessment of the AEF in action, see the conclusions to Mark Ethan Grotelueschen, *The AEF Way of War: The American Army and Combat in World War I* (Cambridge: Cambridge University Press, 2007), pp.343–64.

[16]Sheffield, *The Chief*, pp.331.

[17]See Sheffield, *The Chief*; Andrew A. Wiest, *Haig: The Evolution of a Commander* (Washington, DC: Potomac Books, 2005). For a modern book that updates the traditional, unfavourable view of Haig, see J.P. Harris, *Douglas Haig and the First World War* (Cambridge: Cambridge University Press, 2008).

[18]There is an informative website dedicated to Lawrence studies: http://www.telstudies.org/.

[19]Morrow, *Great War in the Air*, p.221.

[20]Christopher Luck, 'The Smuts Report: Interpreting and Misinterpreting the Promise of Air Power', in Gary Sheffield and Peter Gray (eds.), *Changing War: The British Army, the Hundred Days Campaign and the Birth of the Royal Air Force, 1918* (London: Bloomsbury, 2013), p.161.

[21]Both quoted in Morrow, *Great War in the Air*, p.322.

[22]Buckley, *Air Power*, p.58.

[23]Edward Warner, 'Douhet, Mitchell, Seversky: Theories of Air Warfare', in Edward Mead Earle, *Makers of Modern Strategy* (Princeton: Princeton University Press, 1943), p.494.

[24]Hallion, *Strike*, pp.29–32.

Chapter 6

[1]Jeremy Black, *The Age of Total War 1860–1945* (Westport, CT: Praeger, 2006), p.5.

[2]Based on the table in Jay Winter, 'Demography', in John Horne (ed.), *Companion to World War I* (Chichester: Wiley-Blackwell, 2012), p.249 (figures rounded up or down for convenience).

[3]Recent research has suggested the death toll figure might be as high as 10 million: http://www.telegraph.co.uk/history/world-war-one/10577200/WW1-dead-and-shell-shock-figures-signifi-cantly-underestimated.html.

[4]Alan Kramer, *Dynamic of Destruction: Culture and Mass Killing in the First World War* (Oxford: Oxford University Press, 2007), p.2.

[5]Based on tables in Jeffrey Grey, *A Military History of Australia* (Cambridge: Cambridge University Press, 1990), p.119 and table in *Statistics of the Military Effort of the British Empire During the Great War 1914–1920* (London: HMSO, 1922), p.237 (figures rounded up or down for convenience).

[6]Michael Clodfelter, *Warfare and Armed Conflict: A Statistical Reference to Casualty and Other Figures, 1500–2000* (Jefferson, NC: McFarland, 2002), p.479.

[7]Ellis and Cox, *World War I Databook*, pp.269–70; Leo Grebler and Wilhelm Winkler, *The Cost of the World War to Germany and Austria-Hungary* (New Haven, CT: Yale University Press, 1940), p.147; Samuel Dumas and K.O. Vedel-Petersen, *Losses of Life Caused by War* (Oxford: Clarendon Press, 1923), p.165; Jay Winter, 'Surviving the War', in Jay Winter and Jean-Louis Robert, *Capital Cities at War: Paris, London, Berlin 1914–1919*, Vol. I (Cambridge: Cambridge University Press, 1999 [1997]),

pp.519–20. Winter stresses the figure for Germany is 'a very rough and conservative estimate'.

[8] 'Introduction' to John Crawford and Ian McGibbon (eds.), *New Zealand's Great War* (Auckland: Exisle, 2007), pp.16–17.

[9] Winter, 'Demography', pp.251–52; J.M. Winter, *The Great War and the British People* (Basingstoke: Macmillan, 1985), pp.92, 99.

[10] Guy C. Dempsey, *Albuera 1811: The Bloodiest Battle of the Peninsular War* (London: Front Line, 2008), p.285; Kramer, *Dynamic*, p.2.

[11] Richard Overy, *The Bombing War: Europe 1939–1945* (London: Allen Lane, 2013), pp.21–22, 194, 477.

[12] Kramer, *Dynamic*, pp.147–50.

[13] Jeffery Taubenberger and David Morens, '1918 Influenza: The Mother of All Pandemics', in *Emerging Infectious Diseases*, Vol.12, No. 1 (2006) at http://wwwnc.cdc.gov/eid/article/12/1/05-0979_article.htm; Spencer C. Tucker, (ed.), *The Encyclopedia of World War I* (Santa Barbara: ABC-CLIO, 2005), pp.576–77.

[14] http://virtualexhibition.1418remembered.co.uk/explore/civilians-on-the-move/exodus-14/the-french-and-belgian-exodus-in-1914.html; P.J. Cahalan, 'The Treatment of Belgian Refugees in England During the Great War' (PhD thesis, McMaster University, 1977), p.iii.

[15] Quoted in Pierre Purseigle, 'The Reception of Belgian Refugees in Europe: A Litmus Test of Wartime Social Mobilisation', in Crawford and McGibbon, *New Zealand's Great War*, p.76.

[16] Spencer C. Tucker (ed.), *The European Powers in the First World War: An Encyclopedia* (New York: Garland, 1996), p.638.

[17] Kramer, *Dynamic*, p.141.

[18] Alan Kramer, 'Combatants and Noncombatants: Atrocities, Massacres and War Crimes', in Horne, *Companion*, pp.189–90; John Horne and Alan Kramer, *German Atrocities 1914: A History of Denial* (New Haven, CT: Yale University Press, 2001), pp.38–42.

[19] See Isabel V. Hull, *Absolute Destruction: Military Culture and the Practices of War in Imperial Germany* (Ithaca, NY: Cornell University Press, 2005), figures from p.333.

[20]Horne and Kramer, *German Atrocities,* pp.43, 163.

[21]Stéphane Audoin-Rouzeau and Annette Becker, *1914–1918: Understanding the Great War* (London: Profile, 2002), pp.57–58.

[22]Quoted in Susan R. Grayzel, *Women in the First World War* (Harlow: Pearson, 2002), p.136.

[23]Kramer, *Dynamics,* p.32.

[24]Jens Thiel, 'Between recruitment and forced labour: the radicalization of German labour policy in occupied Belgium and northern France', pp.44–46 and Sophie De Schaepdrijver, 'Military occupation, political imaginations, and the First World War', both in *First World War Studies* Vol. 4, No.1 (2013) p.1.

[25]Dennis Williams, 'War of Liberation: British Second Army and Coalition Warfare in Flanders in the Hundred Days', in Gary Sheffield and Peter Gray (eds.), *Changing War: The British Army, the Hundred Days Campaign and the Birth of the Royal Air Force, 1918* (London: Bloomsbury, 2013), p.105.

[26]*Frankfurter Zeitung*, 31 July 1914, quoted in Jeffrey Verhey, *The Spirit of 1914: Militarism, Myth and Mobilization in Germany* (Cambridge: Cambridge University Press, 2000), pp.46–7.

[27]Jon Lawrence, 'Public space, political space' in Jay Winter and Jean-Louis Robert, *Capital Cities at War: Paris, London, Berlin 1914–1919* Vol. II (Cambridge: Cambridge University Press, 2007), pp.282–84.

[28]Peter Simkins, *Kitchener's Army: The Raising of the New Armies, 1914–16* (Manchester: Manchester University Press, 1988), pp.64, 75.

[29]Lawrence, 'Public space', pp.285–7; David Lloyd George, *War Memoirs*, abridged edition (London: Odhams, 1938) p.39; Catriona Pennell, *A Kingdom United: Popular Responses to the Outbreak of the First World War in Britain and Ireland* (Oxford: Oxford University Press, 2012) p.39. Adrian Gregory, *The Last Great War: British Society and the First World War* (Cambridge: Cambridge University Press, 2008), pp.9–39 is essential reading.

[30]Lawrence, 'Public space', pp.287; Hew Strachan, *To Arms* (Oxford: Oxford University Press, 2001), pp. 154–55; Jean-Jacques

Becker, *The Great War and the French People* (Leamington Spa: Berg, 1985) pp.3–4.

[31]Strachan, *To Arms,* pp. 110, 124–4, 129–30, 157–59.

[32]Christian Wolmar, *Blood, Iron & Gold: How Railways Transformed the World* (London: Atlantic, 2010 [2009]), pp.270–71.

[33]Simkins, *Kitchener's Army,* p.109.

[34]Quoted in Grayzel, *Women,* p.4.

[35]Reinhard J. Sieder, 'Behind the Lines: working-class family life in wartime Vienna', in Richard Wall and Jay Winter (eds.), *The Upheaval of War: Family, Work and Welfare in Europe, 1914–1918* (Cambridge: Cambridge University Press, 1988), p.117.

[36]Kevin Jefferys, *Politics and the People: A History of British Democracy since 1918* (London: Atlantic Books, 2007) pp.14–16. While historians no longer regard the extension of the franchise to women primarily as a reward for work, it would be unwise to completely discount it as a factor.

[37]Grayzel, *Women,* pp.101, 106–09, 118.

[38]Richard Bessel, 'Mobilizing German Society for War', in Chickering and Förster, *Great War, Total War,* p.444.

[39]Elspeth Johnstone, 'Home from Home on the Western Front, 1914–1918: Women's Contribution to Morale', in Celia Lee and Paul Strong (eds.), *Women in War: From Home Front to Front Line* (Barnsley: Pen and Sword, 2012), p.38; Roger Chickering, *The Great War and Urban Life in Germany: Freiburg, 1914–1918* (Cambridge: Cambridge University Press, 2007), p. 294.

[40]Jeremy Black, *The Great War and the Making of the Modern World* (London: Continuum, 2011), p.117; Strachan, *To Arms,* p.905; Stevenson, *1914–1918,* pp.220.

[41]Rosalind Ormiston, *First World War Posters* (London: Flame Tree, 2013), pp.24–25; Stevenson, *1914–1918,* pp.222–23.

[42]Ian F.W. Beckett, *Ypres: The First Battle 1914* (Harlow: Pearson, 2004) pp.76–77, 185–87.

[43]Simkins, *Kitchener's Army,* pp.xiv, 79, 88.

⁴⁴Grey, *Military History of Australia*, p.93; A.B. Gaunson, *College Street Heroes: Old Sydneians in the Great War* (Sydney: Sydney Grammar School Press, 1998), p.9.

⁴⁵Paul Baker, *King and Country Call: New Zealand, Conscription and the First World War* (Auckland: Auckland University Press, 1988), p.15.

⁴⁶Ian Miller, '"A Privilege to Serve": Toronto's Experience with Voluntary Enlistment in the Great War', in Yves Tremblay, *Canadian Military History Since the 17th Century* (Ottawa: Department of National Defence, 2000), pp.145, 151.

⁴⁷Robert Holland, 'The British Empire and the Great War, 1914–1918', in Judith M. Brown and Wm. Roger Louis, *The Oxford History of the British Empire: The Twentieth Century* (Oxford: Oxford University Press, 1999), p.126.

⁴⁸Alvin Jackson, *Home Rule: An Irish History 1800–2000* (Oxford: Oxford University Press, 2003), pp.145.

⁴⁹Charles Townshend, *Easter 1916: The Irish Rebellion* (London: Penguin, 2006 [2005]), pp.160–61.

⁵⁰Jackson, *Home Rule*, pp.143–44.

⁵¹Theo Balderston, 'Industrial Mobilization and War Economies' in Horne, *Companion*, p.217, 229.

⁵²Holger H. Herwig, *The First World War: Germany and Austria-Hungary*, 1914–1918 (London: Edward Arnold, 1997), pp.233–34, 236–37, 240–41.

⁵³Peter Gatrell, *Russia's First World War: A Social and Economic History* (Harlow: Pearson Longman, 2005), pp.108–26; Eric Lohr, 'Russia' in Horne, *Companion*, pp.482–4.

⁵⁴Pierre-Cyrille Hautcoeur, 'Was the Great War a watershed? The Economics of World War I in France', in Stephen Broadberry and Mark Harrison, *The Economics of World War I* (Cambridge: Cambridge University Press, 2005), p.173; Balderston, 'Industrial Mobilization', pp.218, 226; Leonard V. Smith, Stéphane Audoin-Rouzeau and Annette Becker, *France and the Great War 1914–*

1918 (Cambridge: Cambridge University Press, 2003), pp.62–3, 64–65.

⁵⁵Smith, Audoin-Rouzeau and Becker, *France and the Great War,* p.63.

⁵⁶Alan G.V. Simmonds, *Britain and World War One* (Abingdon: Routledge, 2012), pp.40–41.

⁵⁷J.M. Bourne, *Britain and the Great War 1914–1918* (London: Edward Arnold, 1989), pp.188–91.

⁵⁸Stephen Broadberry and Peter Howlett, 'The United Kingdom during World War I: business as usual?' in Broadberry and Harrison, *Economics of World War One,* pp.210, 212.

⁵⁹J.M. Bourne, *Who's Who in World War One* (London: Routledge, 2001), p.176.

⁶⁰Roger Chickering, *Imperial Germany and the Great War, 1914–1918* (Cambridge: Cambridge University Press), pp.37–40.

⁶¹Martin Kitchen, *The Silent Dictatorship* (London: Croom Helm, 1977), pp.272–4, 277–78; Chickering, *Imperial Germany,* pp.76–82; William J. Astore and Dennis E. Showalter, *Hindenburg: Icon of German Militarism* (Dulles, VA: Potomac Books, 2005), pp.41 (quote), 49.

⁶²Richard Bessel, *Germany After the First World War* (Oxford: Oxford University Press, 1995), pp.41–42.

⁶³Herwig, *First World War,* pp.374–81.

⁶⁴Gatrell, *Russia's First World War,* pp.169–72.

⁶⁵Sieder, 'Behind the Lines: working-class family life in wartime Vienna', pp.111, 112, 125, 126 (quote from p.111).

⁶⁶Quoted in Belinda J. Davis, *Home Fires Burning: Food, Politics and Everyday Life in World War I Berlin* (Chapel Hill: University of North Carolina Press, 2000). p.1.

⁶⁷C. Paul Vincent, *The Politics of Hunger: the Allied Blockade of Germany, 1915–1919* (Athens, OH: Ohio University Press, 1985), p.21.

⁶⁸Quoted in Avner Offner, *The First World War: An Agrarian Interpretation* (Oxford: Oxford University Press, 1989 [1988]), p.54.

⁶⁹Quoted in Davis, *Home Fires,* pp.180–1.

⁷⁰Quoted in Chickering, *Great War,* p.268.

⁷¹Chickering, *Imperial Germany,* pp.41, 44–45.

[72]Chickering, *Imperial Germany* p.41;Vincent, *Politics of Hunger*, p.17.

[73]Offner, *First World War*, p.54.

[74]Winter, 'Surviving', pp.517–18.

[75]Thierry Bonzon and Belinda Davis, 'Feeding the Cities', in Winter and Robert, *Capital Cities,* I, pp.310, 321, 340; Leonard V. Smith, 'France', in Horne, *Companion,* pp.419–20.

[76]Jay Winter, 'Demography', in Horne, *Companion*, p.255.

[77]Quote and figures are from David Reynolds, *America: Empire of Liberty* (London. Penguin, 2010 [2010]), p.303.

[78]Quoted in Kathleen Burk, *Old World, New World: The Story of Britain and* America (London: Abacus, 2009 [2007]), p.438.

[79]Burk, *Old World, New World,* pp.443–44.

[80]Jennifer D. Keene, *Doughboys, the Great War and the Remaking of America* (Baltimore: Johns Hopkins University Press, 2003), p.2.

[81]Gatrell, *Russia's First World War,* pp.42, 197–201, 108–26; Eric Lohr, 'Russia' in Horne, *Companion*, pp.484–87. Quote from report: Grayzel, *Women*, p.151.

[82]Grey, *Military History of Australia*, pp.114–15.

[83]Adrian Gregory, 'Military Service Tribunals, 1916–1918' in Jose Harris, *Civil Society in British History: Ideas, Identities, Institutions,* (Oxford: Oxford University Press, 2003), pp.179, 182.

[84]Eliot A. Cohen, *Supreme Command: Soldiers, Statesmen and Leadership in Wartime* (New York: The Free Press, 2002), p.61; Black, *Great War,* p.163.

[85]David Robin Watson, *Georges Clemenceau: A Political Biography* (London: Eyre Methuen, 1974), pp.285–86.

[86]John Horne, 'Remobilizing for 'total war'', in John Horne (ed.), *State, society and mobilization in Europe during the First World War* (Cambridge: Cambridge University Press, 1997) pp.196–97; Watson, *Georges Clemenceau,* pp.285–86.

[87]See John Horne, *Labour at War* (Oxford: Oxford University Press, 1991).

[88]Lucy Masterman, *C.F.G. Masterman. A Biography* (London: Cass, 1968), p. 274.

[89] I am indebted to Professor Stephen Badsey for allowing me to consult two shortly to be published papers on First World War propaganda.

[90] Elizabeth O'Neill, *The War 1915–1916: A History and an Explanation For Boys and Girls* (London: T.C. & E.C. Jack, 1916), p.41. I am indebted to my former student Caitriona McCartney for this reference.

[91] Ormiston, *First World War Posters*, pp.102, 105, 123; Joseph Darracott and Belinda Loftus, *First World War Posters* (London: Imperial War Museum, 1972) pp.45, 67.

[92] Quoted in Horne, *Labour at War*, pp.300–1.

[93] John Brophy and Eric Partridge, *The Long Trail: What the British Soldier Sang and said in the Great War of 1914–18* (London: Andre Deutsch, 1965), pp.88, 134; quote from Matthew Stibbe, *German Anglophobia and the Great War, 1914–1918* (Cambridge: Cambridge University Press, 2001), p.14.

[94] David Stevenson, *The First World War and International Politics* (Oxford: Oxford University Press, 1988), pp.89–91.

[95] Quoted in Z.A.B. Zeman, *A Diplomatic History of the First World War* (London: Weidenfeld and Nicolson, 1971), p.87.

[96] Brian Bond, *The Pursuit of Victory* (Oxford: Oxford University Press, 1996), p.105; Stevenson, *International Politics* p.95; *idem*, 'War Aims and Peace Negotiations' in Hew Strachan (ed.), *The Oxford Illustrated History of the First World War* (Oxford: Oxford University Press, 1998), pp.205–7.

[97] David French, *The Strategy of the Lloyd George Coalition 1916–18* (Oxford: Clarendon, 1995), pp.202–5; Lloyd George, *War Memoirs* Vol. II, pp.1510–17.

[98] Albert Fried (ed.), *A Day of Dedication: The Essential Writings and Speeches of Woodrow Wilson* (New York: Macmillan, 1965), pp.281–7, 319–20; French, *Strategy*, p.274; A.J.P. Taylor, *The First World War* (Harmondsworth: Penguin, 1978 [1963]), p.206.

[99]Diary notes of Oberst von Thaer, 1 October 1918 at http://www.heu.ox.ac.uk/mirrors/mirrors/w...ib.byu.edu:80/~rdh/wwi/1918/thaereng.html. For the last days of Imperial Germany see Herwig, *First World War*, pp.425–46 and Michael Geyer, 'People's War: The German Debate About a *Levée en masse* in October 1918', in Daniel Moran and Arthur Waldron (eds.), *The People in Arms: Military Myth and National Mobilization since the French Revolution* (Cambridge: Cambridge University Press, 2003).

[100]Geyer, 'People's War', p.124.

[101]John Wheeler-Bennett, *Hindenburg: The Wooden Titan* (London: Macmillan, 1967), p.197.

Epilogue

[1]Quoted in Alan Sharp, *The Versailles Settlement: Peacemaking in Paris, 1919* (New York, St. Martin's Press, 1991), p.87.

[2]Margaret MacMillan, *Peacemakers: Six Months that Changed the World* (London: John Murray, 2001), p.7.

[3]Quoted in Sharp, *Versailles Settlement*, p.189.

[4]Michael Howard, 'A Thirty Years' War? The Two World Wars in Historical Perspective', *Transactions of the Royal Historical Society* 6th Series Vol. III (London, RHS, 1993) p.176; Zara Steiner, *The Lights That Failed: European International History 1919–1923* (Oxford: Oxford University Press, 2005), pp.606, 632.

[5]Eric Hobsbawm, *The Age of Extremes* (London: Michael Joseph, 1994).

[6]Deborah Cohen, *The War Come Home: Disabled Veterans in Britain and Germany, 1914–1939* (Berkeley, CA: University of California Press, 2001).

[7]Quoted in David Fromkin, *A Peace to End All Peace: The Fall of the Ottoman Empire and the Creation of the Modern Middle East* (New York: Avon Books, 1989), p.297.

[8]David Reynolds, *The Long Shadow: The Great War and the Twentieth Century* (London: Simon and Schuster, 2013), p.98.

[9]Maldwyn A. Jones, *The Limits of Liberty: American History 1607–1980* (Oxford: Oxford UP, 1983), p.423.

[10]The historiography of the military history of the Second World War is truly vast and cannot be covered here. The following comments on the 1939–45 war have been informed by reading, among very many other books, Richard Overy, *Why the Allies Won* (London: Pimlico, 2006); Paul Addison and Angus Calder (eds.), *Time to Kill: The Soldier's Experience of War in the West 1939–45* (London: Pimlico, 1997); and Gerhard L. Weinberg, *A World at Arms: A Global History of World War II* (Cambridge: Cambridge University Press, 1994).

[11]Steiner, *Lights*, p.1.

Timeline

1870–71	Franco-Prussian War	
1888	Kaiser Wilhelm II ascends the German throne	
1890	Otto von Bismarck dismissed as German Chancellor	
1892–94	France and Russia become allies	
1898	Fashoda Crisis brings Britain and France close to war over Sudan	
1899–1902	Second South African (or Boer) War	
1904	France and Britain sign *Entente Cordiale*	
1904–05	Russo-Japanese War	
1905–06	First Moroccan Crisis	
1908	Austria-Hungary annexes Bosnia-Herzegovnia	
1911	Second Moroccan Crisis	
1912	8 December	So-called 'War Council' held in Berlin
1912–13	First Balkan War	
1913	Second Balkan War	

1914	28 June	Archduke Franz Ferdinand assassinated in Sarajevo
1914	5 July	Germany issues 'blank cheque' of unconditional support for Austria–Hungary
1914	23 July	Austria–Hungary issues ultimatum to Serbia
1914	28 July	Austria–Hungary declares war on Serbia
1914	30 July	Russia mobilises
1914	1 August	Germany declares war on Russia
1914	3 August	Germany declares war on France
1914	4 August	Germany invades Belgium; Britain declares war on Germany
1914	7 August–13 September	Battle of the Frontiers
1914	23 August	Battle of Mons
1914	23 August–11 September	Battle of Lemberg
1914	26–30 August	Battle of Tannenberg
1914	5–12 September	First Battle of the Marne
1914	19 October–22 November	First Battle of Ypres
1914	29 October	Ottoman Empire enters the war
1914	1 November	Battle of Coronel

1914	8 December	Battle of the Falkland Islands
1915	18 February	Germany announces first campaign of unrestricted submarine warfare
1915	22 April–25 May	Second Battle of Ypres
1915	25 April	Allied landings on Gallipoli peninsula
1915	9 May–18 June	Allied spring offensive on Western Front
1915	23 May	Italy declares war on Austria-Hungary
1915	25 September–18 October	Allied autumn offensive on Western Front
1916	21 February–18 December	Battle of Verdun
1916	31 May	Battle of Jutland
1916	4 June–20 September	Brusilov Offensive
1916	1 July–18 November	Battle of the Somme
1917	1 February	Second German unrestricted submarine warfare campaign begins
1917	15 March	Czar Nicholas II abdicates ('February' Revolution in Russia)
1917	6 April	United States of America enters the war
1917	9 April–17 May	Battle of Arras

1917	16 April–9 May	Nivelle Offensive
1917	1–19 July	Kerensky Offensive
1917	31 July–2 December	Third Battle of Ypres (Passchendaele)
1917	7–8 November	Bolsheviks seize power in Russia ('October' Revolution)
1917	20 November–7 December	Battle of Cambrai
1917	9 December	British capture of Jerusalem
1918	8 January	President Wilson announces the 'Fourteen Points'
1918	3 March	Treaty of Brest-Litovsk signed
1918	21 March–5 April	German *Michael* Offensive
1918	7–29 April	German *Georgette* Offensive (Battle of the Lys)
1918	15 July–6 August	Second Battle of the Marne
1918	8–11 August	Battle of Amiens
1918	15–30 September	Successful Allied offensive in Salonika
1918	19–25 September	Battle of Megiddo
1918	26–29 September	Allied Grand Offensive
1918	30 October	Ottoman Empire signs armistice with the Allies and drops out of the war

1918	24 October–3 November	Battle of Vittorio Venito
1918	3 November	Austro-Hungarian Empire signs armistice with the Allies and drops out of the war
1918	9 November	Kaiser Wilhelm II abdicates and goes into exile
1918	11 November	Signing of Armistice with Germany ends fighting on Western Front
1919	28 June	Treaty of Versailles is signed

Index

Reference to illustrations are in *italic*.